Exploring the Principles of Reflective Practice in ELT

Reflective Practice in Language Education
Series Editor: Thomas S. C. Farrell, Brock University

This series covers different issues related to reflective practice in language education and includes an introductory book which introduces these areas. The other books in the series clarify the different approaches that have been taken within reflective practice and outline current themes that have emerged in the research on various topics and methods of reflection that have occurred.

Published:

Reflective Practice in ELT
Thomas S. C. Farrell

Cooperative Learning through a Reflective Lens
George M. Jacobs, Anita Lie, and Siti Mina Tamah

Micro-Reflection on Classroom Communication: A FAB Framework
Hansun Zhang Waring and Sarah Chepkirui Creider

Reflecting on Leadership in Language Education
Edited by Andy Curtis

Reflective Practice in TESOL Service-Learning
Cynthia J. Macknish

Using Video to Support Teacher Reflection and Development in ELT
Laura Baecher, Steve Mann, and Cecilia Nobre

Forthcoming:

English Language Teacher Beliefs
Farahnaz Faez and Michael Karas

Language Teacher Identity and Reflective Practice
Zia Tajeddin

Surviving the Induction Years of Language Teaching: The Importance of Reflective Practice
Thomas S. C. Farrell

Teachers Reflecting on Boredom in the Language Classroom
Mirosław Pawlak, Mariusz Kruk, and Joanna Zawodniak

The Reflective Cycle of the Teaching Practicum
Fiona Farr and Angela Farrell

Exploring the Principles of Reflective Practice in ELT

Research and Perspectives from Turkey

Edited by Bahar Gün and Evrim Üstünlüoğlu

SHEFFIELD UK BRISTOL CT

Published by Equinox Publishing Ltd.
UK: Office 415, The Workstation, 15 Paternoster Row, Sheffield, South Yorkshire S1 2BX
USA: ISD, 70 Enterprise Drive, Bristol, CT 06010

www.equinoxpub.com

First published 2023

British Library Cataloguing-in-Publication Data
A catalogue record for this book is available from the British Library.

ISBN-13 978 1 80050 296 3 (hardback)
978 1 80050 297 0 (paperback)
978 1 80050 298 7 (ePDF)
978 1 80050 360 1 (ePub)

Library of Congress Cataloging-in-Publication Data

Names: Gün, Bahar, editor. | Üstünlüoğlu, Evrim, editor.
Title: Exploring the principles of reflective practice in ELT : research and perspectives from Turkey / edited by Bahar Gün and Evrim Üstünlüoğlu.
Description: Sheffield, South Yorkshire ; Bristol, CT : Equinox Publishing Ltd., 2023. | Series: Reflective practice in language education | Includes bibliographical references and index. | Summary: "This book aims to shed light on the ways in which Reflective Practice is exploited in the Turkish context, by introducing the research and practical applications in different language education settings"-- Provided by publisher.
Identifiers: LCCN 2022053077 (print) | LCCN 2022053078 (ebook) | ISBN 9781800502963 (hardback) | ISBN 9781800502970 (paperback) | ISBN 9781800502987 (pdf) | ISBN 9781800503601 (epub)
Subjects: LCSH: English language--Study and teaching--Turkey. | Reflective teaching--Turkey. | LCGFT: Essays.
Classification: LCC PE1128.A2 E95 2023 (print) | LCC PE1128.A2 (ebook) | DDC 428.0071/0561--dc23/eng/20230302
LC record available at https://lccn.loc.gov/2022053077
LC ebook record available at https://lccn.loc.gov/2022053078

Typeset by S.J.I. Services, New Delhi, India

Contents

Series Editor's Preface

Exploring the Principles of Reflective Practice in ELT: Research and Perspectives from Turkey, edited by Bahar Gün and Evrim Üstünlüoğlu, is an excellent collection of different reflective practice studies conducted in Turkey. In many ways, this book is an extension and development of many of the concepts introduced in the first book in this series that I wrote, *Reflective Practice in ELT*. In fact, the main premise of all the chapters in this collection is that they are specifically linked to the six principles of reflective practice that I outlined in the book. These concepts are that reflective practice is (1) is holistic, (2) is evidence-based, (3) involves dialogue, (4) bridges principles and practices, (5) requires an inquiring disposition, and (6) is a way of life. All the authors in *Exploring the Principles of Reflective Practice in ELT* refer to these six principles in some manner while conducting their reflective practice research and use these principles to guide their discussion. The book is structured around three different contexts: pre-service teacher education context, in-service education context, and self-reflection. The chapters also explore different types of reflection: digital reflection, collaborative reflection, lesson study as a reflective practice, reflections on a Reflective Teaching and Learning Program, and trainer self-reflection.

More specifically, the book begins with an introduction by the editors followed by seven chapters that outline various studies on reflective practice in a Turkish context in different educational settings. The final chapter provides concluding remarks by the editors. Chapter 1, 'Reflection and Collaboration in EFL Teacher Professional Development in Turkey: A Systematic Review' by Serhat Başar, Esat Kuzu, & İrem Çomoğlu, provides a meta-synthesis exploring the implementation of reflective practice studies in ELT in Turkey that sets the scene for the remaining chapters by outlining clear implications for the pre-service education practicum programs, in-service education of tertiary-level teachers, as well as the reflective practices for EFL teacher educators. Chapter 2, 'Pre-Service EFL Teachers' Reflective Thinking Levels and Cognitive Presence in Online Learning Settings: A Correlational Study' by Ceyhun Yükselir & Saadet Korucu-Kış, explores pre-service teachers' reflective inquiry skills, specifically focusing on digital technologies, and how developing reflective thinking in an online-education setting can improve cognitive presence. Chapter 3, 'Engaging in Systematic Digital Reflection: A Case of Pre-Service English Teachers' by Ali Öztüfekçi & Kenan Dikilitaş, examines reflection for pre-service teachers, namely, the use of Information and Communications Technology (ICT) to encourage teachers to become reflective practitioners. Chapter 4, 'Reflective Practice Groups in ELT: An Emergent Model for Professional Development' by Burak Aydın & Irem Çomoğlu, explores collaborative reflection through 'Reflective Practice Groups' (RPGs), and investigates the effects of such reflection on teachers' professional development in an in-service training program. Chapter 5, 'Mediating Reflective Practice through Lesson Study: The Case of an EFL Teacher' by Özgehan Uştuk & İrem Çomoğlu, describes how reflective practice helps one EFL teacher engaged in 'Lesson Study' (LS), by developing and improving her teaching practice. As well as providing insights on reflective practice in LS, the chapter also highlights the importance of teacher discourse in understanding teacher reflection in language teaching. Chapter 6, 'Payoffs and Pitfalls of Reflective Practice as Perceived by Novice EFL Teachers' by İlknur Bayram & Özlem Canaran, focuses on teachers' reflections on a Reflective Teaching and Learning Program (RTLP). Specifically, they explore the perceptions of a group of novice EFL teachers on an RTLP in an in-service teacher education setting. Chapter 7, 'A Blended Reflection Cycle for Trainers: A Case Study' by Mehmet Haldun Kaya, explores the notion of 'reflection-on-action', and he describes his instrumental single case study on a 'Blended Reflection Cycle for Trainers' with the aim of improving both his own training activities and reflective skills. He emphasizes in this chapter a very important concept: that reflection is equally important for teacher trainers as for teachers.

The editors maintain that this collection is a call to action for all ELT professionals, whether experienced, novice, or student teachers, leaders, managers, or teacher educators, who wish to invest in their own professional development by engaging in reflective practice. They hope that the reader will find inspiration by learning about colleagues' collective reflective practice experiences in the Turkish context. As the editors have noted, there are a remarkable number of high-quality reflective practice studies that have been carried out in Turkey and this collection demonstrates that this is true. The seven research articles on reflective practice in ELT outlined in this book have focused on different approaches to reflective practice, from individual to collective reflection, from the perspectives of pre-service teachers and in-service teachers (novice and experienced), as well as from the perspective of teacher trainers. The research results from these articles have implications not only for all stakeholders in Turkey, but also by extension, in EFL settings worldwide.

As such, *Exploring the Principles of Reflective Practice in ELT: Research and Perspectives from Turkey* is suitable for pre-service and in-service language teachers, language teacher educators and administrators wishing to implement reflective practice, as well as for certificate students, MA and PhD students who wish to conduct research on reflective practice in EFL or other contexts, and indeed teachers and teacher educators in different disciplines interested in the concept of service-learning in education. This is truly an excellent addition to Equinox's series on *Reflective Practice in Language Education*.

Thomas S. C. Farrell
Brock University
Series Editor, *Reflective Practice in Language Education*

Acknowledgments

We would like to express our special thanks to the series editor Thomas Farrell who gave us the opportunity to create a book on reflective practice in the Turkish context. We are deeply indebted to him for his constant guidance and advice throughout our editing process.

We also would like to extend our sincere thanks to the chapter authors for their valuable contributions in this book.

We firmly believe this book will be an indispensable addition to the Reflective Practice literature in the field of teacher education.

Bahar Gün and Evrim Üstünlüoğlu
İzmir University of Economics, Turkey

Introduction

Bahar Gün & Evrim Üstünlüoğlu

Professionals in the field of language education are undoubtedly familiar with the terms 'reflection' and 'reflective practice' (RP), as are those in other fields. Today, it is almost impossible to engage in any professional development discussion without referring to these two key concepts.

In presentations, as speakers or audience, we are all familiar with the image of a cat looking into a mirror reflecting a lion's face. This illustration usually generates an interesting discussion about self-image and self-evaluation. This simple but effective 'lion cat mirror' metaphor, and the discussion about its meaning, shows us that there may be many different understandings and interpretations of the term 'reflection.'

Thomas Farrell, in the series *Reflective Practice in Language Education*, of which this book is part, aims to investigate in greater depth the ways in which RP is applied in different countries and contexts, to explore the different understanding of this concept by professionals in a wide variety of ELT settings.

The book at hand, therefore, aims to shed light on the ways in which RP is exploited in the Turkish context, by introducing the research and practical applications in different language education settings. Before presenting the book's thematic structure, it is important to note that in Turkey there is a great amount of knowledge and research in ELT in general, and RP in particular. Extensive publications and national and international conference presentations on reflection-related topics are increasingly common in the country. This book includes examples of this scholarly work, so that ELT professionals in different parts of the globe may benefit from the advances made in context-dependent RP applications in Turkey.

The main premise of all the chapters in the book is based on Farrell's (2019) six principles which state that Reflective Practice

(1) is holistic,
(2) is evidence-based,

(3) involves dialog,
(4) bridges principles and practices,
(5) requires an inquiring disposition, and
(6) is a way of life.

All the authors in the book have made reference to these six principles while conducting their RP research and have used these principles to guide their discussion. The book is structured around three different contexts:

(1) two chapters on pre-service teacher education context,
(2) three chapters on in-service education context, and
(3) one chapter on self-reflection.

The chapters also explore different types of reflection, as follows:

(1) digital reflection (Chapters 2 and 3),
(2) collaborative reflection (Chapter 4),
(3) lesson study as a reflective practice (Chapter 5),
(4) reflections on a Reflective Teaching and Learning Program (Chapter 6), and
(5) trainer self-reflection (Chapter 7).

The first chapter in the book is different in nature from the others in the sense that it is a meta-synthesis exploring the implementation of reflective practice studies in ELT in Turkey. In this study, Başar, Kuzu, & Çomoğlu review 24 RP studies carried out in Turkey between 2010 and 2021. The results of their inductive thematic analysis indicate clear implications for pre-service education practicum programs, in-service education of tertiary-level teachers, as well as reflective practices for EFL teacher educators.

In the second chapter, Yükselir & Korucu-Kış present their study on exploring pre-service teachers' reflective inquiry skills, specifically focusing on digital technologies, and how developing reflective thinking in an online-education setting can improve cognitive presence. Throughout the chapter, the authors seek to understand the relationship between the level of reflective thinking and cognitive presence, and the data analysis clearly points to a positive correlation between the two. The chapter carries important implications for pre-service teacher education contexts, by highlighting the mutual influences of reflective thinking and cognitive presence.

Öztüfekçi & Dikilitaş, in the third chapter, explore a similar aspect of reflection for pre-service teachers, namely, the use of Information and Communications Technology (ICT) to encourage teachers to become reflective practitioners. The authors report on their research into ELT pre-service teachers engaged in online writing tasks, and describe their digital reflections based on the constructive feedback from tutors in an asynchronous course in their curriculum. Potentially relevant to ELT professionals working in similar pre-service settings, the chapter highlights the implications for professional development in terms of fostering teachers' autonomy, enhancing their self-efficacy, and developing their professional identities.

Chapter 4 presents a study sharing perspectives in an in-service teacher education context. In this chapter, Aydın & Çomoğlu explore collaborative reflection through 'Reflective Practice Groups' (RPGs), and investigate the effects of such reflection on teachers' professional development in an in-service training program. The chapter focuses not only on the RP tools used in the process, but also on the insights gained into the value of RPGs as a professional development model. Aydın & Çomoğlu's insightful suggestions and implications may form the basis for ELT institutions applying similar models of in-service teacher training.

Uştuk & Çomoğlu, in Chapter 5, share their study conducted on a different reflective professional development model: Lesson Study (LS). The authors describe how reflective practice helps one EFL teacher engaged in LS, by developing and improving her teaching practice. As well as providing insights on RP in LS, the chapter highlights the importance of teacher discourse in understanding teacher reflection in language teaching. Highly plausible implications are made for the use of LS in the in-service teacher education context, to enable the teachers to reach higher levels of reflection.

Chapter 6 is somewhat different from the others, in that it mainly focuses on teachers' responses to a Reflective Teaching and Learning Program (RTLP). Bayram & Canaran explore the perceptions of a group of novice EFL teachers on an RTLP in an in-service teacher education setting. The authors describe in detail the RTLP, the opportunities for teachers to enhance their reflective skills, and the participants' perceptions about the effectiveness of the program. Bayram & Canaran clearly explain the benefits and the challenges the teachers experienced throughout the program; and make suggestions on how to improve the program based on the feedback from the teachers. Institutions intending to offer an RTLP for their teachers would benefit from the light shed upon the design and conduct of such a professional development (PD) program.

The final chapter of the book is of a completely different nature, as Kaya focuses on the self-reflection of a teacher trainer. He emphasizes that reflection is equally important for teacher trainers as for teachers. In his chapter, Kaya explores the notion of 'reflection-on-action,' and he describes his instrumental single case study on a 'Blended Reflection Cycle for Trainers' with the aim of improving both his own training activities and his reflective skills as a trainer. His qualitative analysis leads him to important implications for teacher trainers around themes including identity change, attitudes of the trainees in training events, and management of the affective domain. This chapter has valuable lessons, not just for teachers, but for teacher trainers whose professional development tends to be neglected in RP studies. Clearly, all teacher trainers and educators, regardless of their level of pedagogical knowledge and experience, need to seek ways to continue to develop professionally.

Readers will find one or two 'reflective breaks' in each chapter, with questions which allow them time to consider their own contexts and their own experiences. These are designed to help readers to directly relate to the studies described in the book, via individual or group reflection, for their own professional development.

This book, overall, is a call to action for all ELT professionals, whether experienced, novice, or student teachers, leaders, managers, or teacher educators, who wish to invest in their own professional development by engaging in reflective practice. We hope that readers will find inspiration from learning about their colleagues' collective RP experiences in the Turkish context. We also hope that, recalling the 'lion cat mirror' metaphor, the book contributes to the diversity of understanding and interpretations of reflective practice, by sharing a variety of perspectives from scholars in Turkey.

REFERENCE

Farrell, T. S. C. (2019). *Reflective practice in ELT*. Equinox Publishing. https://doi.org/10.4324/9781315659824-5

ABOUT THE AUTHORS

Bahar Gün holds BA, MA, and PhD degrees in ELT. Since 2003, she has been working at the İzmir University of Economics (IUE), Turkey, where she is an Assistant Professor. She served as Head of the Teacher Development Unit (TDU) in the School of Foreign Languages (SFL) at IUE between 2006 and 2021, and is currently a member of the TDU that is in charge of in-service teacher training and development programs in the SFL. Her research interests include EFL teacher education in general, and teacher cognition and reflective teaching and learning in particular. She is also a CELTA and ICELT tutor, and an Oxford Teachers' Academy (OTA) trainer. She is the founding president of TESOL Turkey, a Commission on English Language Program Accreditation (CEA) reviewer, and the coordinator of the IATEFL Teacher Training and Education Special Interest Group. She is also a board member of DEDAK, a national agency for the accreditation of language programs in Turkey.

Evrim Üstünlüoğlu received her BA and MA degrees in Teaching English as a Foreign Language, and her PhD in Educational Sciences with a special focus on program development. She has extensive experience, having served as a director, a researcher, and a lecturer for over 30 years. She is a qualified Commission on English Language Program Accreditation (CEA) reviewer, a founding member of DEDAK (a national agency for the accreditation of language programs in Turkey) and TESOL Turkey, and a board member of the IATEFL Leadership and Management Special Interest Group. She has publications in both international and national journals, on quality in higher education, pedagogical competencies of faculty members, observation/reflection, and new approaches in teaching. She has been awarded scholarships to conduct research and to teach as a visiting scholar abroad. Her expertise and interests are quality in education, program development, methodology, and design thinking. She is currently an Associate Professor at the İzmir University of Economics, Turkey.

Chapter 1

Reflection and Collaboration in EFL Teacher Professional Development in Turkey: A Systematic Review

Serhat Başar, Esat Kuzu, & İrem Çomoğlu

1.1. INTRODUCTION

From a traditional perspective, the responsibility for the professional development (PD) of teachers has been put on others rather than on teachers themselves (Tanış & Dikilitaş, 2018; Vangrieken et al., 2017). These kinds of PD programs are generally one-shot activities, which fail to be productive because teachers' adopting new teaching approaches and improving their practice is something that requires time. By drawing attention to this issue, Evans (2019) highlights that teachers need time to internalize new ideas and ways of thinking so that these can become part of their practice; and that they gain exposure to such ideas or perspectives through interaction with co-workers as well as through the effect of many unrecognizable factors. Similarly, Zepeda (2012) argues that learning to teach is an everlasting process that can never be completed. In this respect, traditional methods in PD have been inadequate as they generally do not necessitate teachers' prolonged engagement in development programs. Recently, PD approaches have become more teacher-oriented, inquiry-based, and collaborative (Johnson, 2006). Collaborative reflective practice which facilitates teachers to share their teaching practices, experiences, and ideas and to critically discuss them can be a fruitful method to enhance the professional development of teachers. Farrell (2012) suggests that reflection 'enables teachers to stop, look, and discover where they are at that moment and then decide where they want to go (professionally) in the future' (p. 7). Collaboration, in this process, plays a key role in that alternative perspectives can be gained by teachers through negotiation with others (Van Gyn,

1996) and the problem can be analysed from multiple perspectives, which enables teachers to see the underlying and hidden aspects of the problem.

Research regarding the professional development of English as a Foreign Language (EFL) teachers has focused on Collaborative Reflective Practice (CRP) implementations in pre-service and in-service teacher education in various parts of the world. In this study, we present a meta-synthesis of studies that are based on the implementation of PD models promoting collaborative reflective practices of EFL teachers in Turkey between 2010 and 2021. Our aim was to carry out a systematic review of the literature to provide a broad interpretation of how PD programs involving CRPs make contributions to the professional development of EFL teachers and in what ways CRPs in teacher education in Turkey can be improved.

1.2. LITERATURE REVIEW

With the realization that teaching is a complex and challenging process, the importance attributed to professional development has gradually increased. It is now evident that traditional PD models are inadequate because they follow a top-down process where the needs of teachers are ignored. One-shot institutional-based training programs such as seminars and workshops are often ineffective as teachers generally are unable to transfer what they have covered in these seminars and workshops into their practice (Joyce & Showers, 2002). Moreover, these kinds of applications have faced criticism for preventing teachers from taking full advantage of their learning (Fiszer, 2004). When the topics of PD programs are determined by administrators, it causes disagreement between administrators and teachers (Elliott, 2017). Therefore, a gap seems inevitable between the theory which teachers are equipped with through education programs and practice which is what they implement in their teaching. With the introduction of post-method pedagogy, the narrow understanding of teacher education as limited to elements of the classroom has been rejected and it is recognized that the particular, the practical, and the possible are intertwined, resulting in a dynamic relationship where a holistic approach to an entity functions better than a combination of fragmented approaches to the parts (Kumaravadivelu, 2001). Thus, a search has begun for alternative ways to bridge the gap between theory and practice, and help teachers continuously improve themselves and their teaching methods. Reflective practice (RP), which was first mentioned by Dewey (1933), has been perceived as a promising method to support teachers' continuous professional development. Reflection is seen as an essential component of learning (Day, 1993) and crucial for teacher education (Clarà, 2015). According to Moon (2013), reflection is a process that combines the notions of learning and thinking, that is, the aim of reflecting is to learn something. The intention of reflective practice, as a result, is to learn from teaching. Reflective practice, thus, entails retrospective and introspective processes where teachers constantly question what they do and why they do it.

Murphy (2014) categorizes the purposes of reflective practice as follows: (1) to improve our understanding of teaching and the learning process, (2) to broaden our repertoire of strategic options as language teachers, (3) to take ownership of our own theories of language teaching as informed by teaching practice, and (4) to enhance the quality of learning opportunities we are able to provide in language classrooms. Additionally, Jay & Johnson (2002) describe three components of reflection as description, comparison, and criticism. According to Jay & Johnson, descriptive reflection involves the description of the matter for reflection, while comparative reflection is about reframing the matter in the light of alternative views, research, or other people's perspectives, and critical reflection is related to considering the implications of the matter and developing a fresh perspective.

Schön (1983) categorized reflection into two types: reflection-in-action and reflection-on-action. Reflection-in-action deals with teachers reflecting while they teach; reflection-on-action is looking back and thinking about the lesson they have completed. In this respect, reflection-on-action takes place after the action has transpired. Later, Killion & Todnem (1991) added reflection-for-action as another kind of reflection, in which reflecting is related to thinking about the future teaching process and anticipating what might occur in a future lesson. It also includes reflecting on past teaching experiences in advance of a lesson, and learning from them.

Farrell (2019) proposes six principles of reflective practice. The first principle is that reflective practice is holistic. It focuses on the intellectual, cognitive, and metacognitive aspects of practice as well as its spiritual, moral, and non-cognitive aspects. It recognizes the inner life of a teacher, and it is embedded in the context of the teacher's everyday life inside and outside of the classroom. The second principle is that reflective practice is evidence-based. It is a kind of rigorous and disciplined systematic inquiry. We need to have evidence to be clear about what we reflect on, in order to make informed decisions and understand our actions. In this way, we can also make a distinction between what we do and what we think we do. Third, reflective practice involves dialog. This principle builds on the previous one, in that dialog should be included in an empirical and data-driven approach, being necessary for reflective practice since it facilitates clarification, questioning, and understanding that was not possible through individual or self-reflection (Mann & Walsh, 2017). The fourth principle suggests that reflective practice bridges principles and practices. Reflective practice combines a teacher's principles, philosophy, beliefs, and theory with their practices in the classroom. This is important because focusing only on what teachers do in the classroom and not paying attention to what is in their heads will result in an inadequate understanding of the process. Farrell (2019), in this context, suggests that teaching is like an iceberg because the hidden part is the largest. According to the fifth principle, reflective practice requires an inquiring disposition. Reflection is not just about collecting and examining data. It requires teachers to question everything inside and outside the class which might affect their practices. In order to have such a disposition, teachers should develop certain attitudes to their reflections. As Dewey (1933) suggests, these attitudes include open-mindedness, wholeheartedness, and responsibility. Finally, the sixth principle proposes that reflective practice is a way of life. That is, teachers should not restrict reflection to their teaching and the time they spend at school. Reflection should guide them in their careers and in their daily life. They should continue to think about every issue related to their practice.

Scholars have developed some frameworks for reflection to help teachers follow a systematic reflection process. Grimmet et al. (1990), for example, suggested a basic framework of reflection including three levels: technical, deliberative, and dialectical. At the technical level, they proposed that reflection serves as a mediation of actions. At the deliberative level, weighting among competing perspectives is included in reflection; and at the dialectical level, theoretical knowledge is reconstructed to help teachers transform their practice. Later, Farrell (2015) improved on his previous framework and presented a descriptive and more sophisticated framework for reflecting on practice which includes five stages/levels: philosophy, principles, theory, practice, and beyond practice. The first stage of the framework, philosophy, accepts the teacher as a human being and proposes that teachers' professional practices are affected by their philosophy that has been shaped since their birth. Principles, on the other hand, are related to reflections on teachers' beliefs, assumptions, and conceptions concerning teaching and learning. The third stage, theory, means that teachers can develop their theory which is influenced by their reflections on their principles and philosophy. Reflection on practice starts as teachers observe their actions in the teaching process and students' reactions (non-reactions). Teachers can reflect before, during, or after the teaching. Finally, beyond practice, the last stage, requires teachers to reflect on issues outside of their practice. That is, they need to consider and question social, political, and moral issues that might affect their teaching inside and outside of the classroom, which is also called critical reflection.

Language teachers may reflect on their practices in different ways. According to Farrell (2019), reflection can take weak or strong forms. In the weak form, language teachers sometimes evaluate different aspects of their teaching in an informal way, and this does not contribute to professional development (Wallace, 1996). Strong reflection, on the other hand, is evidence-based. In this respect, it entails systematic data collection to provide an accurate picture of what is happening inside the classroom (Farrell, 2019). Moreover, regarding modes of reflection, Murray (2010) makes a distinction between individual and collaborative reflection. Individual reflection is a teacher's struggle to reflect on their teaching through the data collected from their teaching, while collaborative reflection refers to teachers' sharing their reflection experiences with each other (Turhan & Kırkgöz, 2021). Collaborative reflection has been increasingly drawing attention in language teaching. Reflective practice is now regarded as a social activity (Greene & Magliaro, 2004; Hernández-Ramos, 2004). Therefore, meeting to share experiences and critically think about them to enhance teachers' professional development is seen as crucial. Kraft (2002) highlights that collaborative reflection creates an atmosphere where teachers can monitor their teaching practice through sharing their experiences and gaining awareness about their expectations and assumptions as well as questioning themselves to renew and revise their perspectives. Freeman (1989) also states that while teachers might not realize when they do effective things, a collaborator can draw attention to that aspect of teaching practice, which can trigger a change in the teachers' awareness.

Collaboration should not be perceived as just meeting with other teachers. Murray (2015) pinpoints the importance of collaboration, stating: 'it requires providing teachers with the opportunity to examine, critique, and support one another's work in a safe and supportive environment' (p. 23). In this sense, collaboration is a complex and challenging procedure. Collaboration also provides teachers with the necessary external perspective as well as alternative ideas from colleagues (Loh et al., 2017). Additionally, collaborators might help improve the practice with suggestions (Parsons & Stephenson, 2005).

Communities of practice are very useful ways to encourage collaborative reflective practice. In these communities, people can come together with the aim of sharing and questioning their practices in an active, reflective, collaborative way. They can focus on overcoming the complexities and difficulties of teaching, critically discuss their practice and experiences, and provide alternative perspectives for other collaborators' experiences. In this respect, various kinds of communities of practice can be mentioned. Lesson study (LS), teacher study groups (TSG), critical friends groups (CFG), professional learning communities (PLC), and collaborative action research (CAR) are some of the most commonly utilized ways to create collaborative reflective practice atmospheres.

Reflective Break

- Have you ever engaged in collaborative reflective activities in pre-service education? If so, in what ways have you benefited from them in your teaching?
- What is the role of collaboration in your professional development practices?
- How would you like to integrate collaborative reflection into your professional development?

1.3. METHOD

In this study, we employed a meta-synthesis method of inquiry for the review of qualitative findings in a systematic way in order to make new interpretations that could pave the way for new perspectives (Nye et al., 2016). Adopting a systematic review perspective enabled us to limit the scope of the inquiry to the predetermined criteria of our topic, which helped us to identify the studies more objectively and comprehensively (Chong, 2019). As our topic of interest was based upon collaborative reflection practices among teachers between 2010 and 2021 in Turkey, we predetermined a list of criteria to make relevant decisions on the inclusion or exclusion of the studies for the meta-synthesis.

We mainly focused on research articles published in research journals, yet we included one book chapter based on a research study and one full-text conference proceedings in the synthesis because they were closely related to our topic.

- We focused on the qualitative findings of the studies we selected.
- Studies conducted between 2010 and 2021 were included to shed light on the recent state of CRPs of EFL teachers in Turkey.
- Publications that were only based on the attitudes, beliefs, or perceptions of teachers were not included. We only considered on research studies that were based on the implementation of a PD model including collaborative reflection.

During our search, we used Google Scholar, ERIC, Scopus, and ULAKBİM with the keywords: 'collaborative reflection,' 'collaborative reflective practices,' 'collaborative professional development,' 'lesson study,' 'teacher study groups,' 'critical friends groups,' 'professional learning communities,' 'communities of practice,' and 'collaborative action research.' Our search yielded a total of 24 studies for inclusion in our study.

To analyse the qualitative findings, we carried out an inductive thematic analysis (Braun & Clarke, 2006) by using the codes to reach overarching categories and themes. We read all the studies several times to make our codes fit into relevant subcategories that would constitute the overarching themes. Each theme and related subcategories were finalized after we reached a consensus on the analysis.

1.4. RESULTS

Our search revealed 24 studies between the years 2010 and 2021 that were in line with the scope of our research: Collaborative Reflective Practices (CRPs) in EFL teacher education in Turkey. We grouped these research studies into three major themes considering the target group of reflective practices: (1) CRPs in pre-service teacher education, (2) CRPs in in-service teacher education, and (3) CRPs by teacher educators. While the number of studies focusing on pre-service teachers is 9, 13 studies have been conducted for reflective practices of in-service teachers at various levels. As to the reflective practices of teacher educators, there are only 2 studies in the Turkish context (see Table 1.1).

Table 1.1. An overview of studies on CRPs in Turkey between the years 2010 and 2021.

Target Group	Level	Number of Studies
Pre-service	Practicum	7
	Teaching language skills course	2
In-service	Tertiary	10
	Secondary	2
	Primary	1
Teacher educator self-study		2
Total number of studies		24

1.4.1. Collaborative Reflective Practices in Pre-Service Teacher Education in Turkey

Having reviewed the studies conducted between 2010 and 2021, we found 9 studies integrating collaborative reflective practices into the scope of initial teacher education programs (see Table 1.2). The main focus is on the collaborative reflective practices that took place in the form of peer reflection in pairs/groups or team reflection including the supervisor, mentor, and the pre-service teachers. Analysing these studies in terms of the target group and the context led us to group these studies into two subcategories: collaborative reflective practices in practicum and in teaching language skills courses. In 7 of these studies (Bener & Yıldız, 2019; Çomoğlu & Dikilitaş, 2020; Kırmızı & Tosuncuoğlu, 2019; Mumford & Dikilitaş, 2020; Tavil & Güngör, 2017; Turhan & Kırkgöz, 2021; Yalçın Arslan, 2019), collaborative reflective practice was implemented within the practicum course for fourth-grade students. The 2 other studies were carried out within the context of a teaching skills course taught in the third year of the program (Güngör, 2016; Karakaş & Yükselir, 2021).

Table 1.2. Summary of the CRP studies in pre-service education.

Target Group	Means of Reflection	Purpose	Authors
Pre-service	Collaborative reflective practices (including reflective journals) on video-recorded **practicum** practices and video-recordings of novice teachers in post-lesson conferences	To investigate the effect of video-recording of novice teachers on pre-service teachers' professional knowledge and practices	Tavil & Güngör (2017)
Pre-service	Lesson study as a PD model (including research lessons, observations, and reflections in a **practicum** program)	To analyse how engaging collaboratively in a lesson study as a PD model influences pre-service teachers' professional development	Yalçın Arslan (2019)
Pre-service	An online community of practice as a component of a **practicum** program (including blog-based reflective activities and peer reflections through comments)	To investigate how blog entries lead to reflection among pre-service teachers and what affordances of blogs promote reflection	Bener & Yıldız (2019)
Pre-service	Collaborative reflection on the video-recorded lessons taught in the **practicum** as a group including the pre-service teacher, the supervisor, and the mentor	To explore the initial reflective practices of pre-service teachers and determine the professional development needs based on these reflections	Kırmızı & Tosuncuoğlu (2019)
Pre-service	A peer **practicum** program including pairs and groups co-reflecting on their practicum experiences through verbal records	To provide an alternative practicum (practicum as peers) and investigate how co-reflection with peers and mentoring support from peers develop the sense of self as a teacher	Çomoğlu & Dikilitaş (2020)

Pre-service	Reflection practices through online interaction in a hybrid **practicum** course including a teacher research project	To explore how online spoken and written interactions with the teacher educator promote a higher level of reflection among pre-service teachers based on a practicum course including a teacher research project	Mumford & Dikilitaş (2020)
Pre-service	Collaborative reflection on **practicum** observations in pairs through co-reflective practices	To investigate how critically pre-service teachers as pairs co-reflect on their practicum experiences retrospectively and how reflective practice changes their views on language teaching	Turhan & Kırkgöz (2021)
Pre-service	Self and peer reflection on video-recorded micro-teaching sessions in a **skill course**	To investigate how pre-service teachers monitor and evaluate themselves through reflective practice and bridge the gap between their theoretical understandings and in-class practices	Güngör (2016)
Pre-service	A reflective practice group as a component of a **skill course** (including reflections on video-recorded micro-teaching sessions and group discussions)	To explore to what extent video-recorded micro-teaching sessions and structured group discussions promote reflective practice and peer reflection	Karakaş & Yükselir (2021)

Using video-recorded lessons taught by pre-service teachers in practicum, Kırmızı & Tosuncuoğlu (2019) attempted to analyse how these pre-service teachers employ reflective practices through video-recordings in a group meeting including the pre-service teacher, university supervisor, and the mentor teacher in the practicum school. Their study revealed that pre-service teachers could share their experiences in a dialogic way with the help of reflective practices; nonetheless, they need more information to be involved in reflective practice. Likewise, Tavil & Güngör (2017) conducted a quasi-experimental study in which both experimental and control groups reflected on their video-recorded practicum lessons; however, the experimental group also reflected on the video-recorded lessons of a group of novice teachers working in different regions of Turkey. The findings revealed that the understandings of pre-service teachers regarding professional development improved through collaborative reflection by considering the role of larger socio-economic and cultural factors in teaching. By making use of co-reflective practices in pairs, Turhan & Kırkgöz (2021) intended to identify how pre-service teachers utilize retrospective co-reflection on their practicum experiences and to what extent they can critically reflect on their observations through co-reflective writing and retrospective interviews. The findings indicated that the pre-service teachers engaging in this collaborative reflective practice had changed views toward teaching; however, their reflective practices lacked a high level of criticality. With a similar focus on the role of collaborative reflection, Çomoğlu & Dikilitaş (2020) designed an alternative peer practicum program intending to engage pre-service teachers in co-reflection on their practicum observations and experiences in pairs or groups by keeping a verbal record of these co-reflection sessions. This study aimed to explore how these co-reflective practices and peer mentoring contribute to the pre-service teachers' sense of self, and revealed that teachers could develop this by gaining a perspectival understanding and providing psychological support to construct knowledge together.

In another practicum context, Yalçın Arslan (2019) conducted a lesson study as a PD model for the practicum students to identify the takeaways of engaging in a lesson study requiring them to research, observe, and co-reflect. The study showed that the pre-service teachers who took part reported substantial gains in their professional growth as future teachers, benefiting their learners, and increasing their content-related knowledge. Similarly, Bener & Yıldız (2019) formed an online community of practice whose members were fourth-grade practicum students, and they aimed to investigate how writing blog entries leads to collaborative reflection among pre-service teachers. The results indicated that blogging yielded a medium or high level of reflection in most cases, and it provided some affordances such as peer feedback and a sense of community, which resulted in extended reflective practices among students. Mumford & Dikilitaş (2020) also designed a practicum course, which required three pre-service teachers to engage in teacher research and online spoken/written interactions with the teacher educator based on their research observations and assigned readings. The findings of the study demonstrated that pre-service teachers benefited from spoken and written interactions that facilitated engaging in reflective practices; however, only one teacher was able to make use of a higher level of reflection. The reason for failure in employing critical reflection was related to some factors stemming from the attitudes towards technology and reflective practices.

In the teaching language skills course in the third year of the program, Güngör (2016) organized video-recorded micro-teaching sessions, which was followed by self-reflection and peer reflection on the video-recordings, and self-reflection diaries. Even though this study was mainly based on self-reflective practices, peer reflection was also a component of pre-service teachers' reflective practices. In this sense, Güngör (2016) aimed to investigate how pre-service teachers reflect on their teaching practices and how they bridge the gap between their theoretical knowledge and instructional practices in a simulated teaching context, which revealed that participating in reflective practice increased pre-service teachers' awareness and preparedness for classroom actualities. The other study conducted by Karakaş & Yükselir (2021) attempted to identify how becoming involved in reflective practice through video-recorded micro-teaching sessions, reflection on practices, and peer reflection in guided group discussions promotes pre-service teachers' reflective practices and peer reflection. This reflective program was found to be quite beneficial since the participants made some changes in their practices as a result of reflective thinking practices as a group and they were able to employ critical thinking on their practices.

1.4.2. Collaborative Reflective Practices in In-Service Teacher Education in Turkey

At the in-service level, several studies have been conducted to promote teachers' professional development through various reflection practices such as lesson study and critical friends groups. The studies identified at this level have been mainly implemented for tertiary-level EFL teachers (n=10), followed by secondary-level EFL teachers (n=2), and primary-level EFL teachers (n=1) (see Table 1.3).

The studies in the tertiary level have been grouped into three subcategories: studies including a PD program supported with collaborative reflection (5), LS (3), and CFG (2) (see Table 1.3). By including a PD program supported with action research process and reflective practice, Arslan & Başağa (2010) aimed to investigate the influence of such a PD program on four experienced EFL teachers. Even though the teachers did not work together as a group, they made use of collaborative reflective practices with the researchers throughout the program, which resulted in increased awareness about teaching practices, a higher criticality level in their professional perspectives, and increased collaboration with their colleagues. Mede (2010) attempted to identify how collaboration in pairs benefited two experienced EFL teachers through peer observations, verbal and written peer reflection, and group discussions with the researcher. The findings show that both teachers gained from this PD program, and they were able to improve their instructional practices and perspectives towards collaboration in the light of the reflective practices they conducted collaboratively.

Table 1.3. Summary of the CRP studies in in-service education (tertiary-level).

Target Group	Means of Reflection	Purpose	Authors
In-service (tertiary level)	A reflective development program as a PD model (including critical reflection on teaching and action research)	To explore the takeaways of a PD program supported with reflective practice and action research	Arslan & Başağa (2010)
In-service (tertiary level)	Collaborative reflection on in-class problems in pairs	To explore how collaborative reflection on in-class problems promotes teachers' beliefs and practices	Mede (2010)
In-service (tertiary level)	A reflective PD model to recruit **novice teachers** with the help of experienced teachers (including peer observations and feedback sessions)	To analyse the efficiency of an existing INSET mentoring program from the perspectives of both **novice** and experienced teachers	Tomak & Karaman (2013)
In-service (tertiary level)	Reflective practice-oriented online discussions as a component of a graduate course (including reflection-on/in/for action)	To investigate how teachers engage in reflection on, in, and for action through an online reflective discussion	Burhan Horasanlı & Ortaçtepe (2016)
In-service (tertiary level)	Critical friends groups as a PD model (including a PD program supported with observations and reflective essays)	To analyse teachers' perceptions and practices regarding the use of authentic materials in their classes based on their discussions in a CFG, and how this process influences their PD	Günbay & Mede (2017)
In-service (tertiary level)	Critical friends group as a PD model (including reflective journals, meetings)	To investigate how working in a CFG collaboratively and in an inquiry-based way makes contributions to the professional growth of teachers	Aktekin (2019)
In-service (tertiary level)	Lesson study as a PD model (including teacher workshops, group discussions, and observations)	To investigate the benefits and challenges of lesson study regarding PD of teachers in addition to suggestions made by teachers	Karabuğa & İlin (2019)

In-service (tertiary level)	Lesson study as PD model (including observations, reflective reports, and group discussions)	To explore how teachers engage in various phases (planning, implementation, analysis, and reporting) of lesson study, and how it affects their PD	Bayram & Bıkmaz (2021)
In-service (tertiary level)	A reflective PD program to integrate technology into practices through evidence-based multimodal reflective practices (including self/peer reflection and group discussions)	To investigate how engaging in an evidence-based multi-modal reflective practice changes teachers' integration of technology into their lessons and their reflective practices	Kaya & Adıgüzel (2021)
In-service (tertiary level)	Lesson study as a PD model (including audio-diaries and group discussions on lesson study cycles)	To investigate how lesson study as a PD model yields reflective practices, and how teachers transform their practices through reflection	Uştuk & De Costa (2021)

Two other studies included online collaborative reflection (Burhan Horasanlı & Ortaçtepe, 2016; Kaya & Adıgüzel, 2021). Burhan Horasanlı & Ortaçtepe (2016) designed an online PD program for nine tertiary-level EFL teachers taking a graduate course on an EFL master's program. The teachers wrote self-reflections on assigned topics by considering their teaching experiences and beliefs in addition to interactive peer reflections on what the others wrote through an online platform. This study revealed that the teachers successfully made use of reflection in, on, and for action through the collaborative online discussions. Likewise, Kaya & Adıgüzel (2021) made use of an online PD program involving training on evidence-based multimodal reflection tools, self/peer reflection, and group discussions. Having learned and utilized these evidence-based multimodal reflection tools, followed by collaborative reflections on their practices and views, the participant teachers reported a positive change in their practices and views regarding technology integration and evidence-based multimodal reflective practice.

Another study including the analysis of an existing PD model that involves peer reflection based on observations was conducted by Tomak & Karaman (2013). This study intended to identify the efficiency of an existing PD program designed for the collaboration of experienced teachers and novice teachers in order to familiarize them with the preparatory school. Even though both experienced and novice teachers stated that they benefited from this program, they also reported that it did not meet their expectations due to lack of observations and comprehensive reflective practices in recorded lessons.

As for the studies on the implementation of LS at the tertiary level, Karabuğa & İlin (2019) conducted a study including reflective group discussions. The results show that even though the participants found it demanding because of the amount of time and effort they had to spend and the difficulty of reflecting on peers, they stated that LS made prominent contributions to their knowledge, practices, beliefs, and professional growth in the end. Likewise, to explore how teachers experience LS stages (planning, implementation, analysis, and reporting) and how it affects their professional development, Bayram & Bıkmaz (2021) conducted a study with four experienced EFL teachers. The findings revealed that the teachers had difficulty in finding a topic, designing a lesson, and researching stages. Nonetheless, they also reported that taking part in LS collaboratively led to a substantial increase in their teacher knowledge, collaboration, and researching skills. Also, the study by Uştuk & De Costa, (2021) investigated how four experienced EFL teachers benefited from LS and transformed their practices through reflection. LS practices of teachers accompanied by audio-diaries kept for reflective thinking and collaborative discussions as a group revealed that reflective practices played a major role in the LS process, and this paved the way for both individual and collaborative reflective practices. Reflective practices performed in the LS also supported the transformative agency of the teachers by fostering their empowerment and leading to reflection-as-action, which is described as a more holistic perspective viewing reflection as an action itself in a systematic way.

The final PD model implanted at the tertiary level is CFG. Günbay & Mede (2017) formed a CFG and analysed how eight experienced EFL teachers collaborated and worked on a particular issue: the use of authentic materials in class and what they thought about the use of these materials in class. Using reflective journals and group discussions in CFG, the study shows that CFG improves teachers' instructional practices, collaboration among colleagues, and student participation in the class. Similarly, Aktekin (2019) designed a CFG model for six EFL teachers, exploring how a CFG, including reflection tools such as journals and group discussions, makes an impact on teachers' collaborative professional development. The results show that CFG fosters their professional development, and helps teachers build better relationships through collaboration and improve classroom practices by collaboratively focusing on instructional problems.

Compared to the tertiary level, the number of studies on CRP is relatively limited for EFL teachers working at the secondary and primary levels in Turkey (Table 1.4). For instance, at the secondary level, Songül et al. (2018) formed an online community of practice whose members conducted a lesson study including observations and reflective group discussions. This collaborative PD practice helped teachers to go through cognitive change regarding their knowledge base for technology and instructional strategies, reflection and evaluation skills, and language proficiency. With a similar target group, Bintaş & Dikilitaş (2019) designed a CFG model requiring reflective practices such as reflective journals and group discussions. Collaborative reflection in CFG promoted teacher learning, which enhanced their instructional practices and relatedly student learning in the class. As for the only study at the primary level, Kırkgöz (2013) conducted a collaborative action research project including weekly collaborative meetings with six novice EFL teachers. The findings show that the action research process and collaborative reflection promote teachers' professional growth and enhance their understanding of the new concepts, which in return leads to instructional changes in the class. Yet, the teachers reported some challenges such as trust issues at the initial stage of the study, procedural challenges about the action research process, and critical reflection practices.

Table 1.4. Summary of the CRP studies in in-service education (secondary and primary level).

Target Group	Means of Reflection	Purpose	Authors
In-service (secondary level)	An online professional learning community conducting lesson study as a PD model (including reflective discussions, observations, and webinars)	To investigate how an online lesson study program requiring working collaboratively and reflectively contributes to the professional development of teachers	Songül et al. (2018)
In-service (secondary level)	Critical friends groups as a PD model (including teacher learning through reflective practices based on group discussions and reflective essays)	To identify how engaging in a CFG promotes teacher learning and their reflective practices	Bintaş & Dikilitaş (2019)
In-service (primary level)	Collaborative action research preceded by training on action research and new curricular concepts with **novice teachers** (including collaborative meetings and reflective journals)	To investigate the role of collaborative action research in **novice teachers'** professional development and their knowledge and classroom practices in addition to the challenges the teachers face	Kırkgöz (2013)

1.4.3. Collaborative Reflective Practices by Teacher Educators in Turkey

As reflective practices in EFL teacher education cannot be confined to only pre-service and in-service teachers, we extended the scope of our research to include collaborative reflective practices conducted by teacher educators. We have identified two studies drawing attention to reflective practices of teacher educators (Table 1.5). Engin (2013) conducted a study focusing on teacher educator–pre-service teacher interactions in post-observation feedback sessions in a practicum program. In this study, Engin engaged in dialogic reflection with the teachers and critically examined his own feedback sessions as a trainer. Likewise, Aydın (2016) critically reflected on her performance as a teacher educator through keeping a reflective journal and video-recording her lessons, a process which she called 'a self-critical friendship.' Aydın (2016) revealed that engaging in this kind of reflective practice by collaborating with a self-critical friend (herself) increased her awareness and promoted her professional growth as a teacher educator.

Table 1.5. Summary of the CRP studies conducted by teacher educators.

Target Group	Means of Reflection	Purpose	Authors
Teacher educator	A reflective practice on the interactions between a teacher educator and the trainees in post-observation feedback sessions within a practicum program	To analyse which ways in trainer-trainee interaction yield better understandings for trainees, and to monitor a teacher educator's performance through reflection	Engin (2013)
Teacher educator	A 'self-critical friendship': a teacher educator's reflective practice on her own diaries and video-recorded lessons	To analyse to what extent a teacher educator's teaching practices converge with the stated personal theories transmitted to pre-service teachers, and to raise self-awareness to minimize mismatches	Aydın (2016)

1.5. DISCUSSION AND CONCLUSION

In this study, we particularly aimed to review and analyse the studies integrating collaborative reflective practices, at least as one component of the professional development program adopted by EFL teachers and teacher educators in Turkey. As a result of scrutiny and analysis of the studies, we came up with three major categories: CRPs in pre-service teacher education, CRPs in in-service teacher education, and CRPs by teacher educators. We also made use of subcategories for the first two major categories in order to gain a better understanding of the distribution of the studies in accordance with the particular model employed for the teachers. Even though the number of studies conducted within the scope of CRPs is relatively limited, the findings mainly show that PD programs involving CRPs result in professional growth and more specifically a substantial improvement in teachers' perspectives, instructional practices, and collaboration skills. Engaging in CRPs mostly paved the way for transformational changes in classroom practices, increased teacher knowledge, raised awareness for classroom actualities, and renewed teachers' perspectives towards professional development. However, it was also noted that teachers may face some challenges stemming from a lack of knowledge and training about reflective thinking and the procedural demand of the reflective tasks. In this regard, the discussion below first focuses on CRPs based on the three major categories stated above, followed by a more holistic evaluation of CRPs in Turkey from the perspective of collaborative PD and the role of reflective practices in PD.

Using a variety of PD models to enact CRP among pre-service teachers, the studies conducted with pre-service EFL teachers made substantial contributions to their professional development. Inclusion of some PD models such as lesson study (Yalçın Arslan, 2019), online community of practice (Bener & Yıldız, 2019), teacher research (Mumford & Dikilitaş, 2020), and peer practicum (Çomoğlu & Dikilitaş, 2020) can help pre-service teachers to become familiar with CPD models (Day, 1999) before they start their teaching career. Familiarizing pre-service teachers with such models may play a prominent role in encouraging them to sustain reflective practices beyond their practices (Farrell, 2019) by adopting this perspective in other aspects of their lives. Additionally, co-reflective practices occurring among peers (Kırmızı & Tosuncuoğlu, 2019; Turhan & Kırkgöz, 2021) can also be considered functional in promoting 'interthinking', which is conceptualized as a joint dialogic activity to make sense of experiences (Johnson & Golombek, 2016). Also, using the lessons video-recorded by novice teachers for practicum students (Tavil & Güngör, 2017) can serve as fruitful reflection tools to enable pre-service teachers to practice reflection at the critical level by focusing on a wider social, political, and cultural context (Day, 1993; Hatton & Smith, 1995; Valli, 1997) since the real-life teaching context may offer an opportunity to reflect on how theories are implemented in an actual case.

Even though CRPs in pre-service education yielded some benefits for pre-service teachers, the studies were mostly conducted with fourth-grade practicum students, which indicates a lack of reflective practices in pre-service education before graduation. Reflective practice and reflective thinking are not confined to reflection on particular practices since they aim to transform the routine way people think and take actions by liberating their mind (Dewey, 1933). Integration of reflective practices into pre-service education from an earlier stage might help pre-service teachers to become accustomed to making use of reflective thinking to reconstruct their theoretical knowledge and transform their practices, which is the ultimate level of the reflective framework proposed by Grimmet et al. (1990). As the studies conducted in other courses show (Güngör, 2016; Karakaş & Yükselir, 2021), earlier exposure to CRPs even in simulated teaching contexts can give rise to preparedness for actual teaching, increased awareness, and critical reflection skills, which can end up with better practicum experiences.

With regard to the studies conducted for in-service EFL teachers, most of them have been implemented at the tertiary level, the reason for which might be attributed to the fact that EFL instructors at the tertiary level have a stronger tendency to engage in research or inquiry-oriented studies since they work in a university context. Besides, having a master's degree is a prerequisite for admission to the university as an EFL instructor in Turkey. The studies reviewed demonstrate that CRPs can be delivered in a variety of forms such as online platforms (Burhan Horasanlı & Ortaçtepe, 2016; Kaya & Adıgüzel, 2021), pair reflection (Mede, 2010), action research process (Arslan & Başağa, 2010), lesson study (Bayram & Bıkmaz, 2021; Karabuğa & İlin, 2019; Uştuk & De Costa, 2021), and critical friends groups (Günbay & Mede, 2017; Aktekin, 2019). Through such PD models where 'interthinking' takes place (Johnson & Golombek, 2016), in-service teachers can experience reflective thinking more efficiently. These PD models are bound to provide an appropriate context in which teachers can employ reflective thinking by complying with the five components of Farrell's (2004) reflective practice framework. Considering these components, these PD models offer various activities for reflection, provide ground rules that maintain collaboration for reflective practices, require teachers to spend a certain amount of time on their reflection, enable teachers to benefit from external input coming from their colleagues, and help them build trust towards each other, which facilitates reflective practice by lowering anxiety (Farrell, 2004). In this sense, these kinds of process-oriented bottom-up PD models rather than product-oriented short-term PD activities (Crandall, 2000) can foster reflective thinking and collaboration by providing social mediation among peers (Johnson & Golombek, 2011).

Despite the substantial benefit of these practices at the tertiary level, it can also be seen that teachers may have difficulty in getting used to the inquiry-oriented practices to be used for reflection. The reason why teachers find this challenging might stem from the lack of research knowledge and skills which can be integrated into teacher education programs to prepare teachers for inquiry-oriented PD both theoretically and practically. We also found that the number of studies conducted for novice EFL teachers at the tertiary level is dramatically limited in Turkey although those teachers are in serious need of sustained PD due to lack of reflective practice in their pre-service education and lack of teaching experience (Farrell, 2016).

As for the studies conducted for secondary- and primary-level EFL teachers, using an online professional learning community (Songül et al., 2018), CFG (Bintaş & Dikilitaş, 2019), and collaborative action research with novice teachers (Kırkgöz, 2013) reveals that these PD models foster both collaboration and reflective practice. However, these studies also reveal that teachers have challenges concerning research procedures, trust issues, and critical reflection practices (Kırkgöz, 2013), which again pinpoints the need for theoretical and practical preparation towards reflection on the part of teachers (Farrell, 2019).

The reviewed studies including EFL teacher educators in Turkey make it clear that there are few attempts by teacher educators to reflect on their practices either individually or collaboratively. While Engin (2013) analysed trainer–trainee interactions from a sociocultural perspective to identify scaffolding levels, Aydın (2016) employed the concept of self-critical friendship to shed light on her practices. However, these studies lack collaboration with colleagues which might function as a meditation space for triggering reflective practices of dialogic nature within a group (Farrell, 2018). As teacher educators play a substantial role in determining teacher education practices, they can collaboratively work in communities of practice to improve their own practices and also cooperate with school teachers and pre-service teachers through partnerships based on collaborative teacher research practices, as suggested by Menter & Flores (2021).

All in all, the reviewed studies concerning CRPs in EFL teacher education in Turkey reveal that reflective practice carried out in collaboration with others gives rise to teacher professional growth, positive transformation of beliefs and practices, and better reflection and collaboration skills. However, CRPs require a more holistic perspective that puts the teacher into the focus as a person, together with non-cognitive aspects of teaching and learning such as emotions and feelings (Farrell, 2015). A holistic framework including five levels: teachers' philosophy (self-knowledge of the teacher as a person), principles (beliefs about teaching), theory (constructing theory of practice), practice (implementation of the theory and reflection on it before, during, and after the practice), and beyond practice (critical reflection on the effects of larger social, political, and cultural factors on practices) is needed (Farrell, 2015). We can basically infer from the studies in Turkey that CRPs encourage reflection at the principles, theory, and practice levels; nevertheless, it is hard to say that such practices include philosophy and beyond practice levels. Integrating the philosophy level can induce more in-depth reflection on the teacher as a person and enable teachers to critically reflect on how their personal histories impact their teaching (Farrell, 2015). Likewise, critically reflecting on practices from the beyond practice level can increase teachers' awareness about how macro-level social, political, and cultural factors influence their teaching and learning practices (Farrell, 2015), which might result in transformational changes in beliefs and practices in the long run.

Considering the six principles of reflective practices put forward by Farrell (2019), the studies in Turkey mostly encompass four of these principles: evidence-based reflection, dialogic collaborative reflection, integration of principles and practices, and an inquiring disposition. However, the first principle and the final principle seem to be missing. Thus, offering more space where teachers can reflect on their inner worlds in relation to their profession can yield a broader perspective to identify the associations between personal life and teaching career. To provide such a space for transformation, several PD models such as lesson study (Lewis & Hurd, 2011), teacher study groups (Francis et al., 1994), and collaborative action research (Burns, 1999; Dikilitaş & Griffiths, 2017) can be utilized. Even though LS, TSG, and similar communities of practices such as CFG and PLC studies have been conducted for professional development of teachers in Turkey, there is an obvious need for CAR studies since engaging in action research collaboratively enables teachers to transform their formal individual thinking (Burns, 1999). Additionally, lack of follow-up studies in Turkey raises the question that CRPs might not have ended up with a new way of thinking that can be sustained throughout life. Whether engaging in CRPs has transformed teachers' perspectives towards PD and their instructional practices in the long term is not explicitly explored. Hence, there is a need for follow-up studies to investigate whether these PD practices have lifelong effects on teachers and to ensure that these activities have not turned into traditional one-shot seminars.

To conclude, considering the drawbacks of traditional PD practices based on top-down policies and one-shot seminars that were mostly irrelevant to teacher needs, there have been substantial attempts to transform EFL teacher education in Turkey through collaborative PD models promoting collaboration among peers/colleagues, collaborative reflection, inquiry-oriented practices, and reflective practices. These attempts evidently have given rise to increased awareness and improved practices for teachers; however, there are still some steps to be taken to broaden the scope of collaborative reflective practices efficiently. In this regard, pre-service teachers should be offered more CRPs not only in the practicum but throughout their pre-service education. There is also a need for more CRPs for novice teachers teaching at all levels, including secondary- and primary-level teachers. This is necessary in order to familiarize them with collaborative reflection and explore how they benefit from these practices. Finally, considering the limited number of studies addressing teacher educators who have prominent roles in both pre-service and in-service teacher education, it is essential that they make use of CRPs to monitor and evaluate their practices to increase the quality of teacher education they frame and implement.

Reflective Break

- How do you think pre-service education courses before the practicum could offer collaborative reflective practices for prospective teachers?
- In what ways do you think you collaborate with your colleagues and/or students?

REFERENCES

Aktekin, N. C. (2019). Critical friends group (CFG): Inquiry-based professional development model for Turkish EFL teachers. *Eurasian Journal of Educational Research, 19*(81), 1–20. https://doi.org/10.14689/ejer.2019.81.1

Arslan, R. Ş., & Başağa, N. (2010). A study in the dissemination of reflective practice among English language instructors at tertiary level. *Pamukkale Üniversitesi Eğitim Fakültesi Dergisi (Pamukkale University Faculty of Education Journal), 28*, 11–26.

Aydın, B. (2016). Self-critical friendship: A self-study of a pre-service English language teacher trainer in Turkey. *Eğitimde Kuram ve Uygulama (Journal of Theory and Practice in Education), 12*(4), 962–978.

Bayram, İ., & Bıkmaz, F. (2021). Implications of lesson study for tertiary-level EFL teachers' professional development: A case study from Turkey. *SAGE Open, 11*(2), 1–15. https://doi.org/10.1177/21582440211023771

Bener, E., & Yıldız, S. (2019). The use of blog activities to promote reflection in an ELT practicum. *Australian Journal of Teacher Education (Online), 44*(8), 38–56. https://doi.org/10.14221/ajte.2019v44n8.3

Bintaş, K., & Dikilitaş, K. (2019). Critical friends group and its impact on teachers and he learning process. In D. Polly, C. Martin, & K. Dikilitaş (Eds.), *Handbook of research on educator preparation and professional learning* (pp. 281–304). IGI Global. https://doi.org/10.4018/978-1-5225-8583-1.ch016

Braun, V., & Clarke, V. (2006). Using thematic analysis in psychology. *Qualitative Research in Psychology, 3*(2), 77–101. https://doi.org/10.1191/1478088706qp063oa

Burhan Horasanlı, E., & Ortaçtepe, D. (2016). Reflective practice-oriented online discussions: A study on EFL teachers' reflection on, in and for-action. *Teaching and Teacher Education, 59*, 372–382. https://doi.org/10.1016/j.tate.2016.07.002

Burns, A. (1999). *Collaborative action research for English language teachers*. Cambridge University Press.

Chong, S. W. (2019). A systematic review of written corrective feedback research in ESL/EFL contexts. *Language Education & Assessment*, *2*(2), 70–95. https://doi.org/10.29140/lea.v2n2.138

Clarà, M. (2015). What is reflection? Looking for clarity in an ambiguous notion. *Journal of Teacher Education*, *66*(3), 261–271. https://doi.org/10.1177/0022487114552028

Çomoğlu, İ., & Dikilitaş, K. (2020). Learning to become an English language teacher: Navigating the self through peer practicum. *Australian Journal of Teacher Education*, *45*(8), 23–40. http://dx.doi.org/10.14221/ajte.2020v45n8.2

Crandall, J. (2000). Language teacher education. *Annual Review of Applied Linguistics*, *20*, 34–55. https://doi.org/10.1017/S0267190500200032

Day, C. (1993). Reflection: A necessary but not sufficient condition for professional development. *British Educational Research Journal*, *19*(1), 83–93. https://doi.org/10.1080/0141192930190107

Day, C. (1999). *Developing teachers: The challenges of lifelong learning*. Falmer Press.

Dewey, J. (1933). *How we think: A restatement of the relation of reflective thinking to the educative process*. DC Heath and Company.

Dikilitaş, K., & Griffiths, C. (2017). *Developing language teacher autonomy through action research*. Springer. https://doi.org/10.1007/978-3-319-50739-2

Elliott, J. C. (2017). The evolution from traditional to online professional development: A review. *Journal of Digital Learning in Teacher Education*, *33*(3), 114–125. https://doi.org/10.1080/21532974.2017.1305304

Engin, M. (2013). Trainer talk: Levels of intervention. *ELT Journal*, *67*(1), 11–19. https://doi.org/10.1093/elt/ccs048

Evans, L. (2019). Implicit and informal professional development: What it 'looks like', how it occurs, and why we need to research it. *Professional Development in Education*, *45*(1), 3–16. https://doi.org/10.1080/19415257.2018.1441172

Farrell, T. S. C. (2004). *Reflective practice in action: 80 reflection breaks for busy teachers*. Corwin Press.

Farrell, T. S. C. (2012). Reflecting on reflective practice: (Re)Visiting Dewey and Schön. *TESOL Journal*, *3*(1), 7–16. https://doi.org/10.1002/tesj.10

Farrell, T. S. C. (2015). *Promoting teacher reflection in second language education: A framework for TESOL professionals*. Routledge. https://doi.org/10.4324/9781315775401

Farrell, T. S. C. (2016). TESOL, a profession that eats its young! The importance of reflective practice in language teacher education. *Iranian Journal of Language Teaching Research*, *4*(3), 97–107.

Farrell, T. S. C. (2018). *Research on reflective practice in TESOL*. Routledge. https://doi.org/10.4324/9781315206332

Farrell, T. S. C. (2019). *Reflective practice in ELT*. Equinox Publishing. https://doi.org/10.4324/9781315659824-5

Fiszer, E. P. (2004). *How teachers learn best: An ongoing professional development model*. Scarecrow Education.

Francis, S., Hirsh, S., & Rowland, E. (1994). Improving school culture through study groups. *Journal of Staff Development, 15*, 36–39.

Freeman, D. (1989). Teacher training, development, and decision making: A model and related strategies for language teacher education. *TESOL Quarterly, 23*(1), 27–45. https://doi.org/10.2307/3587506

Greene, H. C., & Magliaro, S. G. (2004). A computer-mediated community of learners in teacher education. In C. Vrasidas & G. V. Glass (Eds.), *Current perspectives on applied information technologies* (pp. 51–67). Information Age Publishing.

Grimmett, P. P., MacKinnon, A. M., Erickson, G. L., & Riecken, T. J. (1990). Reflective practice in teacher education. In R. T. Clift, W. R. Houston, & M. C. Pugach (Eds.), *Encouraging reflective practice in education: An analysis and issues of programs* (pp. 20–38). Teachers College Press.

Günbay, E. B., & Mede, E. (2017). Implementing authentic materials through critical friends group (CFG): A case from Turkey. *The Qualitative Report, 22*(11), 3055–3075. https://doi.org/10.46743/2160-3715/2017.2744

Güngör, M. N. (2016). Turkish pre-service teachers' reflective practices in teaching English to young learners. *Australian Journal of Teacher Education, 41*(2), 137–151. http://dx.doi.org/10.14221/ajte.2016v41n2.9

Hatton, N., & Smith, D. (1995). Reflection in teacher education: Towards definition and implementation. *Teaching and Teacher Education, 11*(1), 33–49. https://doi.org/10.1016/0742-051X(94)00012-U

Hernández-Ramos, P. (2004). Web logs and online discussions as tools to promote reflective practice. *The Journal of Interactive Online Learning, 3*(1), 1–16.

Jay, J. K., & Johnson K. L. (2002). Capturing complexity: A typology of reflective practice for teacher education. *Teaching and Teacher Education, 18*(1), 73–85. https://doi.org/10.1016/S0742-051X(01)00051-8

Johnson, K. E. (2006). The sociocultural turn and its challenges for second language teacher education. *TESOL Quarterly, 40*(1), 235–257. https://doi.org/10.2307/40264518

Johnson, K. E., & Golombek, P. R. (2011). *Research on second language teacher education: A sociocultural perspective on professional development.* Routledge.

Johnson, K. E., & Golombek, P. R. (2016). *Mindful L2 teacher education: A sociocultural perspective on cultivating teachers' professional development.* Routledge. https://doi.org/10.4324/9781315641447

Joyce, B., & Showers, B. (2002). *Student achievement through staff development.* Association for Supervision and Curriculum Development.

Karabuğa, F., & İlin, G. (2019). Practicing lesson study in a Turkish education context: Considering the challenges, suggestions, and benefits from EFL teachers' perspectives. *International Journal for Lesson and Learning Studies, 8*(1), 60–78. https://doi.org/10.1108/IJLLS-05-2018-0036

Karakaş, A., & Yükselir, C. (2021). Engaging pre-service EFL teachers in reflection through video-mediated team micro-teaching and guided discussions. *Reflective Practice, 22*(2), 159–172. https://doi.org/10.1080/14623943.2020.1860927

Kaya, M. H., & Adıgüzel, T. (2021). Technology integration through evidence-based multimodal reflective professional training. *Contemporary Educational Technology, 13*(4), ep323. https://doi.org/10.30935/cedtech/11143

Killion, J., & Todnem, G. (1991). A process for personal theory building. *Educational Leadership, 48*(7), 14–16.

Kırkgöz, Y. (2013). A school-university collaborative action research teacher development programme: A case of six Turkish novice teachers of English. *Asian EFL Journal, 71*, 3–56.

Kırmızı, Ö., & Tosuncuoğlu, I. (2019). Becoming reflective practitioners: A case study of four beginning pre-service EFL teachers in Turkey. *English Language Teaching, 12*(4), 127–138. https://doi.org/10.5539/elt.v12n4p127

Kraft, N. P. (2002). Teacher research as a way to engage in critical reflection: A case study. *Reflective Practice, 3*(2), 175–189. https://doi.org/10.1080/14623940220142325

Kumaravadivelu. B. (2001). Toward a post-method pedagogy. *TESOL Quarterly, 35*(4), 537–560. https://doi.org/10.2307/3588427

Lewis, C., & Hurd, J. (2011). *Lesson study step by step: How teacher learning communities improve instruction*. Heinemann.

Loh, J., Hong, H., & Koh, E. (2017). Transforming teaching through collaborative reflection: A Singaporean case study. *Malaysian Journal of ELT Research, 13*(1), 1–11.

Mann, S., & Walsh, S. (2017). *Reflective practice in English language teaching: Research-based principles and practices*. Routledge. https://doi.org/10.4324/9781315733395

Mede, E. (2010). The effects of collaborative reflection on EFL teaching. *Procedia – Social and Behavioral Sciences, 2*(2), 3888–3891. https://doi.org/10.1016/j.sbspro.2010.03.610

Menter, I., & Flores, M. A. (2021). Connecting research and professionalism in teacher education. *European Journal of Teacher Education, 44*(1), 115–127. https://doi.org/10.1080/02619768.2020.1856811

Moon, J. A. (2013). *A Handbook of reflective and experiential learning: Theory and practice*. Routledge. https://doi.org/10.4324/9780203416150

Mumford, S., & Dikilitaş, K. (2020). Pre-service language teachers reflection development through online interaction in a hybrid learning course. *Computers & Education, 144*, 103706. https://doi.org/10.1016/j.compedu.2019.103706

Murphy, J. M. (2014). Reflective teaching: Principles and practices. In M. Celce-Murcia, D. M. Brinton, & M. A. Snow (Eds.), *Teaching English as a second or foreign language*, 4th ed. (pp. 613–628). National Geographic Learning.

Murray, A. (2010). Empowering teachers through professional development. *English Teaching Forum, 48*(1), 2–11.

Murray, E. (2015). Improving teaching through collaborative reflective teaching cycles. *Investigations in Mathematics Learning, 7*(3), 23–29. https://doi.org/10.1080/24727466.2015.11790343

Nye, E., Melendez-Torres, G. J., & Bonell, C. (2016). Origins, methods and advances in qualitative meta-synthesis. *Review of Education, 4*(1), 57–79. https://doi.org/10.1002/rev3.3065

Parsons, M., & Stephenson, M. (2005). Developing reflective practice in student teachers: Collaboration and critical partnerships. *Teachers and Teaching: Theory and Practice, 11*(1), 95–116. https://doi.org/10.1080/1354060042000337110

Schön, D. (1983), *The reflective practitioner: How professionals think in action*. Temple Smith.

Songül, B. C., Delialioğlu, Ö., & Özköse Bıyık, Ç. (2018). An investigation of Turkish EFL teachers' development through an online professional development program. In J. C. Yang, M. Chang, L. H. Wong, & M. M. T. Rodrigo (Eds.), *Proceedings of the 26th International Conference on Computers in Education* (pp. 647–656). Asia-Pacific Society for Computers in Education, Manila.

Tanış, A., & Dikilitaş, K. (2018). Turkish EFL ınstructors' engagement in professional development. *Eurasian Journal of Applied Linguistics, 4*(1), 27–47. https://doi.org/10.32601/ejal.460628

Tavil, Z. M., & Güngör, M. N. (2017). A sociocultural perspective on the development of Turkish pre-service teachers' competences and qualifications. *Pedagogy, Culture & Society, 25*(2), 263–277. http://dx.doi.org/10.1080/14681366.2016.1252788

Tomak, B., & Karaman, A. C. (2013). Mentoring in a professional development program for novice teachers at a state university in Turkey: A qualitative inquiry. *The International Journal of Research in Teacher Education, 4*(2), 1–13.

Turhan, B., & Kırkgöz, Y. (2021). A critical and collaborative stance towards retrospective reflection in language teacher education. *European Journal of Teacher Education*, 1–19. https://doi.org/10.1080/02619768.2021.1917545

Uştuk, Ö., & De Costa, P. I. (2021). Reflection as meta-action: Lesson study and EFL teacher professional development. *TESOL Journal, 12*(1), e00531. https://doi.org/10.1002/tesj.531

Valli, L. (1997). Listening to other voices: A description of teacher reflection in the United States. *Peabody Journal of Education, 72*(1), 67–88. https://doi.org/10.1207/s15327930pje7201_4

Van Gyn, G. H. (1996). Reflective practice: The needs of professions and the promise of cooperative education. *Journal of Cooperative Education, 31*, 103–131.

Vangrieken, K., Meredith, C., Packer, T., & Kyndt, E. (2017). Teacher communities as a context for professional development: A systematic review. *Teaching and Teacher Education, 61*, 47–59. https://doi.org/10.1016/j.tate.2016.10.001

Wallace, M. (1996). Structured reflection: The role of the professional project in training ESL teachers. In D. Freeman & J. C. Richards (Eds.), *Teacher learning in language teaching* (pp. 281–294). Cambridge University Press.

Yalçın Arslan, F. (2019). The role of lesson study in teacher learning and professional development of EFL teachers in Turkey: A case study. *TESOL Journal, 10*(2), e00409. https://doi.org/10.1002/tesj.409

Zepeda, S. J. (2012). *Professional development: What works*, 2nd ed. Routledge.

ABOUT THE AUTHORS

Serhat Başar works as an English lecturer at the İzmir Institute of Technology, Turkey. He completed his undergraduate and MA programs in the Foreign Language Education Department of Boğaziçi University, and is a PhD candidate in the English Language Teaching Department of Dokuz Eylül University, İzmir. His fields of interest include language teacher cognition, teacher education, and professional development of EFL teachers.

Esat Kuzu is a research assistant and PhD student in the ELT Department of Dokuz Eylül University, İzmir, Turkey. He completed his undergraduate program in the Foreign Language Education Department of Boğaziçi University and his MA in the ELT Department of Çukurova University. He is interested in research on program evaluation, ecological literacy, and professional development of EFL teachers.

İrem Çomoğlu is an Associate Professor at Dokuz Eylül University, Faculty of Education, English Language Teaching Department, Izmir, Turkey. She has published widely in national and international journals and books. Her research focuses on teacher learning and development in TESOL and teacher research mainly from a qualitative research paradigm.

Chapter 2

Pre-Service EFL Teachers' Reflective Thinking Levels and Cognitive Presence in Online Learning Settings: A Correlational Study

Ceyhun Yükselir & Saadet Korucu-Kış

2.1. INTRODUCTION

Preparing would-be teachers to become reflective practitioners is contingent upon cultivating reflective mindsets in them. The growth of reflective mindsets, in parallel, relies on equipping candidate teachers with inquiring dispositions (Farrell, 2019). In this regard, initial teacher education programs occupy a critical role in training teachers willing to question their learning processes and practices. To become reflective practitioners and reflective thinkers in teacher education programs, teacher candidates need to possess the disposition for reflection and decision-making to have more effective classes (Cochran-Smith & Villegas, 2015; Parsons & Brown, 2002; Zeichner & Liston, 2013). In the literature, there are numerous studies attempting to define the main characteristics of the teaching disposition. Most of these studies (e.g., Peterson, 2016; Schulte & Edwards, 2008) devote attention to the necessary steps to make teaching effective, such as developing mindfulness, understanding values/behaviors, and having the temperament to improve the quality of teaching, all of which are closely associated with the construct of reflective thinking.

In today's ever-technologizing world, cognitive presence is proposed as a means to foster reflective thinking in pre-service teachers in online learning environments. Defined as 'the extent to which learners are able to construct and confirm meaning through sustained reflection and discourse in a critical community of inquiry' (Garrison et al., 2001, p. 11), cognitive presence is concerned with thinking processes and aims to foster higher-level thinking skills such as reflection and critical inquiry (Sadaf & Olesova, 2017). According to Garrison (2003), the promotion of cognitive presence in asynchronous online learning environments is possible through attending to aspects supportive of higher-order learning skills together with collaboration and reflection.

Garrison (2016) states that 'a community of learners is composed of participants who assume the roles of both teacher and learner while engaging in discourse with the specific purposes of facilitating inquiry, constructing meaning, and validating understanding that in turn metacognitively develop the ability and predisposition for further learning' (p. 23). According to Yang (2009), a community of practice has an ability to form a platform to share and exchange knowledge and find new information based on personal needs, thereby enabling learners to take responsibility in the community and deal with problems. Garrison (2016) states that cognitive presence, which is created through communication, collaboration, and discussion in a community, is linked with critical thinking and it is based on the reflective thinking/inquiry model (consisting of the stages of pre-reflection, reflection, and post-reflection) formulated by Dewey (1933). In a similar vein, Guthrie (2010) states that cognitive presence offers 'a comprehensive framework that reinforces the development of critical thinking skills within a context of reflective pedagogies' (p. 5). Garrison et al. (2000) also mention that 'cognitive presence is a vital element in critical thinking, a process and outcome that is frequently presented as the ostensible goal of all higher education' (p. 89). From all these perspectives, the achievement of cognitive outcomes, that is cognitive presence, and the meaningful learning process are the ultimate goals of a community of inquiry (Vaughan & Garrison, 2005). In this chapter, we therefore focus on the interplay between pre-service EFL teachers' reflective inquiry skills on cognitive presence rather than social presence and teaching presence, as Redmond (2014) states that 'reflection is a key concept which cognitive presence originates' (p. 50).

Reflective thinking and critical thinking can be conceptualized to foster higher-order learning skills in academic settings and there is agreement among scholars that thinking level is an influential element to engage learners in problem-solving, decision-making, questioning, and identifying their strengths and weaknesses especially in higher education contexts (Choy & Cheah, 2009; Ersözlü & Arslan, 2009; Facione & Facione, 1996). Based on the tenets of self-monitoring and self-awareness, a fundamental prerequisite for providing higher-order thinking skills to equip learners with cognitive skills is to be connected with critical thinking and reflective thinking; that is, if learners develop certain reflective abilities, they can be proactive to monitor and self-regulate their own learning (Elder & Richard, 2004; Ghanizadeh, 2011, 2017). Taken from this stance, assessing cognitive presence with reflective thinking skills in practical inquiry focuses on higher-order learning skills rather than personalized learning outcomes (Garrison et al., 2001).

Although it is not standard practice in teacher education programs in Turkey (Tezgiden Cakcak, 2015), a number of studies have been conducted to promote the adoption of reflective practice due to its promising potential in enhancing instructional practices. These studies investigated reflective practice-oriented discussions in terms of reflection types (Burhan-Horasanlı & Ortaçtepe, 2016), reflective practice tools (Unlu & Kulekci, 2020), opportunities and challenges of reflective practice (Korucu-Kis & Kartal, 2019), implications of graduate research on reflective practices in ELT programs (Korucu-Kis & Demir, 2019), video-mediated micro-teaching to promote reflection (Eröz-Tuğa, 2013; Karakaş & Yükselir, 2021; Yeşilbursa, 2011), the quality of self-reflection through reflection training (Gün, 2011), reflective practices in teaching English to young learners through micro-teaching sessions (Güngör, 2016), and the characteristics of critical reflections of English language teacher candidates (Turhan & Kirkgoz, 2018). All of these studies aimed to train teacher candidates to become reflective practitioners and were conducted in face-to-face classrooms.

However, online learning is becoming increasingly prevalent in higher education contexts due to the opportunities created by digital technologies. Attempts to develop reflective habits of mind in teacher candidates should be maintained in these unique environments as well. The extant literature (Boulton & Hramiak, 2012; Galikyan & Admiraal, 2019; Shea & Bidjerano, 2009) hypothesizes that one of the ways to develop reflective mindsets in pre-service teachers in online settings is to engage them in activities that will foster cognitive presence in online learning experiences. Considering that no previous study has investigated reflective thinking levels and cognitive presence of EFL pre-service teachers in online learning settings in Turkey and there is no statistically based study investigating the hypothesized relationship between reflective thinking levels and cognitive presence, this study aims to fill these gaps by responding to the following research questions:

1. What is the level of reflective thinking among pre-service EFL teachers in online learning environments?
2. What level of cognitive presence do pre-service EFL teachers report regarding their online learning experiences?
3. How do pre-service EFL teachers' reflective thinking levels and cognitive presence correlate?

2.2. LITERATURE REVIEW

2.2.1. Reflective Thinking

Reflective practice is an intentional and systematic inquiry on the actions focusing on intelligence and rational deeds rather than routine thoughts, which Dewey (1933) called reflective inquiry. Viewing reflective practice as a rigorous and disciplined activity, Farrell (2019) states that Dewey's work is an attempt to cultivate a 'thinking citizenry' in a developed society focusing on intellectual and rational actions/practices. In this context, Grayling (2002) stated that 'the best thing any education can bequeath is the habit of reflection and questioning' (p. 179). According to Farrell (2015), reflection in teaching environments means for teachers to engage in their beliefs and practices with a critical eye. Looking retrospectively and taking the theoretical consideration about reflections into account in the field of teacher education and language teaching/learning, most scholars refer to John Dewey (1933) and Donald Schön (1983), two distinguished researchers studying similar concepts of reflective thinking. However, Fendler (2003) regards the definitions proposed by the two distinguished scholars as contradictory. He states that, while Dewey's approach to reflection is more rational and works in proximity of professionalism, Schön's tendency is intuitive and personal which focuses on teaching experience practice. Thus, reflective thinking has become quite common and apparent in both general education and the TESOL field. In order to understand reflective thinking and inquiry better, it would be necessary to examine the frameworks adapted by pioneering figures (Dewey, 1933; Schön, 1983; Freire, 1970) in reflective inquiry. For example, Dewey (1933) regards reflective inquiry as thinking, Schön (1983) as a way of knowing, and Freire (1970) as critical consciousness in political, social, and cultural contexts. From this argument, it seems that the implementations and understandings of RP and inquiry differ from each other theoretically in the literature, which can sometimes create confusion and ambiguity, but show their dynamic features as well in education.

As mentioned above, reflective thinking practice in the field of education is mostly based on the studies of Dewey (1933) and Schön (1983). Reflective thinking can be considered as an assessment of the outcome or consequences of actions in achieving a task, during the task or after its completion. It can also be deemed as directing one's own future actions in academic performance through questioning and critical thinking. Based on the theoretical ideas of Mezirow (1998), reflective thinking can be divided into four phases: habitual action, understanding, reflection, and critical reflection (Leung & Kember, 2003). Habitual action, which Schön (1983) called *knowing-in-action*, is an activity that can be managed through little conscious thought, and it mostly emerges as a result of frequent repetition. The second phase, understanding, means achieving learning with existing knowledge and meaning. Dewey (1933) regarded the reflection phase as the leading and prominent step in reflective thinking, which engages in learning experiences, assumptions, and appreciations in our mindsets and intellectual activities. The last phase, critical thinking, is concerned with higher-order learning skills, making us aware of the learning settings in which we perceive all possibilities such as what we feel, act, and do. This leads us into developing a deep learning approach for academic performance, including a change or transformation in personal beliefs and ideas and what we do in our teaching practice (Farrell, 2015; Kember et al., 2000; Mezirow, 1998; Phan, 2008, 2009). In the previous literature, there are certain studies (Afshar & Rahimi, 2016; Ersözlü & Arslan, 2009; Ghanizadeh, 2017; Phan, 2009) that focus on learners' academic success and metacognition abilities positively in view of the role of reflective thinking skills.

In the teacher education context, Walsh & Mann (2015) conducted a study to promote data-led and evidence-based reflection. They argue that although reflective thinking has been evident in each area of the educational field for a long time, there are not concrete instances and implementations to figure out how reflection creates a knowledge base for the researchers and practitioners. In another study, Mann & Walsh (2013) state that reflection has a considerable place in professional education; however it is 'not sufficiently data-led; too often presented as an individual process which fails to value collaboration or participation in a community of practice; dominated by written forms of reflection at the expense of potentially more beneficial spoken forms and insufficiently detailed about the nature of reflective tools' (p. 293). Farrell (2015, 2019) also points out that teachers are encouraged to make use of data to reveal informed decisions about their practice, rather than carry out instructional and routine actions in an evidence-based approach to reflective practices through gathering data from different sources.

With respect to the development of a reflective disposition, Dewey (1933) suggests the possession of three sets of attitudes by practitioners. These characteristics in reflective inquiry are called *open-mindedness* (being free from biased thoughts), *wholeheartedness* (taking a wholehearted attitude to a project/idea), and *responsibility* (taking responsibility for the consequences). Later, Dewey added a fourth disposition, *directness* (faith and belief in human action) to engage practitioners in thinking and inquiry (Lyons, 2010). According to Farrell (2019), these three reflective dispositions/attitudes have a considerable role in promoting teachers' informed decisions and thereby making them effective reflective practitioners in gathering data and observing their teaching and learning philosophy, theories, practices, and experiences.

2.2.2. Cognitive Presence

Computer-mediated communication (CMC), which aims at delivering educational courses through computer conferencing, has been used extensively in higher education contexts in the realm of online learning. In this regard, Garrison et al. (2000) conducted a study investigating a conceptual framework for CMC which attempts to critically inquire about computer conferencing. The researchers outlined the core elements available in the Community of Inquiry (CoI) framework, as *social presence*, *cognitive presence*, and *teaching presence*.

Several studies have been carried out to find out the effectiveness and validity of the CoI framework in online learning environments (Akyol & Garrison, 2011; Arbaugh et al., 2008; Satar & Akcan, 2018) and the results of these studies have revealed that this framework can play an effective role in promoting online teaching and learning experiences (Meyer, 2003; Pawan et al., 2003). These studies have also shown that the CoI framework provides a platform for cognitive presence to be analysed in understanding metacognitive processes. Similarly, Lipman (2003) suggests that community of inquiry is a platform in which 'students listen to one another with respect, build on one another's ideas, challenge one another to supply reasons for otherwise unsupported opinions, assist each other in drawing inferences from what has been said, and seek to identify one another's assumptions' (p. 20). From this perspective, it is clear that CoI requires learners to acquire the features of autonomous and self-regulated learning, to take action and give feedback in negotiating with peers, sharing and exchanging ideas. It is a fact that internet and computer technology have an effect on designing the academic curriculum in higher education with the help of professional development programs (Çelik, 2013). In online learning environments, the CoI framework, through supporting higher-order learning with three components (social presence, cognitive presence, and teaching presence), has shown its usefulness in encouraging quality interaction and analytical discourse, and deep learning (Garrison et al., 2001; Garrison & Cleveland-Innes, 2005; Morueta et al., 2016).

In line with this, Garrison (2016) also introduces the Practical Inquiry (PI) model, which is based on experience, in order to comprehend the tenets of cognitive presence in educational settings, consisting of four phases: *triggering*, *exploration*, *integration*, and *resolution* (see Figure 2.1). All of the phases are intertwined with each other to create engagement in PI and construct meaning, knowledge, and collaboration with others. It is worth noting that the integration and resolution phases in PI are highly reflective phases and learners become more reflective practitioners once they confront challenges (Akyol et al., 2009). Redmond (2014) states that reflection can be coded in the resolution phase as it requires higher-order learning and critical thinking skills and thus adds a reflective contribution to cognitive presence and helps researchers and educators promote reflective processes.

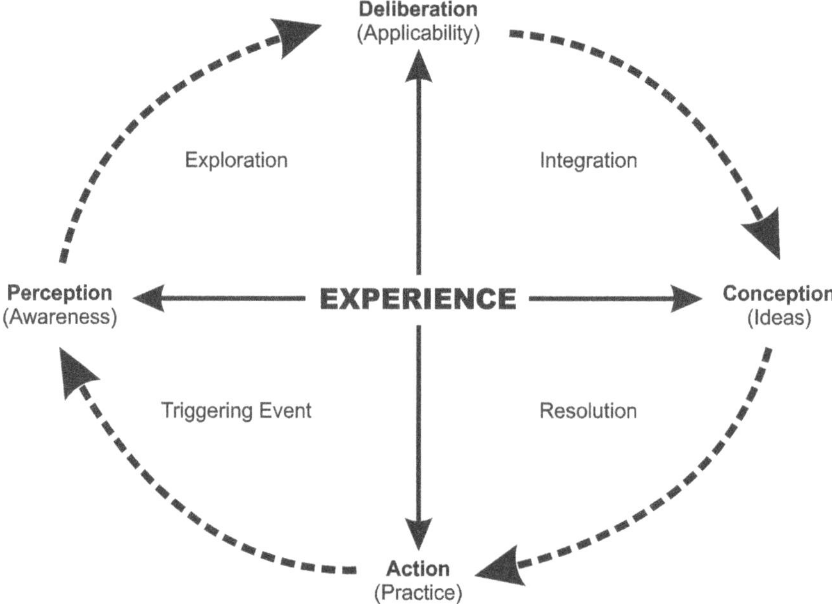

Figure 2.1. Practical Inquiry model (Garrison et al., 2000, p. 99).

In online learning settings, research has shown that the CoI framework is effective in enhancing teaching and learning experiences (Meyer, 2003; Pawan et al., 2003). To illustrate this, Kanuka & Garrison (2004) carried out a study exploring the cognitive presence in online learning to foster higher-order learning skills in using asynchronous text-based internet technology. They found that constructs such as discourse, collaboration, management, reflection, etc. are helpful to promote learning skills in online learning. In another study (Akyol & Garrison, 2011), students' level of cognitive presence in online discussions in a graduate course both in online and blended learning was found to be relatively high. On the other hand, this study also found that the resolution phase of PI was the least active phase in the same context within the blended learning due to time limitations in the courses. Sağlam et al. (2020) investigated the role of the CoI framework in online communities and found that promoting social presence enriches the effectiveness of cognitive presence in online communities, thereby fostering higher-order skills.

2.3. METHOD

Given that no study in Turkey to date has investigated reflective thinking levels and cognitive presence of EFL pre-service teachers in online learning settings, and the extant literature takes for granted that reflection promotes cognitive presence, there is a need for statistically based studies. Therefore, this study adopted a descriptive and correlational research design to investigate EFL pre-service teachers' reflective thinking levels and cognitive presence, and to provide evidence for the relationship between these two significant constructs of online learning environments. According to Creswell (2012), the explanatory form of correlational research enables one to estimate the degree of association between variables.

2.3.1. Participants and Context

This study was undertaken at a Turkish state university at the beginning of Spring 2021. Participants in the study were a convenience sample (Dörnyei, 2007) of 117 pre-service teachers in their second year of a four-year English language teaching program, who were taking their courses online due to the Covid-19 pandemic. Of the respondents, 41 were male and 76 were female. The mean age of the pre-service teachers was 21.5 years. A web-based survey consisting of a demographic section and two existing scales, namely, Questionnaire for Reflective Thinking and Community of Inquiry Index, was designed and conducted. The participants responded to the questionnaire considering their learning experiences in language acquisition (LA) courses. This course is one of the compulsory core courses that aims to help EFL pre-service teachers develop a thorough understanding of how languages are learned, and what external and internal factors influence this learning process. Pre-class reading assignments, in-class discussions, and reflections by pre-service teachers on their own language learning experiences with regard to the theories covered constitute the activities undertaken in these courses. Before the participants responded to the survey, informed consent was sought. They read an information screen briefing them about the aim of the study and assuring them about the confidentiality of the data. In cases where consent was granted, the survey proceeded.

2.3.2. Instruments

The *Questionnaire for Reflective Thinking* was originally developed by Kember et al. (2000) and adapted into Turkish by Basol & Gencel (2013). The instrument consists of 4 scales (i.e., habitual action, understanding, reflection, and critical reflection) and 16 items. It is used to measure levels of reflective thinking and rated by learners using a 5-point Likert scale. The overall alpha value for the Turkish version was found to be 0.77, which indicates a reasonable internal consistency of the instrument.

The *Community of Inquiry Index* was developed by Arbaugh et al. (2008) and adapted into Turkish by Öztürk (2012). The instrument measures three constructs: teaching presence, social presence, and cognitive presence. In line with the purposes of the study, the subscale of cognitive presence was used and rated by learners using a 5-point Likert scale. Achieving high levels of cognitive presence often constitutes the main goal of online learning environments and the subscale of cognitive presence includes 12 items measuring 'the extent to which learners are able to construct and confirm meaning through sustained reflection and discourse in a critical community of inquiry' (Garrison et al., 2001, p. 11). The internal consistency value for the subscale of cognitive presence was within the acceptable range (α=0.75).

2.3.3. Data Analysis

The data obtained from students' responses to questionnaires were analysed using SPSS 22.0 statistical software. Descriptive statistics (i.e., mean and standard deviation) were used to assess the level of reflective thinking and cognitive presence for the sample. Pearson's correlation coefficient was used to calculate the correlation between the variables. Before calculating the correlations, the normality and homoscedasticity of the data were verified using the skewness and kurtosis values and graphical analysis of residuals respectively.

2.4. FINDINGS

The research questions of the study are used to organize the study findings. Initially, descriptive statistics concerning the participants' cognitive presence and levels of reflective thinking in online learning environments are presented, and the correlation coefficient values are subsequently reported to show the association of the study variables.

Table 2.1 displays the means and standard deviations for the scale of cognitive presence. The results of descriptive analysis show that the mean and standard deviation scores for the scale of cognitive presence are 3.80 and 0.42 respectively. These findings indicate that students' level of cognitive presence is above average in online learning settings.

Table 2.1. Mean and standard deviation values for the items in the cognitive presence scale.

CP	N	x̄	SD
Problems posed increased my interest in course issues.	117	3.76	0.89
Course activities piqued my curiosity.	117	3.45	0.99
I felt motivated to explore content-related questions.	117	3.70	0.87
I utilized a variety of information sources to explore problems posed in this course.	117	4.10	0.55
Brainstorming and finding relevant information helped me resolve content-related questions.	117	4.06	0.52
Online discussions were valuable in helping me appreciate different perspectives.	117	3.68	0.83
Combining new information helped me answer questions raised in course activities.	117	3.91	0.71
Learning activities helped me construct explanations/solutions.	117	3.74	0.68
Reflection on course content and discussions helped me understand fundamental concepts in this class.	117	3.97	0.51
I can describe ways to test and apply the knowledge created in this course.	117	3.50	0.72
I have developed solutions to course problems that can be applied in practice.	117	3.63	0.75
I can apply the knowledge created in this course to my work or other non-class related activities.	117	4.07	0.67
Total		3.80	0.42

Despite a narrow range between the mean scores of the items of cognitive presence, the three most and three least agreed items among the subscales are as follows: 'I utilized a variety of information sources to explore problems posed in this course' ($\bar{x}$=4.10, SD=.55), 'I can apply the knowledge created in this course to my work or other non-class related activities' ($\bar{x}$=4.07, SD=.67), and 'Brainstorming and finding relevant information helped me resolve content related questions' ($\bar{x}$=4.06, SD=.52); 'Course activities piqued my curiosity' ($\bar{x}$=3.45, SD=.99), 'I can describe ways to test and apply the knowledge created in this course' ($\bar{x}$=3.50, SD=.72), and 'I have developed solutions to course problems that can be applied in practice' ($\bar{x}$=3.63, SD=.75). These results indicate that online learning experiences pre-service teachers engage in generate higher-level learning to a moderate degree.

As to the reflective thinking levels among pre-service teachers, the mean values for the subscales of reflective thinking range from 3.16 to 4.04 and there is a narrow range between the standard deviation scores (SD=0.46 and SD=0.71). As shown in Table 2.2, the highest scores are measured in the subscales of 'Reflection' (4.04) and 'Understanding' (3.97). The participants have the lowest scores on the measures of 'Habitual action' (3.16) and 'Critical reflection' (3.23). To give a general picture of the students' responses, the mean total of the reflective thinking scale was also calculated and found to be 3.60 with a standard deviation of 0.36. The overall scores for the scale indicate an above average reflection on online learning activities.

Table 2.2. Mean and standard deviation values of the subscales of reflective thinking levels.

	N	$\bar{x}$	SD
Habitual action	117	3.16	0.64
Understanding	117	3.97	0.47
Reflection	117	4.04	0.46
Critical reflection	117	3.23	0.71
Total reflective thinking	117	3.60	0.36

The subscales of 'Understanding' and 'Reflection' involve the most agreed items in the survey. As seen in Table 2.3, the items 'To pass this course you need to understand the content' ($\bar{x}$=4.28, SD=.76), 'This course requires us to understand concepts taught by the lecturer' ($\bar{x}$=4.23, SD=.46), and 'I sometimes question the way others do something and try to think of a better way' ($\bar{x}$=4.23, SD=.46) have the highest mean scores among others. On the other hand, the least agreed items in the survey are observed in the subscales of 'Habitual action' and 'Critical reflection'. The items 'This course has challenged some of my firmly held ideas' ($\bar{x}$=2.83, SD=1.03), 'If I follow what the lecturer says, I do not have to think too much on this course' ($\bar{x}$=2.93, SD=0.96), and 'In this course we do things so many times that I started doing them without thinking about it' ($\bar{x}$=3.16, SD=0.89) have the lowest mean scores among others. These results indicate that the experiences pre-service teachers go through in online learning settings encourage them to engage in thoughtful action and assume an inquiring disposition rather than take unconscious actions. Yet, they mostly fail in engaging pre-service teachers in transformational experiences through which they can critically review their presuppositions.

Table 2.3. Mean and standard deviation values for the items in the reflective thinking levels scale.

Habitual action	N	x̄	SD
When I am working on some activities, I can do them without thinking about what I am doing.	117	3.18	0.90
In this course we do things so many times that I started doing them without thinking about it.	117	3.16	0.89
As long as I can remember handout material for examinations, I do not have to think too much.	117	3.37	1.15
If I follow what the lecturer says, I do not have to think too much on this course.	117	2.93	0.96
Understanding			
This course requires us to understand concepts taught by the lecturer.	117	4.23	0.46
To pass this course you need to understand the content.	117	4.28	0.76
I need to understand the material taught by the teacher in order to perform practical tasks.	117	3.99	0.77
In this course you have to continually think about the material you are being taught.	117	3.38	0.90
Reflection			
I sometimes question the way others do something and try to think of a better way.	117	4.22	0.57
I like to think over what I have been doing and consider alternative ways of doing it.	117	4.08	0.62
I often reflect on my actions to see whether I could have improved on what I did.	117	4.11	0.65
I often re-appraise my experience so I can learn from it and improve for my next performance.	117	3.74	0.80
Critical reflection			
As a result of this course, I have changed the way I look at myself.	117	3.41	0.95
This course has challenged some of my firmly held ideas.	117	2.83	1.03
As a result of this course, I have changed my normal way of doing things.	117	3.34	0.91
During this course I discovered faults in what I had previously believed to be right.	117	3.34	0.92

As to the correlation between total reflective thinking and cognitive presence, a positive high correlation (r=0.608) is observed (Büyüköztürk, 2016) and the variables correlate significantly (p<.01). This means that as reflective thinking increases, so does the level of cognitive presence and vice versa. When the association between the subscales of habitual action, understanding, reflection, and critical reflection and the scale of cognitive presence is investigated, significant positive relationships can be observed between the variables, yet at differing levels. While weak correlations are identified between cognitive presence and the subscales of habitual action (r=.299, p<.01) and understanding (r=.272, p<.01), meaningful correlations (Dörnyei, 2007) exist between cognitive presence and the measures of reflection (r=.515, p<.01) and critical reflection (r=.454, p<.01).

Table 2.4. The correlation between cognitive presence and levels of reflective thinking.

	r	CP
Cognitive presence	Pearson Correlation	1
	Sig. (2-tailed)	
	N	117
Habitual action	Pearson Correlation	.299**
	Sig. (2-tailed)	.001
	N	117
Understanding	Pearson Correlation	.272**
	Sig. (2-tailed)	.003
	N	117
Reflection	Pearson Correlation	.515**
	Sig. (2-tailed)	.000
	N	117
Critical reflection	Pearson Correlation	.454**
	Sig. (2-tailed)	000
	N	117
Total reflective thinking	Pearson Correlation	.608**
	Sig. (2-tailed)	000
	N	117

Note: **Correlation is significant at the 0.01 level.

2.5. DISCUSSION AND CONCLUSION

Training reflective practitioners depends on developing pre-service EFL teachers' reflective thinking skills. The development of these skills can be made possible by including such activities as classroom action research, lesson study projects, critical networks, collaboration, peer observation, and video-based journaling in teacher education programs (Cirocki & Farrell, 2017; Widodo & Ferdiansyah, 2018). Though there have been some studies to explore if Turkish students are taking part in reflective thinking activities in face-to-face settings, there is a dearth of research investigating to what extent these skills are improved in online courses in Turkey, where online learning activities are getting more and more common. Moreover, the previous literature has suggested that using activities that promote reflective thinking in online courses will contribute to the development of cognitive presence, an indicator of whether high-level learning is achieved in online settings or not.

Language teaching activities about reflection/reflective practice should include not only systematic data-gathering but also the practice of informed decision-making. Thus, reflective dispositions including open-mindedness, responsibility, and wholeheartedness are required to engage learners in reflective activities both in and out of the classes (Farrell, 2015, 2019). It can also be suggested that considering the increased awareness and attention to studies regarding reflective practices all over the world (Farrell, 2016), online learning communities have the potential to impact teachers' continuing professional development by means of contributing to reflection (Zhang et al., 2017). In addition, bringing reflection as an indicator into cognitive presence could enlarge the scope of self-assessment of learning contributions and outcomes, especially in the higher cognitive levels of the resolution phase in online learning experiences (Redmond, 2014).

There are three main conclusions based on the findings of the study. First, the participants' cognitive presence was found to be above average (3.80). Since cognitive presence plays an active role in developing an reflective inquiring disposition in pre-service teachers, course contents should be designed to foster reflective practice including such activities as problem-solving, creating, analysing, and evaluating that stimulate higher-order thinking (for example) as well as strategies like role-play, question and answer, video-recording, digital photography (photovoice), blogging, and reflective journals (Cirocki & Farrell, 2017; Darabi et al., 2011; Farrell, 2018a; Kuswandono, 2014; Richards & Farrell, 2005). Furthermore, using online discussion questions, especially resolution questions based on the model of practical inquiry can also help learners utilize and develop cognitive presence in online learning (Sadaf & Olesova, 2017).

Second, the participants' level of reflective thinking was also found to be above average (3.60). Since training reflective practitioners depends on the development of a reflective disposition in pre-service teachers, courses in teacher education programs should involve activities of questioning, considering alternative ways to resolve issues, and thinking over past experiences to encourage reflective thinking among teacher candidates. Pre-service teachers should be assisted to become thoughtful and critical thinkers by means of scaffolding; that is to say, the comments should not be given in a direct way (Zhu, 2014). In Turkey, even though reflection is not a standard practice, many teacher educators made successful attempts at promoting the idea of reflectivity among pre-service teachers (Eröz-Tuğa, 2013; Gün, 2011; Turhan & Kirkgoz, 2018; Yesilbursa, 2011). In parallel with this, the findings of the study show that the values of habitual action and understanding were found to be low, which are on average 3.16 and 3.97, respectively. On the other hand, the values of reflection dimensions (mean=4.04) were found to be high. As mentioned earlier, critical reflection includes self-observation, self-assessment, and self-evaluation which help the reconstruction of professional knowledge in teacher education (Farrell, 2018b). However, studies conducted in the Turkish context have shown that learners cannot reach the level of critical reflection (e.g., Ayan & Seferoğlu, 2011; Yesilbursa, 2011). Even if learners achieve criticality, they seem to be lacking abstract thinking in reconstructing and reaching conclusions (Turhan & Kirkgoz, 2018), which is in line with the findings obtained from the subscale of critical reflection (mean=3.23) in the current study.

Third, a meaningful and positive relationship was found between reflective thinking and cognitive presence. Although this relationship was presented as a hypothesis in the previous literature (Leung & Kember, 2003; Mezirow, 1998; Redmond, 2014), there was no statistically based study dealing with this issue in the pre-service EFL context. Thus, the findings of this study contribute to the literature providing statistically based evidence. At the same time, developing learners' reflective disposition in online learning settings depends on the design of the course content in a way that develops learners' higher-order thinking levels. Similarly, the activities that develop reflection such as questioning, considering alternative ways to resolve issues, and thinking over past experiences also contribute to cognitive presence. The findings of the study suggest a meaningful and positive relationship between reflective thinking and cognitive presence. They also suggest that designing online learning settings that promote cognitive presence contributes to the training of reflective practitioners. Thus, it can be stated that preparing teachers to become reflective practitioners is one of the prominent themes in TESOL education and continuing professional development (Cirocki & Farrell, 2019; Cirocki & Widodo, 2019; Larrivee, 2008). In order to take various roles as reflective practitioners, teachers are required to have certain characteristics such as self-perception, self-reflection, self-assessment, self-direction, and self-adjustment for the purpose of facilitating future learning (Qinhua et al., 2016). In conclusion, integrating reflective thinking activities with cognitive presence in online learning settings in the Turkish pre-service EFL context can be promoted to foster learners' higher-order learning skills and, thus, help them become critical thinkers and reflective practitioners in the language learning process.

Limitations and Further Research: The study has certain limitations that should be considered when interpreting the results. First, the sample size should be kept in mind as well as the fact that participants were limited to one state university and one course. Second, only two measures were employed to collect quantitative data. Third, any causal implications obtained as a result of correlation analyses should be read with caution and should be further studied in longitudinal designs using various tools to enrich the findings, obtain triangulation, and provide a comprehensive view. Further research, exploring the relationship between reflective thinking skills and cognitive presence, could be conducted by using mixed-methods research design, investigating and observing more courses with different variables such as social presence and teaching presence of pre-service ELT teaching programs.

Reflective Break

Based on the results of this study, we have suggested that training reflective practitioners depends on developing pre-service EFL teachers' reflective thinking skills. Our findings have also revealed that there is a meaningful and positive relationship between reflective thinking and cognitive presence.

- To what extent do you agree with our suggestion?
- How do you think reflective thinking skills can promote cognitive presence in online learning settings?
- How do you think higher-order learning skills foster criticality and enable pre-service teachers to become critical thinkers and reflective practitioners?

REFERENCES

Afshar, H. S., & Rahimi, M. (2016). Reflective thinking, emotional intelligence, and speaking ability of EFL learners: Is there a relation? *Thinking Skills and Creativity*, *19*, 97–111. https://doi.org/10.1016/j.tsc.2015.10.005

Akyol, Z., & Garrison, D. R. (2011). Understanding cognitive presence in an online and blended community of inquiry: Assessing outcomes and processes for deep approaches to learning. *British Journal of Educational Technology*, *42*(2), 233–250. https://doi.org/10.1111/j.1467-8535.2009.01029.x

Akyol, Z., Arbaugh, J. B., Cleveland-Innes, M., Garrison, D. R., Ice, P., Richardson, J. C., & Swan, K. (2009). A response to the review of the community of inquiry framework. *International Journal of E-Learning & Distance Education*, *23*(2), 123–136. Athabasca University Press.

Arbaugh, J. B., Cleveland-Innes, M., Diaz, R. S., Garrison, D. R., Ice, P., Richardson, J. C., & Swan, K. (2008). Developing a community of inquiry instrument: Testing a measure of the community of inquiry framework using a multi-institutional sample. *The Internet and Higher Education*, *11*(3–4), 133–136. https://doi.org/10.1016/j.iheduc.2008.06.003

Ayan, D., & Seferoğlu, G. (2011). Using electronic portfolios to promote reflective thinking in language teacher education. *Educational Studies*, *37*(5), 513–521. https://doi.org/10.1080/03055698.2010.539782

Basol, G., & Gencel, I. E. (2013). Reflective thinking scale: A validity and reliability study. *Educational Sciences: Theory and Practice*, *13*(2), 941–946.

Boulton, H., & Hramiak, A. (2012). E-reflection: The development of reflective communities of learning for trainee teachers through the use of shared online web logs. *Reflective Practice*, *13*(4), 503–515. https://doi.org/10.1080/14623943.2012.670619

Burhan-Horasanlı, E., & Ortaçtepe, D. (2016). Reflective practice-oriented online discussions: A study on EFL teachers' reflection on, in and for-action. *Teaching and Teacher Education*, *59*, 372–382. https://doi.org/10.1016/j.tate.2016.07.002

Büyüköztürk, Ş. (2016). *Veri Analizi El Kitabı*. Pegem Akademi, Ankara.

Celik, S. (2013). Internet-assisted technologies for English language teaching in Turkish universities. *Computer Assisted Language Learning*, *26*(5), 468–483. https://doi.org/10.1080/09588221.2012.692385

Choy, S. C., & Cheah, P. K. (2009). Teacher perceptions of critical thinking among students and its influence on higher education. *International Journal of Teaching and Learning in Higher Education*, *20*(2), 198–206.

Cirocki, A., & Farrell, T. S. C. (2017). Reflective practice for professional development of TESOL practitioners. *The European Journal of Applied Linguistics and TEFL*, *6*(2), 5–23.

Cirocki, A., & Farrell, T. S. C. (2019). Professional development of secondary school EFL teachers: Voices from Indonesia. *System*, *85*, 102111. https://doi.org/10.1016/j.system.2019.102111

Cirocki, A., & Widodo, H. P. (2019). Reflective practice in English language teaching in Indonesia: Shared practices from two teacher educators. *Iranian Journal of Language Teaching Research*, *7*(3), 15–35.

Cochran-Smith, M., & Villegas, A. M. (2015). Framing teacher preparation research: An overview of the field, part 1. *Journal of Teacher Education*, *66*(1), 7–20. https://doi.org/10.1177/0022487114549072

Creswell, J. W. (2012). *Educational research: Planning, conducting, and evaluating quantitative and qualitative research*. Prentice Hall.

Darabi, A., Arrastia, M. C., Nelson, D. W., Cornille, T., & Liang, X. (2011). Cognitive presence in asynchronous online learning: A comparison of four discussion strategies. *Journal of Computer Assisted Learning, 27*(3), 216–227. https://doi.org/10.1111/j.1365-2729.2010.00392.x

Dewey, J. (1933). *How we think: A restatement of the relation of reflective thinking to the education process*. DC Heath and Company.

Dörnyei, Z. (2007). *Research methods in applied linguistics*. Oxford University Press.

Elder, L., & Richard P. (2004). Critical thinking and the art of close reading, part IV. *Journal of Developmental Education, 28*(2), 36–37.

Eröz-Tuğa, B. (2013). Reflective feedback sessions using video recordings. *ELT Journal, 67*(2), 175–183. https://doi.org/10.1093/elt/ccs081

Ersözlü, Z. N., & Arslan, M. (2009). The effect of developing reflective thinking on metacognitive awareness at primary education level in Turkey. *Reflective Practice, 10*(5), 683–695. https://doi.org/10.1080/14623940903290752

Facione, N. C., & Facione. A. P. (1996). Externalizing critical thinking in knowledge development and clinical judgment. *Nursing Outlook, 44*(3), 129–136. https://doi.org/10.1016/S0029-6554(06)80005-9

Farrell, T. S. C. (2015). *Promoting teacher reflection in second language education: A framework for TESOL professionals*. Routledge. https://doi.org/10.4324/9781315775401

Farrell, T. S. C. (2016). Anniversary article: The practices of encouraging TESOL teachers to engage in reflective practice: An appraisal of recent research contributions. *Language Teaching Research, 20*(2), 223–247. https://doi.org/10.1177/1362168815617335

Farrell, T. S. C. (2018a). *Research on reflective practice in TESOL*. Routledge. https://doi.org/10.4324/9781315206332

Farrell, T. S. C. (2018b). *Reflective language teaching: Practical applications for TESOL teachers*. Bloomsbury Publishing. https://doi.org/10.5040/9781350021389

Farrell, T. S. C. (2019). *Reflective practice in ELT*. Equinox Publishing. https://doi.org/10.4324/9781315659824-5

Fendler, L. (2003). Teacher reflection in a hall of mirrors: Historical influences and political reverberations. *Educational Researcher, 32*(3), 16–25. https://doi.org/10.3102/0013189X032003016

Freire, P. (1970). *Pedagogy of the oppressed*. Seabury.

Galikyan, I., & Admiraal, W. (2019). Students' engagement in asynchronous online discussion: The relationship between cognitive presence, learner prominence, and academic performance. *The Internet and Higher Education, 43*, 100692. https://doi.org/10.1016/j.iheduc.2019.100692

Garrison, D. R. (2003). Cognitive presence for effective asynchronous online learning: The role of reflective inquiry, self-direction and metacognition. *Elements of Quality Online Education: Practice and Direction, 4*(1), 47–58.

Garrison, D. R. (2016). *E-learning in the 21st century: A community of inquiry framework for research and practice*. Taylor & Francis.

Garrison, D. R., Anderson, R. T., & Archer, W. (2000). Critical inquiry in a text-based environment: Computer conferencing in higher education. *The Internet and Higher Education, 2*(2–3), 87–105. https://doi.org/10.1016/S1096-7516(00)00016-6

Garrison, D. R., Anderson, R. T., & Archer, W. (2001). Critical thinking, cognitive presence, and computer conferencing in distance education. *American Journal of Distance Education, 15*(1), 7–23. https://doi.org/10.1080/08923640109527071

Garrison, D. R., & Cleveland-Innes, M. (2005). Facilitating cognitive presence in online learning: Interaction is not enough. *The American Journal of Distance Education, 19*(3), 133–148. https://doi.org/10.1207/s15389286ajde1903_2

Ghanizadeh, A. (2011). An investigation into the relationship between self-regulation and critical thinking among Iranian EFL teachers. *The Journal of Technology & Education, 5*(3), 213–221.

Ghanizadeh, A. (2017). The interplay between reflective thinking, critical thinking, self-monitoring, and academic achievement in higher education. *Higher Education, 74*(1), 101–114. https://doi.org/10.1007/s10734-016-0031-y

Grayling, A. C. (2002). *Meditations for the humanist: Ethics for a secular age.* Oxford University Press.

Gün, B. (2011). Quality self-reflection through reflection training. *ELT Journal, 65*(2), 126–135. https://doi.org/10.1093/elt/ccq040

Güngör, M. N. (2016). Turkish pre-service teachers' reflective practices in teaching english to young learners. *Australian Journal of Teacher Education, 41*(2), 137–151. https://doi.org/10.14221/ajte.2016v41n2.9

Guthrie, K. L. (2010). Reflective pedagogy: Making meaning in experiential based online courses. *Journal of Educators Online, 7*(2), 1–21. https://doi.org/10.9743/JEO.2010.2.2

Kanuka, H., & Garrison. D. R. (2004). Cognitive presence in online learning. *Journal of Computing in Higher Education, 15*(2), 21–39. https://doi.org/10.1007/BF02940928

Karakaş, A., & Yükselir, C. (2021). Engaging pre-service EFL teachers in reflection through video-mediated team micro-teaching and guided discussions. *Reflective Practice, 22*(2), 159–72. https://doi.org/10.1080/14623943.2020.1860927

Kember, D., Leung, D., Jones, A., Yuen Loke, A., McKay, J., Sinclair, K., & Tse H. (2000). Development of a questionnaire to measure the level of reflective thinking. *Assessment & Evaluation in Higher Education, 25*(4), 381–395. https://doi.org/10.1080/713611442

Korucu-Kis, S., & Demir, Y. (2019). A review of graduate research on reflective practices in English language teacher education: Implications. *Issues in Educational Research, 29*(4), 1241–1261. http://www.iier.org.au/iier29/korucu-kis.pdf

Korucu-Kis, S., & Kartal, G. (2019). No pain no gain: Reflections on the promises and challenges of embedding reflective practices in large classes. *Reflective Practice, 20*(5), 637–653. https://doi.org/10.1080/14623943.2019.1651715

Kuswandono, P. (2014). University mentors' views on reflective practice in microteaching: Building trust and genuine feedback. *Reflective Practice, 15*(6), 701–717. https://doi.org/10.1080/14623943.2014.944127

Larrivee, B. (2008). Development of a tool to assess teachers' level of reflective practice. *Reflective Practice, 9*(3), 341–360. https://doi.org/10.1080/14623940802207451

Leung, D., & Kember, D. (2003). The relationship between approaches to learning and reflection upon practice. *Educational Psychology, 23*(1), 61–71. https://doi.org/10.1080/01443410303221

Lipman, M. (2003). *Thinking in education*. Cambridge University Press. https://doi.org/10.1017/CBO9780511840272

Lyons, N. (2010). *Handbook of reflection and reflective inquiry: Mapping a way of knowing for professional reflective inquiry*. Springer Science & Business Media. https://doi.org/10.1007/978-0-387-85744-2

Mann, S., & Walsh, S. (2013). RP or RIP: A critical perspective on reflective practice. *Applied Linguistics Review, 4*(2), 291–315. https://doi.org/10.1515/applirev-2013-0013

Meyer, K. A. (2003). Face-to-face versus threaded discussions: The role of time and higher-order thinking. *Journal of Asynchronous Learning Networks, 7*(3), 55–65. https://doi.org/10.24059/olj.v7i3.1845

Mezirow, J. (1998). On critical reflection. *Adult Learning Quarterly, 48*(3), 185–198. https://doi.org/10.1177/074171369804800305

Morueta, R. T., López, P. M., Hernando Gómez, A., & Harris, V. W. (2016). Exploring social and cognitive presences in communities of inquiry to perform higher cognitive tasks. *The Internet and Higher Education, 31*, 122–131. https://doi.org/10.1016/j.iheduc.2016.07.004

Öztürk, E. (2012). An adaptation of the community of inquiry index: The study of validity and reliability. *Elementary Education Online, 11*(2), 409–422.

Parsons, R. D., & Brown Kimberlee, S. (2002). *Teacher as reflective practitioner and action researcher*. Wadsworth Learning.

Pawan, F., Paulus, T. M., Yalcin, S., & Chang, C. F. (2003). Online learning: Patterns of engagement and interaction among in-service teachers. *Language Learning & Technology, 7*(3), 119–140.

Peterson, B. R. (2016). The development of a disposition for reflective practice. In Anita G. Welch and Shaljan Areepattamannil (Eds.), *Dispositions in teacher education* (pp. 3–30). Sense Publishers. https://doi.org/10.1007/978-94-6300-552-4_1

Phan, H. P. (2008). Unifying different theories of learning: Theoretical framework and empirical evidence. *Educational Psychology, 28*(3), 325–340. https://doi.org/10.1080/01443410701591392

Phan, H. P. (2009). Exploring students' reflective thinking practice, deep processing strategies, effort, and achievement goal orientations. *Educational Psychology, 29*(3), 297–313. https://doi.org/10.1080/01443410902877988

Qinhua, Z., Dongming, M., Zhiying, N., & Hao, X. (2016). *Adult competencies for lifelong learning*, Vol. 9. River Publishers.

Redmond, P. (2014). Reflection as an indicator of cognitive presence. *E-Learning and Digital Media, 11*(1), 46–58. https://doi.org/10.2304/elea.2014.11.1.46

Richards, J. C., & Farrell, T. S. C. (2005). *Professional development for language teachers: Strategies for teacher learning*. Ernst Klett Sprachen. https://doi.org/10.1017/CBO9780511667237

Sadaf, A., & Olesova, L. (2017). Enhancing cognitive presence in online case discussions with questions based on the practical inquiry model. *American Journal of Distance Education*, *31*(1), 56–69. https://doi.org/10.1080/08923647.2017.1267525

Sağlam, A., Göktürk, L., & Dikilitaş, K. (2020). Evaluating an online professional learning community as a context for professional development in classroom-based research. *TESL-EJ*, *24*(3), 1–17.

Satar, H. M., & Akcan, S. (2018). Pre-service EFL teachers' online participation, interaction, and social presence. *Language Learning & Technology*, *22*(1), 157–183.

Schön, D. A. (1983). *The reflective practitioner: How professionals think in action*. Basic Books.

Schulte, L. E., & Edwards, S. (2008). The development and validation of the diversity dispositions index. *Teacher Education Faculty Publications*, *5*(3), 11–19. https://digitalcommons.unomaha.edu/tedfacpub/17/

Shea, P., & Bidjerano, T. (2009). Community of inquiry as a theoretical framework to foster 'epistemic engagement' and 'cognitive presence' in online education. *Computers & Education*, *52*(3), 543–553. https://doi.org/10.1016/j.compedu.2008.10.007

Tezgiden Cakcak, S. Y. (2015). Preparing teacher candidates as passive technicians, reflective practitioners or transformative intellectuals? Doctoral dissertation, Middle East Technical University, Ankara. http://etd.lib.metu.edu.tr/upload/12618876/index.pdf

Turhan, B., & Kirkgoz, Y. (2018). Towards becoming critical reflection writers: A case of English language teacher candidates. *Reflective Practice*, *19*(6), 749–762. https://doi.org/10.1080/14623943.2018.1539651

Unlu, Z., & Kulekci, E. (2020). Reflective practice tools in ESL: Two retrospective evaluations. *Applied Linguistics Review*, *11*(1), 109–127. https://doi.org/10.1515/applirev-2017-0075

Vaughan, N., & Garrison, D. R. (2005). Creating cognitive presence in a blended faculty development community. *The Internet and Higher Education*, *8*(1), 1–12. https://doi.org/10.1016/j.iheduc.2004.11.001

Walsh, S., & Mann, S. (2015). Doing reflective practice: A data-led way forward. *ELT Journal*, *69*(4), 351–362. https://doi.org/10.1093/elt/ccv018

Widodo, H. P., & Ferdiansyah, S. (2018). Engaging student teachers in video-mediated self-reflection in teaching. In Kerry J. Kennedy and J. Chi-Kin Lee (Eds.), *The Routledge handbook of schools and schooling in Asia* (pp. 922–934). Routledge.

Yang, S. H. (2009). Using blogs to enhance critical reflection and community of practice. *Journal of Educational Technology & Society*, *12*(2), 11–21.

Yesilbursa, A. (2011). Reflection at the interface of theory and practice: An analysis of pre-service English language teachers' written reflections. *Australian Journal of Teacher Education*, *36*(3), 50–62. https://doi.org/10.14221/ajte.2011v36n3.5

Zeichner, K. M., & Liston, D. P. (2013). *Reflective teaching: An introduction*, 2nd ed. Routledge. https://doi.org/10.4324/9780203822289

Zhang, S., Liu, Q., & Wang, Q. (2017). A study of peer coaching in teachers' online professional learning communities. *Universal Access in the Information Society*, *16*(2), 337–347. https://doi.org/10.1007/s10209-016-0461-4

Zhu, H. (2014). Reflective thinking on EFL classroom discourse. *Journal of Language Teaching & Research*, *5*(6), 1275–1282. https://doi.org/10.4304/jltr.5.6.1275-1282

ABOUT THE AUTHORS

Ceyhun Yükselir (PhD) is an Associate Professor of English Language Teaching at the Department of English Language and Literature, Osmaniye Korkut Ata University, Turkey, where he teaches Academic Writing, Research Methods, Teaching Language Skills, Literature in Language Teaching, and Linguistics. His research interests include teacher education, reflective teaching, learner autonomy, technology integration in EFL classes, and applied linguistics with ELT focus.

Saadet Korucu-Kış is an Assistant Professor in the English Language Teaching Department of Necmettin Erbakan University, Konya, Turkey. She holds a BA, MA, and PhD in English Language Teaching. Her research interests relate to teacher education, technology-enhanced language learning, instructional design, and reflective practice.

Chapter 3

Engaging in Systematic Digital Reflection: A Case of Pre-Service English Teachers

Ali Öztüfekçi & Kenan Dikilitaş

3.1. INTRODUCTION

As an international phenomenon, technology is an inseparable part of our everyday lives and our efforts to improve teaching and learning (Sandholtz et al., 1997; Voogt et al., 2009). With the increasing importance of technology in education, more online courses are provided in teacher education programs. Despite their potential benefits, pre-service teachers do not prefer such courses (Teo et al., 2008). For various possible reasons, pre-service teachers are often offered courses delivered through traditional, knowledge-transmission-oriented approaches (Mann & Walsh, 2017). However, incorporating online components into teacher preparation is rather important as these provide alternative learning opportunities and promote 'sustained collaborative dialogues' between teacher-educator and pre-service teachers that allow personal and collaborative reflection (Johnson & Golombek, 2016).

Given the affordances of online teacher education courses, we designed and taught an online course to examine the over-time development of an ability to reflect through the course as well as the professional development of the participating pre-service teachers. We argue that it is unrealistic to expect teachers to develop a sense of reflectivity unless they have engaged in exploratory, evaluative, and critical reflective writing on their past learning experiences, observations, and teaching experiences (Collin et al., 2013; Farrell, 2012; Lee, 2004; Jay & Johnson, 2002). An online platform can offer opportunities to create an atmosphere where students engage in digital reflective writing (Kirk & Pitches, 2013; Sura, 2015), but pre-service teachers' preferences towards and participation in such online learning will determine how far this is achieved (Sutherland et al., 2010). In this regard, teacher preparation should help pre-service teachers somewhat in piecing together the theoretical and practical knowledge reflectively (Beauchamp, 2015; Farrell, 2007) and recognizing the interrelationship between the two so that they can put theory into practice once they start in the profession (Sharbain & Tan, 2012). Thus, there are some initiatives that could be conducted with pre-service teachers to help them develop professionally. One such means is to give pre-service teachers online writing tasks connected with what they read and provide them with constructive feedback specifically focused on tips to write reflectively through an asynchronous course. To this end, we addressed the following research question:

> What are the major characteristics of the professional development observed in pre-service EFL teachers as they engage in digital reflection?

Our inquiry into the over-time development of pre-service teachers through an asynchronous course and digital reflection contributes to the relevant literature on pre-service teachers' professional development.

3.2. LITERATURE REVIEW

3.2.1. Pre-Service Teacher Education Programs

Teacher education programs aim at preparing learners to become well-qualified teachers. Among their several goals, a particularly prominent one is to support pre-service teachers' acquisition of professional knowledge, teaching skills, and attitudes. Though teacher education programs are complex, in general they typically encompass the following key components: studies in subject matter, pedagogy and subject-specific pedagogy, as well as teaching practice (e.g., Flores, 2016; Kansanen, 2014; Schmidt et al., 2011). As Flores (2016) points out in relation to such key components, their place in the program and their interaction are varied to better promote pre-service teachers' professional learning. Furthermore, Kansanen (2014) emphasizes that the way such components are used in a program to design an efficacious curriculum remarkably contributes to the quality of pre-service teacher education preparation. One of the critical points identified is the question of whether the learning content of the different components can be integrated into a coherent structure so that pre-service teachers' learning is supported (Flores, 2016). This question relates to the way the learning opportunities available for pre-service teachers are structured as well as to the level of coherence. For example, pre-service teachers should always be provided with clear links between courses on subject matter and courses on subject-specific pedagogy and general pedagogy in their respective teacher education programs (Kansanen, 2014). Similarly, practical learning opportunities help pre-service teachers to acquire teaching expertise, as they support them in progressing from the stage of teacher novices to advanced beginners (Berliner, 2004) and in starting to become reflective practitioners (Schön, 1983).

Leading researchers and scholars in teacher training suggest that teachers undergo training that initiates active learning, whereby the teachers are at the center of the process and structure the pedagogical knowledge themselves (Cochran-Smith & Lytle, 1999; Little, 2002). This type of training holds important implications for how pre-service teachers become aware of the essence of their chosen profession, develop self-regulating capabilities, and mould their pedagogical knowledge. Researchers (e.g., Beyer & Davis, 2012; Pintrich, 2004) claim that the ability to structure knowledge substantially depends mainly on the learning environment.

3.2.2. E-Learning and Reflection

Contemporary educational settings have begun to put electronic learning (e-learning) environments at the center of their curricula, specifying that such environments offer easy access to hypermedia that provides information by a variety of hypertexts, graphics, animation, and audio or video, which the learner navigates autonomously. Technology-enhanced, student-centered learning environments create contexts within which knowledge and skills are authentically anchored and that provide a range of tools and resources for navigating and manipulating information (Hannafin & Land, 1997). The aforesaid environments 'afford and provide opportunities to seek rather than comply, to experiment rather than to accept, to evaluate rather than to accumulate, and to interpret rather than to adopt' (Hannafin & Land, 1997, p. 175).

An e-learning environment may provide learners with opportunities for active, student-centered learning in which the students themselves decide what to learn, how to learn, whether they understand the material, when to change plans and strategies, and when to increase efforts, based on their own needs and interests (Azevedo & Cromley, 2004). Britt and Gabrys (2001), for instance, argued that in such an environment, learners need to be able to regulate, control, and evaluate their own learning progress. Although the e-learning environment seems to inherently promote the application of self-regulation capabilities, much research has shown that it often leads to little study because learners do not know how to direct themselves to effectively make the best of what the environment has to offer. Many researchers (e.g., Azevedo & Cromley, 2004; Blank, 2000; Hannum, 2001; Kramarski & Mizrachi, 2006; Michalsky et al., 2007) unearthed that learners of all ages fail to apply relevant prior knowledge in e-learning environments. Learners happen to have difficulties in coordinating the numerous representations of information, determining an appropriate learning continuum, planning, using effective strategies, and monitoring their progress. These findings suggest that e-learning environments should incorporate further support for students. Therefore, the presence of a course moderator (e.g., online tutoring) plays a key role as they might help learners move forward with their studies more effectively (Hrastinski et al., 2018; Lapadat, 2002).

In addition to research outlining e-learning environments, much research is devoted to reflectivity development. Reflection is a notion that has gained much popularity in the field of teacher education (Farrell, 2014; Farrell & Jacobs, 2016; Mann & Walsh, 2017). The pioneering work of both Dewey (1910) and Schön (1983) has been influential on subsequent studies; however, there has not been any one single commonly agreed-on definition of reflectivity (Akbari, 2007). Dewey (1910) argued that reflection is the persistent and careful consideration of beliefs and knowledge in light of potential evidence that supports it. Schön (1983), however, conceived of reflection as an individual process that allows teachers to make sense of their experiences. What these two different definitions have in common is that reflection is a thinking process carried out by teachers with the aim of 'assessing, understanding, reframing or giving coherence to situations associated with their professional practice' (Hiver & Whitehead, 2018, p. 3). Unlike traditional models of teacher education relying on top-down transmission of knowledge, reflective practice utilizes a wide array of techniques, including reflective writing (Richards & Farrell, 2005). A shift taking place both in mainstream teacher education and in English language teaching (ELT) has brought about a change in the view of teacher-learning (Yeşilbursa, 2011). Pre-service teacher education is now considered as a socially negotiated process rather than a one-size-fits-all approach to teacher education (Richards, 2008). To this end, reflective writing could be one way for pre-service teachers to reflexively investigate their own professional growth (Richards & Farrell, 2005). As such, Farrell (2019) argues that reflection is an inclusive activity and proposes six principles, namely, (1) reflective practice is holistic, (2) it is evidence-based, (3) it involves dialog, (4) it bridges principles and practices, (5) it requires an inquiring disposition, and (6) it is a way of life. Similarly, Farrell (2015) provides a framework for reflecting on practice, encompassing five major components: philosophy, principles, theory, practice, and beyond practice.

Furthermore, one possible means to effectively incorporate such reflection into teacher preparation would be through digital tools. A body of research studies has proved that digital reflection can improve both pre- and in-service teachers' knowledge concerning cognitive and metacognitive components (e.g., Kleinknecht & Gröschner, 2016; Rosaen et al., 2008; Santagata et al., 2007). In such digital environments, pre-service teachers continuously reflect and are provided with feedback, which is, then, followed by online interaction with peers, mentors, or experts (So et al., 2009). Some other studies have also shown that digital reflection might foster pre-service teachers' self-efficacy and constructivist beliefs (Gröschner et al., 2018; Heemsoth & Kleickmann, 2018). Similarly, for instance, Cacciamani et al. (2012) investigated the concept of reflection in an online environment and found that student participation and presence of a supportive tutor led to success in reflection, which brings about increased agency, higher metacognitive reflective skills and abilities, and knowledge-building. Otherwise, reflection without support and guidance may remain at a superficial level (Wopereis et al., 2010). However, because each individual is different and unique in terms of their responses, it cannot be taken for granted that interaction with the course tutor will lead to greater levels of reflective skills (Gelfuso & Dennis, 2014). Thus, pre-service teachers might develop varying reflection skills and abilities, and the most striking indicator of such development is that of their own articulation of how much they have progressed (Hacker & Barkhuizen, 2008). Similarly, Luo et al. (2017) investigated two cases where pre-service teachers were introduced to Twitter in the hopes of providing them with opportunities to develop a personal learning network through synchronous discussion. The study examined how the pre-service teachers participated in these live chats through pre-activity reflections, student tweets, and post-activity reflections which were analysed both qualitatively and quantitatively. The results indicated that although participants' familiarity with Twitter varied, no participant was reported to have participated in such discussions on Twitter and the vast majority of the participants indicated a positive perception and preference towards continuing with Twitter live chats.

Not surprisingly, then, it can be claimed that metacognition and reflection are relatively synonymous in a non-technical sense and can be used interchangeably by educators (Rhem, 2013). As Duffy, et al. (2009) put it, 'given that metacognition is "thinking of one's thinking", it is a short step to associating metacognition with "reflecting on one's thinking"' (p. 242). However, though it may appear that a teacher who is reflective is also metacognitive, this is not fully supported by existing studies (Hiver & Whitehead, 2018).

The existing literature indicates that reflection is a crucial component of pre-service teacher education (Farrell, 2001; Kumaravadivelu, 2001; Schön, 1983). To specify the situation in Turkey, some studies (Güngör, 2016; Mumford & Dikilitaş, 2020; Yeşilbursa, 2011) examine the reflective practices of pre-service English teachers. Güngör (2016), for instance, aimed to promote reflective practice at the pre-service level in teaching English to young learners through video-recorded micro-teaching sessions, reflective journals, and lesson plans. The findings of the study reported that providing pre-service teachers with reflective tools contributed to their professional development, self-and peer-reflections, and their readiness to teach English to young learners; thus, honing our understanding of the importance of reflection in teacher education. In the study by Mumford & Dikilitaş (2020), the researchers set off to investigate the growth of reflective thinking skills in three pre-service English teachers. Taking an exploratory approach, the researchers offered a hybrid course focusing on reflection development through online engagement. The data were collected through interviews with the participating pre-service teachers, observations of their contributions to online lessons, and their reflective papers. The study found that there were different positions amongst the three participants as regards their attitudes to reflection, and only one of the pre-service teachers was observed to reach higher levels of reflection. However, the study concluded that it is important to understand individual motivations as individuals themselves are key in the promotion of their own reflection, suggesting that 'different trajectories in uptake of reflective practice are inevitable' (Mumford & Dikilitaş 2020, p. 9). As such, the current study examines the over-time developmental characteristics of Turkish pre-service teachers enrolled, at the time of the study, in an asynchronous course offered in an ELT department at a Turkish university. Specifically, our study investigates the effects of digital reflection on English pre-service teachers' professional development in the hope of deepening our understanding of the importance of reflective practice.

3.3. METHOD

Based on the impetus for the study discussed above, our primary purpose was to examine the over-time developmental processes of pre-service teachers registered for a course delivered asynchronously. Specifically, it was sought to investigate the extent to which pre-service teachers develop professionally. In line with the goal of the study, as mentioned above, the following research question was addressed:

> What are the major characteristics of professional development observed in EFL pre-service teachers as they engage in digital reflection?

3.3.1. Research Design

The study employed a qualitative approach to data collection and analysis. More specifically, the qualitative research design was based on grounded theory (Strauss & Corbin, 1998), which helped us induce a pattern of the pre-service teachers' professional development gained through their involvement and participation in the asynchronous course. This grounded theory approach allowed us to capture the major characteristics of pre-service teachers' professional development in an exploratory manner. This is specifically important for our study as we were interested in analysing our data without any preconceptions and in developing themes based on the generated data (i.e., data-driven) through an exploratory perspective. In this regard, grounded theory incorporates a 'systematic approach, a flexible emerging design, and the use of active codes to capture the experiences of the participants' (Creswell, 2012, p. 431).

3.3.2. Context and Participants

Forty-five Turkish pre-service EFL teachers participated in the study. The participating pre-service teachers were senior undergraduate ELT students, who would teach at both primary and secondary levels all across the country after they successfully completed their studies and graduated. In this regard, the first author taught the course and had access to all the participants (i.e., the emic perspective); whereas the second author provided etic perspectives as he engaged in the process of framing this study.

Of the 45 participants, 32 were female and 13 male. The participants whose age ranged from 20 to 21 constituted the largest group, whereas the ones between the ages of 25 and 27 represented the smallest group. These were considered to be appropriate to participate in the study since they had never taken an asynchronous course before. This new experience involved autonomous behaviors, critical and elaborated reflection on testing and assessment issues, and collaborative and joint writing assignments in which they were required to complete relevant readings and research. All participants are referred to here by pseudonyms.

3.3.3. Content of the Course

The study was conducted in a 14-week-long undergraduate course entitled 'Special Topics in ELT' offered in the department of English language teaching at a private (non-profit, foundational) university. This fully online course was designed to discuss the major principles and practices of language testing and assessment and to construct and investigate testing and assessment materials. The course aimed to help pre-service teachers to revisit their own beliefs about testing and assessment, allowing them to elaborate both individually and collaboratively on their beliefs and past learning experiences as well as on the lessons observed through the practicum upon reading the relevant course materials uploaded weekly onto an online platform called 'ItsLearning,' which is a digital learning management system (LMS). This platform gives teachers and students a virtual platform where collaborative learning takes place through tools for individual and group messaging, group projects, course materials, classroom competitions and the like. In this regard, the course included weekly reading and reflection assignments, whereby the participating pre-service teachers had asynchronous interaction with the course tutor and completed both individual and joint digital reflective assignments, followed by online written feedback provided by the tutor, which mainly focused on tips to help pre-service teachers to write more reflectively and critically.

3.3.4. Data Collection

For the purposes of the current study, the data were collected through 12 reflection papers (see Appendix 3.1). The participating pre-service teachers were given weekly guidelines for the tasks and wrote weekly digital reflections in response to different tasks covering various aspects of testing and assessment. Specifically, the participating pre-service teachers completed their reflection papers both individually and collaboratively (i.e., digitally collaborating with other pre-service teachers registered to the same course).

3.3.5. Data Analysis

The data were jointly analysed by both authors through the 'open to selective coding' approach, which helped us capture aspects of pre-service teachers' professional development. Rather than seeking generalizable issues, we aimed to capture participants' voices through thick descriptions via inductive analysis. The data were first open-coded, reducing larger discourse into smaller meaning units, such as sentence fragments, clauses, or phrases. Then these smaller linguistic units were axially coded to reveal the categories of meaning, followed by selective coding, where the central themes emerged and were connected so as to generate the main qualitative findings regarding the major characteristics of professional development as the participants engaged in digital reflection during the course. Despite having a single source of data, we drew on multiple sets of reflective accounts of each pre-service teacher.

An iterative process of reading of the data was also followed to avoid misinterpretation of any kind and to ensure trustworthiness. Having analysed the relevant data individually, we negotiated the final themes through peer debriefing, sharing our thoughts regarding the interpretation process in order to ensure the validity and credibility of the study (Spall, 1998). Detailed coding and analysis were performed until after it was felt that no further categories would emerge in the themes within the data (Seale, 1999).

3.4. FINDINGS

The present study aimed to identify the major characteristics of professional development as the participating pre-service EFL teachers engaged in digital reflection. Our data analysis revealed three main characteristics of professional development for pre-service teachers: fostering autonomy, enhancing self-efficacy, and developing professional identities as motivated teachers (Table 3.1). Furthermore, it was seen that critical and digital reflective writing helped teachers foster autonomy, enhance self-efficacy, and develop motivation. Extracts from the participants' statements provide evidence for these emerging themes. In order to thematize the findings, excerpts are analysed and categorized in accordance with the themes identified.

Table 3.1. Major themes with sub-themes regarding the impact of digital reflective writing.

Fostering Autonomy	Enhancing Self-Efficacy	Developing Professional Identities as Motivated Teachers
Exercise of choice	Self-regulation	Ideal self
Self-directed ownership	Challenging previous experiences and beliefs	Ought-to self

3.4.1. Fostering Autonomy

A key theme that we identified was related to pre-service teachers' autonomy development. Completing their weekly reading assignments as well as digital reflective writing assignments, the vast majority of the pre-service teachers showed a growing sense of autonomy with regard to testing and assessment through exercising their choices and developing self-directed ownership. These are displayed in the following sub-themes.

Exercise of Choice: The participating pre-service teachers throughout the course stated their own preferences towards testing and assessment – indicating a sense of autonomy – to speak their minds as can be seen in the following sample excerpt:

Excerpt 1: Student development

> ... I think that the way to minimise the errors of ranking exams and other exams is through alternative assessment. Compared to traditional assessment techniques, alternative assessment contributes more to student development. (Utku)

As is illustrated in the above-given quote, while reading about testing and assessment and reflecting on what they read, the participating pre-service teachers were observed to state their own preferences towards and perceptions of which type of assessment could better help with student development. Such preferences can be attributed to these pre-service teachers' being able to make personal choices (Zeng, 2013) and their sense of autonomy, which could be related to their capacity to grow and to widen the space of professional freedom (Benson & Haung, 2008). This statement above exemplifies a developing sense of autonomy, which is also reflected by another pre-service teacher who wrote:

Excerpt 2: Authenticity in testing and assessment

> ... in my opinion what authenticity actually refers to in terms of assessment is that the language should be natural, the context should integrate the 'real world', the topics should be meaningful (interesting) for the learners, a proper organisation of some kind should be incorporated, and the tasks should represent 'real-world' tasks. (Yeşim)

The statement above also illustrates how this pre-service teacher articulates her understanding of authenticity in testing and assessment. The use of language indicates how digital reflection has informed the participating pre-service teacher in autonomously taking stances related to her work and professional development.

Self-Directed Ownership: Another sub-theme that was found to be relevant to autonomy development was that of self-directedness in relation to testing and assessment. The vast majority of the participating pre-service teachers had implicit self-suggestions leading them to have some self-directed ownership, as in the following excerpt:

Excerpt 3: Implicit self-suggestion

> ... most of the teachers are giving arguably less importance to listening, but listening is actually one of the skills that teachers should get trained as to how to teach successfully in the classroom. For instance, the teacher should acknowledge where to use intensive, responsive, extensive and selective listening tasks according to the students' needs. (Ahmet)

As can be seen from the statement above, the pre-service teacher takes an exploratory and highly reflective stance, albeit implicit, in self-directed development, which reveals that they are ready to take the initiative and make informed choices based on an awareness of their own needs, interests, and values in terms of testing and assessment. Similarly, another participant highlighted the importance of students' needs by writing:

Excerpt 4: Needs of students

> I believe that the first thing I should do is learn my students' needs and their learning styles. As I mentioned continuously in my previous reflection papers, my high school teachers were not aware of the importance of this aspect of teaching. (Büşra)

The above statement illustrates another characteristic of an autonomous teacher – having the freedom to develop effective ways of teaching for students. The participating pre-service teacher stresses the importance of being aware of students' needs and acting upon them accordingly, which suggests that the asynchronous course and the reading and digital reflective writing assignments helped pre-service teachers to have a growing awareness about possessing the ability to shift gear on students' pace and needs when necessary as well as taking initiatives and actions on their own.

3.4.2. Enhancing Self-Efficacy

Bandura (1986) defined self-efficacy as 'people's judgements of their capabilities to organise and execute the course of action required to attain designated types of performance' (p. 391). In addition, teacher self-efficacy refers to teachers' beliefs about their capabilities to effectively perform a given task to achieve desirable learning outcomes in a given situation (Tschannen-Moran et al., 1998). Inspired by these definitions within the relevant literature, we came up with another key theme upon finalizing the data analysis, which fell into two sub-themes, as follows.

Self-Regulation: Among various sources of efficacy beliefs, the most robust one is thought to be self-reflection; how individuals experience activities and reflect on these activities is of paramount importance to having high-efficacy perceptions. To this end, 35 of the participating pre-service teachers highlighted how important it is to self-reflect on their own understanding and knowledge in relation to testing and assessment, as seen in the following excerpt:

Excerpt 5: Development of reflective teaching

> ... I cannot underestimate the importance of the reflections as they helped me to internalise the concepts through making connections with my own examples and observational notes. Precisely, my practicum visit, field-notes that I kept during these visits, reading through important issues discussed in the articles, receiving feedback from my tutor on my reaction papers all helped me see the importance of reflection and made me realise I am now more eager to reflect on myself, others and my teaching practises. (Kayra)

The quote given above demonstrates some efficacy beliefs, the first of which is related to vicarious experiences, which are gained through observation, while the second is more related to social persuasion, i.e., encouragement received from others about her own abilities and competencies, which seems to relate to the ability of self-regulation.

Challenging Previous Experiences and Beliefs: Another relevant sub-theme that emerged in relation to self-efficacy was related to pre-service teachers' previous experiences and beliefs in language testing and assessment. Thirty-eight of the pre-service teachers explicitly referred to their past experiences in language learning and compared these to their newly emerging experiences as they engaged in digital reflection. Berkay's quote supports this particular finding:

Excerpt 6: Exposure to traditional assessment

> When I was a language learner, I was mostly exposed to traditional assessment, which made me realise that it was all wrong. Based on my own experiences as well as the readings I've done throughout this course, I can say that I will make sure to use alternative assessment tools more to bring the best out of my learners. (Berkay)

The excerpt above highlights the effects of the course on the pre-service teachers in terms of developing self-efficacy relating to testing and assessment; it is observed that the participants somehow linked their past experiences with their new experiences gained through the readings and relevant activities exercised in the course.

3.4.3. Developing Professional Identities as Motivated Teachers

The data analysis revealed that the participating pre-service teachers were also reported to be motivated to reflect on the acquired knowledge through the course in their ideal and ought-to selves (Dörnyei, 2005). The former refers to an ideal image of an individual to be possessed, whereas the latter deals more with 'the attributes that one believes one ought to possess to meet expectations and to avoid possible negative outcomes' (Dörnyei, 2005, p. 106). Inspired by Dörnyei's L2 Motivational Self System, the following sub-themes were induced.

Ideal Self: As is discussed above, ideal self refers to an 'ideal image'. In this regard, our data revealed that 39 of the participating pre-service teachers were rather motivated to refer to their ideal selves, as can be seen in the following excerpt:

Excerpt 7: The impact of the course

> ... now that I have been introduced to different aspects of testing and assessment – things that I have never thought about before – I am even more motivated to take it all to a next level and apply them in my teaching settings. I mean, the assignments I have completed in this course have helped me realise what kind of a teacher I wish to be. I will definitely make use of alternative assessment more than traditional assessment, pay attention to the needs and interest of my students, and shape my teaching practises accordingly. (Emre)

This excerpt illustrates the impact of the course on pre-service teachers' ideal images, which suggests a positive influence of the course on their intended efforts to make 'good' teachers.

Ought-to Self: Although some participants' motivation was triggered through their 'ideal images,' there were others who were observed to be more motivated when they thought of the institutions they would be working at. The following excerpt supports this finding:

Excerpt 8: Working with young learners

> I am planning to work with young learners in the future and based on my observations during my practicum observation, I realised that the best type of assessment that works well with this profile of students

> is alternative assessment rather than traditional assessment. Because I will be working at an institution where I will be teaching young learners, I will have to adapt my teaching and make use of assessment types appropriate for such learners. (Özlem)

The above statement highlights how this pre-service teacher is inclined to meet the expectations of others (e.g., the institution and relevant stake-holders) in a way that she thinks is more appropriate. This, therefore, might suggest that another professional development characteristic that pre-service teachers experienced during their involvement in the asynchronous course is related to their ought-to self in terms of language testing and assessment.

3.5. DISCUSSION

In relation to our research question, we identified three major characteristics of pre-service teachers engaging in digital reflection in our course, each of which had different sub-themes. As such, based on the findings of the present study, it might be argued that pre-service teacher education programs need to give pre-service teachers the opportunity to reflect on the acquired knowledge that is important for professional development, which concurs with previous studies (e.g., Cacciamani et al., 2012; Kramarski & Mizrachi, 2006; Michalsky et al., 2007; Sachs, 2000).

Specifically, due to the asynchronous nature of the course and the digitalized reflection assignments, the participating pre-service teachers were observed to have reflectively developed a sense of autonomy relating to testing and assessment (Wopereis et al., 2010). This finding, in particular, indicates how effective an asynchronous course can be as it gives the participants not only the opportunity to speak their minds per se but to observe their own developmental processes throughout the course, which also concurs with a study by Hacker & Barkhuizen (2008) who argue that course participants are to be given the chance to take some control over their own learning to better observe their progress, thus promoting autonomy. To this end, in contrast to the premises of traditional classroom settings, the current study found that, as against commonly held beliefs, an asynchronous course incorporating digital reflection would contribute to the developmental processes of pre-service teachers, allowing them to control their pace, to collaborate with other course participants, to develop higher levels of reflectivity and the like (Gelfuso & Dennis, 2014). Therefore, it can be argued that it is not only face-to-face classroom settings that promote the professional development of pre-service teachers, but asynchronous courses can also support pre-service teachers and help them prepare for their future teaching practices.

One of the most striking developmental characteristics of the participating pre-service teachers was found to relate to that of motivation, as outlined in Dörnyei's (2005) approach to motivation. The findings pertaining to motivation are of paramount importance as they indicate that the asynchronous course and digital reflection had an impact on pre-service teachers' motivation development especially in the form of reference to their future teaching practices. These findings suggest that if the learning content of different components can be integrated into a coherent structure in an initial teacher education course, course participants' learning is supported (Flores, 2016). In this regard, thanks to the contributing nature of the course assignments (e.g., weekly digital reflective assignments) along with other developmental characteristics, the participating pre-service teachers were seen to be motivated in relation to testing and assessment issues and in considering how they would benefit from their learning process once they started in the profession.

As such, we can argue that the asynchronous course described in this study offers spaces for collaborative and individual engagement which can be thought of as a contributing variable to the professional development of pre-service teachers.

Moreover, we conclude that digital reflection engagement supported through the growing awareness into reflectivity, the self-efficacy promoted by the familiarized genre of reflective writing, along with persuasive constructive feedback and collaborative writing could address many aspects of initial teacher education such as the lack of reflectivity in the pre-service context as well as professional development of pre-service teachers (Ronfeldt & Reininger, 2012). In this regard, the findings of the present study reveal that digital reflection can improve pre-service teachers' knowledge concerning cognitive and metacognitive components as they continuously engage in reflection and are provided with feedback (Kleinknecht & Gröschner, 2016). Therefore, it can be argued that digital reflection offers opportunities for pre-service teachers to have the freedom in organising how they proceed as they go about completing course components (Hiver & Whitehead, 2018). Given the affordances of digital reflection in teacher education programs, the asynchronous nature of online courses is particularly conducive to 'deeper reflection about course contents' (Benigno & Trentin, 2000, p. 260) as it allows learners time to ponder new ideas and consider their responses. As such, incorporating digital reflection in online courses would also encourage and foster deeper levels of reflection because of the asynchronous nature of the courses.

3.6. IMPLICATIONS AND CONCLUSIONS

In line with what has thus far been discussed, the study has a number of implications for pre-service teacher education programs. First and foremost, teacher education programs should start incorporating such learning environments into their curricula, as is discussed by Sharbain & Tan (2012), given how fast the advances in technology have recently been. Additionally, the findings of this study provide instructors and researchers with helpful insights into the effects of an asynchronous course on the professional development of pre-service teachers as they engage in digital reflection, which instructors might consider before introducing such a course to their learners or during the course (Lapadat, 2002). More specifically, teacher education programs should be oriented towards a more transformational model of course delivery (Foote, 2015) involving online components rather than adopting only transmission-oriented, one-size-fits-all, and one-shot approaches (Meyer, 2014), viz., in order for pre-service teachers to develop more professionally and to better reflect on their teaching practices. Overall, this study's findings imply that digital reflection should be considered as an important component of pre-service teacher education.

Reflective Break

Our study found three major characteristics of pre-service teachers engaging in digital reflection: fostering autonomy, enhancing self-efficacy, and developing professional identities as motivated teachers. In light of these characteristics, we would like readers to think about the questions and reflect on them, considering how this study has informed their understanding.

- How do you think engaging in digital written reflection might promote pre-service teachers' professional development?
- How would engagement in collaborative and experiential reflection contribute to over-time developmental processes of pre-service teachers?
- Which learning conditions will best foster and promote pre-service teachers' reflectivity and professional development?

REFERENCES

Akbari, R. (2007). Reflections on reflection: A critical appraisal of reflective practices in L2 teacher education. *System, 35*(2), 192–207. https://doi.org/10.1016/j.system.2006.12.008

Azevedo, R., & Cromley, J. G. (2004). Does training on self-regulated learning facilitate students' learning with hypermedia? *Journal of Educational Psychology, 96*(3), 523–535. https://doi.org/10.1037/0022-0663.96.3.523

Bandura, A. (1986). The explanatory and predictive scope of self-efficacy theory. *Journal of Social and Clinical Psychology, 4*(3), 359–373. https://doi.org/10.1521/jscp.1986.4.3.359

Beauchamp, C. (2015). Reflection in teacher education: Issues emerging from a review of current literature. *Reflective Practice, 16*(1), 123–141. https://doi.org/10.1080/14623943.2014.982525

Benigno, V., & Trentin, G. (2000). The evaluation of online courses. *Journal of Computer Assisted Learning, 16*(3), 259–270. https://doi.org/10.1046/j.1365-2729.2000.00137.x

Benson, P., & Haung, J. (2008). Autonomy in the transition from foreign language learning to foreign language teaching. *DELTA: Documentação de Estudos em Lingüística Teórica e Aplicada, 24*, SPE, 421–439. https://doi.org/10.1590/S0102-44502008000300003

Berliner, D. C. (2004). Describing the behavior and documenting the accomplishments of expert teachers. *Bulletin of Science, Technology & Society, 24*(3), 200–212. https://doi.org/10.1177/0270467604265535

Beyer, C. J., & Davis, E. A. (2012). Learning to critique and adapt science curriculum materials: Examining the development of preservice elementary teachers' pedagogical content knowledge. *Science Education, 96*(1), 130–157. https://doi.org/10.1002/sce.20466

Blank, L. M. (2000). A metacognitive learning cycle: A better warranty for student understanding? *Science Education, 84*(4), 486–506. https://doi.org/10.1002/1098-237X(200007)84:4<486::AID-SCE4>3.0.CO;2-U

Britt, M. A., & Gabrys, G. L. (2001). Teaching advanced literacy skills for the world wide web. *Learning and Teaching on the World Wide Web*, Academic Press, 73–90. https://doi.org/10.1016/B978-012761891-3/50007-2

Cacciamani, S., Cesareni, D., Martini, F., Ferrini, T., & Fujita, N. (2012). Influence of participation, facilitator styles, and metacognitive reflection on knowledge building in online university courses. *Computers & Education, 58*(3), 874–884. https://doi.org/10.1016/j.compedu.2011.10.019

Cochran-Smith, M., & Lytle. S. L. (1999). Relationships of knowledge and practice: Teacher learning in communities. In A. Iran-Nejad & P. D. Pearson (Eds.), *Review of Research in Education* (pp. 249–305). American Educational Research Association, Washington, DC. https://doi.org/10.2307/1167272

Collin, S., Karsenti, T., & Komis, V. (2013). Reflective practice in initial teacher training: Critiques and perspectives. *Reflective Practice, 14*(1), 104–117. https://doi.org/10.1080/14623943.2012.732935

Creswell, J. W. (2012). *Educational research: Planning, conducting, and evaluating quantitative and qualitative research*. Pearson.

Dewey, J. (1910). What is thought? In *How we think: A restatement of the relation of reflective thinking to the educative process*. DC Heath and Company. https://doi.org/10.1037/10903-000

Dörnyei, Z. (2005). *The psychology of the language learner: Individual differences in second language acquisition*. Routledge.

Duffy, G. G., Miller, S., Parsons, S., & Meloth, M. (2009). Teachers as metacognitive professionals. In Douglas J. Hacker, John Dunlosky, & Arthur C. Graesser (Eds.), *Handbook of metacognition in education* (pp. 252–268). Routledge.

Farrell, T. S. C. (2001). Tailoring reflection to individual needs: A TESOL case study. *Journal of Education for Teaching, 27*(1), 23–38. https://doi.org/10.1080/02607470120042528

Farrell, T. S. C. (2007). Failing the practicum: Narrowing the gap between expectations and reality with reflective practice. *TESOL Quarterly, 41*(1), 193–201. https://doi.org/10.1002/j.1545-7249.2007.tb00049.x

Farrell, T. S. C. (2012). Reflecting on reflective practice: (Re)Visiting Dewey and Schön. *TESOL Journal, 3*(1), 7–16. https://doi.org/10.1002/tesj.10

Farrell, T. S. C. (2014). *Promoting teacher reflection in second language education: A framework for TESOL professionals*. Routledge. https://doi.org/10.4324/9781315775401

Farrell, T. S. C. (2015). *Reflective language teaching: From research to practice*. Bloomsbury Publishing.

Farrell, T. S. C. (2019). *Reflective practice in ELT*. Equinox Publishing. https://doi.org/10.4324/9781315659824-5

Farrell, T. S. C., & Jacobs, G. M. (2016). Practising what we preach: Teacher reflection groups on cooperative learning. *The Electronic Journal for English as a Second Language, 19*(4), 1–9.

Flores, M. A. (2016). Teacher education curriculum. In J. Loughran & M. L. Hamiltion (Eds.), *International handbook of teacher education*. Springer Press. https://doi.org/10.1007/978-981-10-0366-0_5

Foote, L. S. (2015). Transformational learning: Reflections of an adult learning story. *Adult Learning, 26*(2), 84–86. https://doi.org/10.1177/1045159515573017

Gelfuso, A., & Dennis, D. V. (2014). Getting reflection off the page: The challenges of developing support structures for pre-service teacher reflection. *Teaching and Teacher Education, 38*, 1–11. https://doi.org/10.1016/j.tate.2013.10.012

Gröschner, A., Schindler, A., Holzberger, D., Alles, M., & Seidel, T. (2018). How systematic video reflection in teacher professional development regarding classroom discourse contributes to teacher and student self-efficacy. *International Journal of Educational Research, 90*, 223–233. https://doi.org/10.1016/j.ijer.2018.02.003

Güngör, M. N. (2016). Turkish pre-service teachers' reflective practices in teaching English to young learners. *Australian Journal of Teacher Education, 41*(2), 9. https://doi.org/10.14221/ajte.2016v41n2.9

Hacker, P., & Barkhuizen, G. (2008). Autonomous teachers, autonomous cognition: Developing personal theories through reflection in language teacher education. In T. Lamb & H. Reinders (Eds.), *Learner and teacher autonomy*. John Benjamins Publishing Company. https://doi.org/10.1075/aals.1.14hac

Hannafin, M. J., & Land, S. M. (1997). The foundations and assumptions of technology-enhanced student-centered learning environments. *Instructional Science, 25*(3), 167–202. https://doi.org/10.1023/A:1002997414652

Hannum, W. (2001). Knowledge management in education: Helping teachers to work better. *Educational Technology*, *41*(3), 47–49.

Heemsoth, T., & Kleickmann, T. (2018). Learning to plan self-controlled physical education: Good vs. problematic teaching examples. *Teaching and Teacher Education*, *71*, 168–178. https://doi.org/10.1016/j.tate.2017.12.021

Hiver, P., & Whitehead, G. (2018). Teaching metacognitively: Adaptive inside-out thinking in the L2 classroom. In A. Haukas, C. Bjorke, & M. Dypedahl (Eds.), *Metacognition in language learning and teaching*. Routledge. https://doi.org/10.4324/9781351049146-13

Hrastinski, S., Cleveland-Innes, M., & Stenbom, S. (2018). Tutoring online tutors: Using digital badges to encourage the development of online tutoring skills. *British Journal of Educational Technology*, *49*(1), 127–136. https://doi.org/10.1111/bjet.12525

Jay, J. K., & Johnson, K. L. (2002). Capturing complexity: A typology of reflective practice for teacher education. *Teaching and Teacher Education*, *18*(1), 73–85. https://doi.org/10.1016/S0742-051X(01)00051-8

Johnson, K. E., & Golombek. P. R. (2016). *Mindful L2 teacher education: A sociocultural perspective on cultivating teachers' professional development*. Routledge. https://doi.org/10.4324/9781315641447

Kansanen, P. (2014). Teaching as a master's level profession in Finland: Theoretical reflections and practical solutions. In Q. MacNamara, J. Murray, & M. Jones (Eds.), *Workplace learning in teacher education*. Springer. https://doi.org/10.1007/978-94-007-7826-9_16

Kirk, C., & Pitches, J. (2013). Digital reflection: Using digital technologies to enhance and embed creative processes. *Technology, Pedagogy and Education*, *22*(2), 213–230. https://doi.org/10.1080/1475939X.2013.768390

Kleinknecht, M., & Gröschner, A. (2016). Fostering pre-service teachers' noticing with structured video feedback: Results of an online-and video-based intervention study. *Teaching and Teacher Education*, *59*, 45–56. https://doi.org/10.1016/j.tate.2016.05.020

Kramarski, B., & Mizrachi, N. (2006). Online discussion and self-regulated learning: Effects of instructional methods on mathematical literacy. *The Journal of Educational Research*, *99*(4), 218–231. https://doi.org/10.3200/JOER.99.4.218-231

Kumaravadivelu, B. (2001). Toward a post-method pedagogy. *TESOL Quarterly*, *35*(4), 537–560. https://doi.org/10.2307/3588427

Lapadat, J. C. (2002). Written interaction: A key component in online learning. *Journal of Computer-Mediated Communication*, *7*(4), JCMC742. https://doi.org/10.1111/j.1083-6101.2002.tb00158.x

Lee, I. (2004). Using dialogue journals as a multi-purpose tool for pre-service teacher preparation: How effective is it? *Teacher Education Quarterly*, *31*(3), 73–97.

Little, J. W. (2002). Locating learning in teachers' communities of practice: Opening up problems of analysis in records of everyday work. *Teaching and Teacher Education*, *18*(8), 917–946. https://doi.org/10.1016/S0742-051X(02)00052-5

Luo, T., Sickel, J., & Cheng, L. (2017). Preservice teachers' participation and perceptions of Twitter live chats as personal learning networks. *TechTrends, 61*(3), 226–235. https://doi.org/10.1007/s11528-016-0137-1

Mann, S., & Walsh, S. (2017). *Reflective practice in English language teaching: Research-based principles and practices*. Routledge. https://doi.org/10.4324/9781315733395

Meyer, K. A. (2014). Student engagement in online learning: What works and why. *ASHE Higher Education Report, 40*(6), 1–114. https://doi.org/10.1002/aehe.20018

Michalsky, T., Zion, M., & Mevarech, Z. R. (2007). Developing students' metacognitive awareness in asynchronous learning networks in comparison to face-to-face discussion groups. *Journal of Educational Computing Research, 36*(4), 395–424. https://doi.org/10.2190/320V-8H4W-1123-44R6

Mumford, S., & Dikilitaş, K. (2020). Pre-service language teachers reflection development through online interaction in a hybrid learning course. *Computers & Education, 144*, 103706. https://doi.org/10.1016/j.compedu.2019.103706

Pintrich, P. R. (2004). A conceptual framework for assessing motivation and self-regulated learning in college students. *Educational Psychology Review, 16*(4), 385–407. https://doi.org/10.1007/s10648-004-0006-x

Rhem, J. (2013). *Using reflection and metacognition to improve student learning: Across the disciplines, across the academy*. Stylus Publishing, LLC.

Richards, J. C. (2008). Second language teacher education today. *RELC Journal, 39*(2), 158–177. https://doi.org/10.1177/0033688208092182

Richards, J. C., & Farrell, T. S. C. (2005). *Professional development for language teachers: Strategies for teacher learning*. Cambridge University Press. https://doi.org/10.1017/CBO9780511667237

Ronfeldt, M., & Reininger, M. (2012). More or better student teaching? *Teaching and Teacher Education, 28*(8), 1091–1106. https://doi.org/10.1016/j.tate.2012.06.003

Rosaen, C. L., Lundeberg, M., Cooper, M., Fritzen, A., & Terpstra, M. (2008). Noticing noticing: How does investigation of video records change how teachers reflect on their experiences? *Journal of Teacher Education, 59*(4), 347–360. https://doi.org/10.1177/0022487108322128

Sachs, J. (2000). The activist professional. *Journal of Educational Change, 1*(1), 77–94. https://doi.org/10.1023/A:1010092014264

Sandholtz, J. H., Ringstaff, C., & Dwyer, D. C. (1997). *Teaching with technology: Creating student-centered classrooms*. Teachers College Press, Teachers College, Columbia University.

Santagata, R., Zannoni, C., & Stigler, J. W. (2007). The role of lesson analysis in pre-service teacher education: An empirical investigation of teacher learning from a virtual video-based field experience. *Journal of Mathematics Teacher Education, 10*(2), 123–140. https://doi.org/10.1007/s10857-007-9029-9

Schmidt, W. H., Cogan, L., & Houang, R. (2011). The role of opportunity to learn in teacher preparation: An international context. *Journal of Teacher Education, 62*(2), 138–153. https://doi.org/10.1177/0022487110391987

Schön, D. A. (1983). *The reflective practitioner: How professionals think in action*. Basic Books.

Seale, C. (1999). Grounding theory. *The Quality of Qualitative Research*, *1*, 87–105. https://doi.org/10.4135/9780857020093.n7

Sharbain, I. H. A., & Tan, K. (2012). Pre-service teachers' level of competence and their attitudes towards the teaching profession. *Asian Journal of Social Sciences & Humanities*, *1*(3), 14–22.

So, W. W., Pow, J. W., & Hing-keung Hung, V. (2009). The interactive use of a video database in teacher education: Creating a knowledge base for teaching through a learning community. *Computers & Education*, *53*(3), 775–786. https://doi.org/10.1016/j.compedu.2009.04.018

Spall, S. (1998). Peer debriefing in qualitative research: Emerging operational models. *Qualitative Inquiry*, *4*(2), 280–292. https://doi.org/10.1177/107780049800400208

Strauss, A., & Corbin, J. (1998). *Basics of qualitative research techniques*. Sage Publications.

Sura, T. (2015). Infrastructure and Wiki pedagogy: A multi-case study. *Computers and Composition*, *37*, 14–30. https://doi.org/10.1016/j.compcom.2015.06.002

Sutherland, L., Howard, S., & Markauskaite, L. (2010). Professional identity creation: Examining the development of beginning preservice teachers' understanding of their work as teachers. *Teaching and Teacher Education*, *26*(3), 455–465. https://doi.org/10.1016/j.tate.2009.06.006

Teo, T., Ching, S. C., Hung, D., & Beng Lee, C. (2008). Beliefs about teaching and uses of technology among pre-service teachers. *Asia-Pacific Journal of Teacher Education*, *36*(2), 163–174. https://doi.org/10.1080/13598660801971641

Tschannen-Moran, M., Hoy, W. A., & Hoy, W. K. (1998). Teacher efficacy: Its meaning and measure. *Review of Educational Research*, *68*(2), 202–248. https://doi.org/10.3102/00346543068002202

Voogt, J., Tilya, F., & Van Akker, J. (2009). Science teacher learning of MBL-supported student-centered science education in the context of secondary education in Tanzania. *Journal of Science Education and Technology*, *18*(5), 429–438. https://doi.org/10.1007/s10956-009-9160-8

Wopereis, Iwan G. J. H., Sloep, P. B., & Poortman, S. H. (2010). Weblogs as instruments for reflection on action in teacher education. *Interactive Learning Environments*, *18*(3), 245–261. https://doi.org/10.1080/10494820.2010.500530

Yeşilbursa, A. (2011). Reflection at the interface of theory and practice: An analysis of pre-service English language teachers' written reflections. *Australian Journal of Teacher Education*, *36*(3). https://doi.org/10.14221/ajte.2011v36n3.5

Zeng, Z. (2013). Pathways to pre-service teachers' professional development: Insights from teacher autonomy. *Proceedings of the 2013 International Academic Workshop on Social Science*. https://doi.org/10.2991/iaw-sc.2013.194

APPENDIX 3.1

Weekly Individual or Collaborative Reflective Papers

1	Reflecting retrospectively on testing and assessment experiences • *Please discuss your English language learning experience with specific reference to how you were assessed and tested.* • *Discuss what testing is and how assessing and teaching are interrelated.*
2	Reflecting on principles of language assessment • *Discuss each principle of language assessment by giving examples from your experiences.* • *Compare and contrast validity and reliability.* • *What makes a test or assessment reliable and valid?* • *Give examples of tests you have taken before and which you think were not reliable and valid.*
3	Reflecting retrospectively on testing and assessment types • *Discuss the test types and write about which of these tests you have taken before, and where, when, and why.* • *What are the advantages and disadvantages you observe when you take a multiple-choice test?* • *What can and can't be measured through tests? Why?* • *How would you ensure appropriate washback to the students when or after they are tested? Give reasons for your explanations.*
4	Reflecting on principles of testing • *Write about the worst and best testing experience you have had so far.* • *Suggest how the testing conditions could have been improved.* • *Select a standardized test you are quite familiar with (perhaps a recent one you have taken) and evaluate the test using five principles of practicality, reliability, validity, authenticity, and washback.*
5	Collaborative reading, writing, and discussing standardisation • *What are the consequences of standards-based and standardized testing? Provide details through examples from your learning experiences.* • *What are the consequences of test-driven teaching and learning? Give anecdotes from your own educational background. Discuss this in your group and list specific consequences that describe your views and the views of your group.*
6	Collaboratively writing on assessment of listening skill • *Describe listening as a skill by narrating your experiences with learning listening too.* • *How are the listening activities implemented in the classroom you are currently observing? Give details.* • *What kinds of assessment practises of listening do the teachers you observe have? Describe the assessment using the terms we have been covering so far.*

7 Collaboratively writing on assessment of speaking skill

- *Identify 5 key characteristics of speaking skill.*
- *Make a list including sentences such as, e.g., listening is a receptive skill which requires learners to be exposed to language use presented through different channels – video, audio, or human talk.*
- *In the light of the characteristics, you have listed above, discuss your experiences with learning to speak English. Each person can write his or her own experiences and then you can synthesize it in a summary paragraph.*
- *How are the speaking activities implemented in the classroom you are currently observing?*
- *Give details about teachers' and students' roles.*
- *How is speaking assessed in the classroom you observe? Evaluate this against the assessment principles of speaking [presented elsewhere]. Each of you in the group could bring in your own observational notes and write jointly.*

9 Collaboratively writing on assessment of reading skill

- *Describe assessment tasks and discuss these tasks with your practicum observational notes.*
- *Interview a reading teacher from one of the schools you can access and ask how they assess reading comprehension (each group member will interview one teacher).*
- *Write a summary of the interview with reference to how they assess reading and why they prefer to do so.*

10 Thinking about assessment tasks to use in the future

- *List the assessment tasks for writing and reflect on each to discuss their effectiveness depending on your English language learning experiences.*
- *Which of these would you consider using in your future teaching practices, and why?*

11 Understanding alternative assessment through own experiences

- *Describe what you understand by 'alternative assessment' and how it is different from 'traditional assessment'.*
- *List alternatives in assessment and discuss their characteristics.*
- *With which of these alternatives have you been assessed? Discuss by giving detailed contextual information of your experiences.*
- *Which of these have you observed or heard in your practicum observations? Describe the procedures followed and how you and students felt during such assessment.*

12 Writing an individual reflective paper on your own development in testing and assessment as a pre-service teacher

- *How has 'integrating your own testing and assessment experiences and observation in the practicum' influenced your becoming reflective and critical over time? Give examples.*
- *How has such a course structure (delivered asynchronously) influenced your learning testing and assessment?*
- *Describe three beliefs that you held before the course regarding testing and assessment and how they have been influenced during the course.*
- *What do you think you will be doing differently when assessing and testing your own students in the future? Give clear examples.*

ABOUT THE AUTHORS

Ali Öztüfekçi is a Lecturer in the Department of Foreign Language Teaching at Bahçeşehir University, İstanbul, Turkey. Currently, he is in the process of writing up his PhD thesis on bilingual pre-service education. He has published articles on early bilingualism, learner autonomy, and World Englishes. His research interests include teacher reflection, early bilingualism, and bilingual teacher education.

Kenan Dikilitaş is a Professor at the University of Stavanger in Norway, where he mentors academics and supports professional development, in particular relating to their (online) teaching practices. He also leads a course in 'Qualitative Research in Higher Education' for doctoral students at the Department of Education. His research interests include (language) teacher education, mentoring and investigating action research, and more recently, developing teaching and learning in digital environments.

Chapter 4

Reflective Practice Groups in ELT: An Emergent Model for Professional Development

Burak Aydın & Irem Çomoğlu

4.1. INTRODUCTION

In recent years, schools in Turkey have transformed into more accountable institutions in response to high expectations from society with regard to quality education. All educational shareholders have been more involved in educational policies and quality learning has been sought more than ever. Consequently, teachers of English language are required to be competent professionals who can fulfill contemporary demands and requirements (Richards, 2008). In particular, language instructors who teach at tertiary-level English preparatory programs in Turkey need to be qualified as they carry out a significant teaching mission. Since this one-year preparatory program is the first year of university education for many students – prior to the commencement of their departmental studies – the instructors need to be qualified enough to prepare learners for the multidimensional linguistic requirements of academic and professional life.

In an effort to ensure the above-mentioned professional quality, lifelong professional development (PD) seems to be crucial for language instructors. PD, as defined by Diaz-Maggioli (2004, p. 5), is 'a career-long process in which educators fine-tune their teaching to meet student needs,' as opposed to short-term theoretical development offered by pre-service training. Supporting the idea of extended improvement for language teachers, Richards (2008) notes that teaching English requires a special type of knowledge gained from academic and practical spheres so these teachers may continually raise their teaching standards. Unfortunately, in Turkey, PD opportunities for language teachers generally consist of short-mode events in which teachers are passive recipients of information while experts are the sources of wisdom (Atay, 2006). This way of professional development is actually traditional, decontextualized, and has little to offer teachers (Day & Sachs, 2004). As Johnstone (2006) puts it, these one-off PD events do not provide development and there is no long-term effect in this sense. Another shortcoming is that seminars, talks, and lectures do not differentiate learning to meet the diversity of teachers' needs (Diaz-Maggioli, 2004).

As opposed to the challenges mentioned above, a visionary understanding of PD is required to offer useful professional learning opportunities to language instructors in Turkey. As Diaz-Maggioli (2004, p. 5) notes, visionary PD is a 'job-embedded commitment that teachers make in order to further the purposes of the profession while addressing their own particular needs.' At this point, there are numerous components proposed by a range of scholars to the end of visionary PD. For Craft (2000), effective development is school-based, which addresses the realities of specific teaching contexts. Similarly, Fullan & Hargreaves (1992) note that effective PD is teacher-centered, prioritizing innovation based on teachers' needs and purposes. In the same vein, Mercer & Gregersen (2020) emphasize teachers' physical, mental, and emotional well-being as a central part of their improvement. According to Guskey (2000) and Johnstone (2006), effective PD is also process-based as opposed to one-shot training with little impact. Moreover, Knight (2002) asserts that PD should be practiced in communities of practice as a part of teachers' collaborative endeavor. Lastly, for Bailey (2006), effective PD should promote teacher autonomy, which can be done through the utilization of effective reflection. Clearly, the one-shot expert form of PD does not correspond with any visionary component above, thus not serving much for teachers' progress.

After a close scrutiny of all these visionary perspectives, we have concluded that effective professional development of language instructors is feasible through a focus on reflection, collaboration, and process, which is inclusive of all the conducive factors promoting successful professional development. More particularly, we think that reflection is a powerful tool to be utilized as a part of teachers' PD, and it is even more favorable when practiced through teacher collaboration and for an extended period of time.

From this point of view, our present study focuses on a process-based and collaborative reflection form, 'Reflective Practice Groups' (RPGs) (Distad & Brownstein, 2004) and delves into its benefits from the perspective of visionary PD. Focusing on a single RPG case, the study aims to yield insights into the field by investigating the intrinsic components of the construct along with its impact on language instructors' PD. Towards this purpose, the study first lays out the literature behind collaborative reflection, encompassing the traits of reflective practice, social-constructivism, and the basics of RPG practice. Then, after the methodology is presented, the findings are displayed within a pattern of emerging themes, leading to a discussion of these findings with regard to the depth of the RPG practice and how it addresses the contemporary understanding of teachers' PD.

4.2. LITERATURE REVIEW

4.2.1. Reflective Practice and Social Constructivism

Reflection, mostly a loosely defined term, is basically a type of thinking different from a routine and impulsive one, according to John Dewey (1933), whose legacy still inspires the field. Reflective activity, for him, is a deep inquiry which facilitates the ability to understand issues in depth. Schön (1983, 1987) is another scholar who specifies the workings of reflective practice, especially for professionals, by emphasizing the ideas of reflection-in-action (thinking consciously about the happenings on the spot) and reflection-on-action (thinking retrospectively about our actions). In addition, Killion & Todnem (1991) put forward the idea of reflection 'for' action, which means planning future practices based on previous experiences. Within this perspective, reflective practice has recently been a very prominent subject for scrutiny and there has been a bulk of interest in it along with its repercussions in teaching.

In specific terms, according to Brookfield (2017, p. 3), reflective practice is actually a 'critical' teaching activity which incorporates a 'sustained and intentional process of identifying and checking the accuracy and validity of our teaching assumptions.' Another specific look towards reflective practice comes from Wallace (1991), who presents how reflective practice actually works in teaching – from knowledge level to competence level – as seen in Figure 4.1.

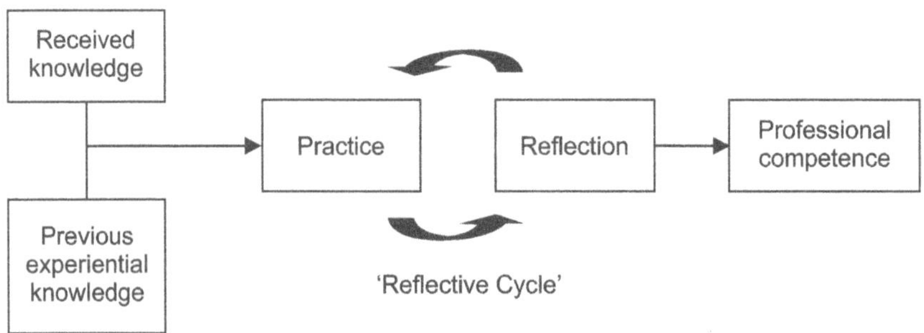

Figure 4.1. Reflective cycle (Wallace, 1991, p. 15).

Reflective practice, as a broad topic of interest, has also been elaborated on in terms of its efficiency in the light of some principles and pathways. For one, Rodgers (2002), after distilling big ideas from Dewey's prose, notes that effective reflection is a continual meaning-making process which is systematic and rigorous; it needs to be practiced in community; and also, one needs to adopt some attitudes to be able to utilize reflection. From another perspective, Farrell (2019) sees reflection as an inclusive activity and puts forward six principles: (1) reflective practice is holistic, (2) is evidence-based, (3) involves dialog, (4) bridges principles and practices, (5) requires an inquiring disposition, and (6) is a way of life. Farrell (2015) also proposes five stages for reflection: (1) philosophy, (2) principles, (3) theories, (4) practices, (5) beyond practice.

The commonality of the tenets of reflection is that it is better practiced in interaction with others as a collaborative act. Relevant to the fact, Van Gyn (1996) notes that collaboration is an integral aspect of reflection and therefore collaborative reflection should always be sought. This calls for the social constructivist learning paradigm, originating from the legacy of Lev Vygotsky (1978), who thinks that learning is a social act since higher-order thinking develops through mediation of thought through social contexts. In particular, social constructivists see learning as a meaning-making activity rather than accumulation of knowledge (Oldfather et al., 1999). More specifically, socially constructed learning happens in communities through the act of intersubjectivity, which means developing self through others (Tudge, 1992). Therefore, collaborative reflection is actually a qualified activity – practiced within a community of practice (Wenger et al., 2002) – which merges the premises of a special thinking style (reflection) and the activity of co-construction of knowledge (social constructivism).

4.2.2. Reflective Practice Groups (RPGs)

As a specific construct for teachers embedding collaborative reflection and social constructivist learning, Reflective Practice Groups (RPGs) are defined as 'a particular way for teachers to regularly and systematically reflect on their practice in a supportive, collegial environment free from evaluation' (Distad & Brownstein, 2004, p. 2). RPG is a professional teacher collaboration which builds on past actions to improve future practices through reflective practice (see Figure 4.2).

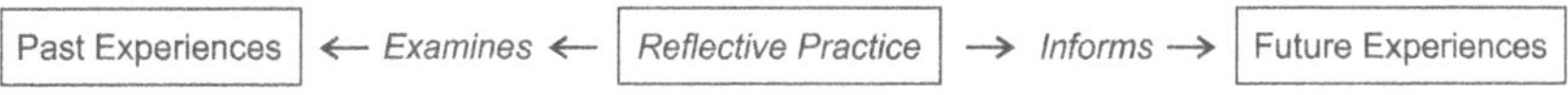

Figure 4.2. RPGs as a bridge between past and future (Distad & Brownstein, 2004, p. 8).

RPGs are formed to facilitate teacher efficacy that feeds into enhanced learning for students through their collaborative and democratic nature. They can take many forms and different names such as dialog, study, or support groups; action research groups, lesson plan groups, teaching-strategy groups, and online chat groups (Distad & Brownstein, 2004). Other names for RPGs include teacher reflection (development) groups (Farrell, 1998, 2001, 2003, 2013), collaborative reflection groups (Glazer et al., 2004), and critical development teams (Diaz-Maggioli, 2004).

These groups are facilitated by the participating teachers who assume a rotational facilitator duty (Distad & Brownstein, 2004) and they are ideally participated in by five to eight teachers (Richards & Farrell, 2005). Farrell (2003, p. 17; 2013, p. 10) proposes the core elements for these teacher groups as below:

- Providing different opportunities for teachers to reflect: utilizing reflective practice tools such as teacher journals, classroom observations, critical friends, and discussions.
- Negotiating some ground rules.
- Making provisions for time such as individual time, activity time, development time, reflection time.
- Providing external input for reflection like classroom instances, experiences, theories.
- Providing low affective state for quality reflection.

Farrell & Jacobs (2016) also put forward some principles for RPGs such as heterogeneous grouping, collaborative skills, group autonomy, maximized interactions, equal opportunities, individual accountability, positive interdependence, and cooperation as values. On the other hand, Diaz-Maggioli (2004) cautions us about some misinterpretations of RPGs, noting that these meetings are not regular staff meetings to discuss school-wide issues, nor an in-service training activity or a complaint session. Apparently, RPGs are solution-oriented, complete, and supportive constructs free from evaluation and judgment.

The literature on RPG generally consists of case studies which mostly yield emergent themes in the field. In fact, different cases surface different themes and attitudes, but the practicality and functionality of RPGs seem intact. Starting with one of the pioneers of the idea, Farrell's (1998) study in Korea focused on three teachers in the process of 16 reflective meetings – under the name of 'Teacher Development Groups.' The study inquired into what teachers talked about, whether the talks were descriptive or critical, and how much reflection developed over time. The results indicated that teachers generally talked about their personal theories and problems in teaching, their talks were descriptive in nature, and not much reflective development occurred in the 16 meetings. The takeaway from the study is that reflection takes time and requires guidance.

Farrell's (2013) study in Canada with three ESL teachers over a two-year period also revealed much about RPG groups. This time the teachers generally talked about the school context, their perception of self as a teacher, and their learners. More importantly, the teachers maintained that the meetings were empowering, promoted self-improvement, raised awareness, and provided support which, as stated, was impossible while working in isolation. In short, Farrell's studies proved the high impact of RPGs in terms of teachers' PD.

Apart from Farrell's seminal research, there are other insightful studies on the effect of the RPG model of development. Christodoulou (2013), in the Greek context, worked with five instructors of English over a 13-week-long guided reflective practice period. He noted the emergent themes as follows: awareness, reflecting on the positive, critical reflection, therapeutic value of the meetings, and reframing practice. He also provided some conclusions after the study, viz., that (1) reflection is transformational, (2) requires time, (3) is a guided process, (4) is appreciative, and (5) requires free will.

Kuh (2015) studied a critical friends group with a variety of participants including coaches, teachers, and para-educators in the USA. The study raised three themes: mutual engagement, joint enterprise, and shared repertoire. The only pitfall of the study was that teachers mostly talked about school-wide issues, as opposed to enhancement of student learning. Similarly, Berkey et al. (1990) studied a variety of participants, inviting teachers, researchers, and administrators to a reflective project named 'Teacher Development and Organizational Change.' According to their findings, for teachers, the project promoted new perspectives; for administrators, it promoted the discovery of teachers' ideas in depth; and for researchers, it helped in giving effective feedback and avoiding judgment in the endeavor.

In the Turkish context, there are a few studies focusing on the RPG construct. Fakazlı & Kuru-Gönen (2017) studied teachers' perceptions of the reflective practice tools (diaries and video-recordings) used in reflective meetings. They worked with eight tertiary-level language instructors for 15 weeks. The findings showed that the teachers enjoyed the use of the tools. They particularly favored teacher diaries for remembering the instances clearly and supported the use of video-recordings since it promoted objectivity for reflection. Burhan-Horasanlı & Ortaçtepe (2016) studied an online discussion community with tertiary-level language instructors. They focused on the reflection types (in, on, for action) and the topics emerging. As the results indicated, teachers were observed to be reflecting 'on' motivation, personal characteristics, autonomy, and language learning. In addition, they reflected 'in' to analyse their beliefs and 'for' some actions to enhance student learning. The researchers noted that reflection is an embedded process – involving the cycle of reflection in, on, and for actions – and that it should be a collaborative process.

As the studies indicate, collaborative reflective practice cases yield positive results in terms of enhancement in teachers' professional knowledge, awareness, skills, and attitude. Based on the fact, our RPG case is likely to reveal other perspectives and add to the knowledge base gleaned from the related literature. In particular, the purpose of our study is to create qualitative data from a tertiary-level English program, which will contribute to the understanding of collaborative and process-oriented reflection in language teachers' PD.

4.3. METHOD

4.3.1. Design

The present study was designed in the qualitative research paradigm and as a single instrumental case study with multiple participants as the first author Burak's master's thesis, which was supervised by Irem, the second author. As Merriam (2009, p. 203) defines it, a case study is 'an intensive, holistic description and analysis of a single, bounded unit.' In case studies, researchers utilize a variety of data collection techniques and tools such as interviews, audio-visual materials, observations, and documents in order to explore a bounded system in depth (Creswell, 2007). Within this understanding, the present study sought a detailed conception of RPG from the meanings derived from the words and actions of the participating teachers by means of close inquiry and deep discoveries. Particularly, the research aimed to find answers to the following questions:

1. How do teachers engage in RPG?
2. What insights can we gain about RPG as a visionary PD model?

4.3.2. Context and Participants

The study was conducted at the school of foreign languages of a foundation university. Five language instructors teaching in a preparatory English program participated in the study and they were sampled on a voluntary basis, in line with the fact that reflective practice is a voluntary activity (Harvey et al., 2020). As for ethical considerations, the site school approved the study through a decision made by its ethics committee and the participants expressed their willingness for the study through signing consent forms. Also, to address privacy concerns, instead of teachers' real names, pseudonyms were utilized in the data. The demographic and academic backgrounds of the teachers can be found in Table 4.1.

Table 4.1. Demographic and academic background of the participants.

Name	Age	Degree	Certification	Teaching Experience	Current Level/ Skill Taught	Administrative Roles
Teacher B	32	BA in English Literature	Pedagogical Education Certificate; Material Development; SIT TESOL Certificate	8 years	Elementary (Repeating students) / Integrated Skills	Program Supervisor (currently)
Teacher G	26	BA in English Literature	SIT TESOL Certificate	4 years	Pre-Intermediate / Integrated Skills, Reading, Writing	–
Teacher J	29	BA in English Literature	SIT TESOL Certificate	7 years	Pre-Intermediate / Integrated Skills, Reading, Listening, Speaking	Program Supervisor (previously)
Teacher M	28	BA in American Culture and Literature	Pedagogical Education Certificate	5 years	Upper-Intermediate / Integrated Skills	Test Administrator (currently)
Teacher S	28	BA & MA in American Culture and Literature	Pedagogical Education Certificate	6 years	Elementary (Repeating students)	Educational Coordinator; Testing, Curriculum and Materials office member (previously)

As can be noted from the table, the participating teachers were all graduates of literature departments, but they held certificates related to the field of English language teaching (ELT). They were of different backgrounds as to their experiences with administrative duties, whereas their teaching experiences were rather homogeneous. The commonality in their profiles is that they had reasonable experience in the field (minimum 4 years) and they were experienced in teaching a variety of levels and skills as well as in working for administration.

The school context is also really important for the findings of this study. The site school was dedicated to teachers' professional development and had a Continuing Professional Development Office having a role to achieve that end. The school adopted a reflective stance to PD, offering the SIT TESOL Certificate Course for the instructors, a course locating experiential learning and reflection at its center (see Certificate in TESOL 2021), and offering teachers a developmental scheme in which they were engaged in a variety of reflective PD activities throughout the academic year. However, until the commencement of our study, the developmental structure of the school had not actually promoted process-based and collaborative reflective practice projects in the academic calendar apart from the summer courses. Our research findings can be interpreted realistically within the view of the aforementioned PD system with its advantages and shortcomings.

4.3.3. Data Collection and Analysis

The data for the study were collected within the 14-week-long RPG meeting process. In other words, the RPG process itself was the source of our data collection. In this period of study, our teachers held 10 weekly meetings – with two introductory pre-RPG meetings in a single week and eight (bi)weekly regular RPG meetings. The meetings lasted 1–2 hours and the topics and dates were selected by the participants. Below, the specific dynamics used in the design of this particular RPG are presented:

- The purpose was raising teacher efficacy and the teachers were free to choose the topics of discussion (Distad & Brownstein, 2004).
- Trust and confidentiality were adopted as the principles (Distad & Brownstein, 2004) along with Farrell's (2003, 2013) aforementioned reflective group elements.
- Both received and experiential knowledge was used (Wallace, 1991) to reflect in, on (Schön, 1983, 1987), and for (Killion & Todnem, 1991) actions; to build on past to inform future (Distad & Brownstein, 2004), by also utilizing Kolb's (2015) Experiential Learning Cycle as a note of reference.
- Reflective practice tools were used to bring data to the meetings – namely, journals, surveys, questionnaires, recordings, and observations (Richards & Lockhart, 1996).
- Each meeting was facilitated by a different teacher in a rotational design (Distad & Brownstein, 2004; Glazer et al., 2004) and the facilitators helped the group initiate and maintain the discussions along with promoting participation and reflection (Eitington, 2002).

In an effort to help a clear understanding of the group meetings, the RPG activity log in Table 4.2 illustrates the details about the meetings, including the dates, the topics of discussion, facilitators, actions, and RP tools utilized.

Table 4.2. RPG activity log.

Meeting Name	Date	Facilitator/Topic	Activity
Pre-RPG Meeting 1 (Introduction)	December 18, 2019	The Researcher	• Introduction to the study – presentation about reflective practice. • Task given: A critical incident to be journaled for an ongoing puzzle.
Pre-RPG Meeting 2 (Brainstorming)	December 20, 2019	The Researcher	• Participants sharing incidents. • Finding common issues, brainstorming more issues, and poster-making.
RPG Meeting 1	December 27, 2019	Teacher S *Student & Teacher Motivation*	• Survey info shared, reflected. • Common topics and categories reached. • RP tools: Student/teacher surveys and literature.
RPG Meeting 2	January 8, 2020	Teacher J *Student Motivation*	• Articles and journals shared, analysed. • Teachers deriving action points to be tried until the next meeting. • RP tools: Reading literature and journaling.
RPG Meeting 3	January 15, 2020	Teacher G *Student Motivation*	• Experiences/insights shared, reflected. • Closure with prominent themes. • RP tools: Journaling.
RPG Meeting 4	February 12, 2020	Teacher M *Teacher Motivation*	• Journal notes shared, reflected. • Closure. • RP tools: Journaling (the factors motivating the teachers in their profession).
RPG Meeting 5	February 19, 2020	Teacher B *Use of L1*	• Articles shared, reflected. • Teacher J sharing a survey. • RP tools: Reading literature, student survey.

RPG Meeting 6	February 28, 2020	Teacher S *Use of L1*	• Survey results (student) and recordings (teachers' use of L1) shared, reflected. • Closure. • RP tools: Surveys and audio-recording.
RPG Meeting 7	March 4, 2020	Teacher M *Time Management (Lesson Planning)*	• Teachers planning a lesson for another teacher (Intermediate level & 50-min lesson). • RP tools: Co-planning.
RPG Meeting 8	March 11, 2020	Teacher B & The Researcher *Time Management & Closure*	• Teacher T (the invitee) sharing reflections upon conducting the planned lesson. • Closure of RPG (writing thank you letters & last remarks).

For the data collection, a variety of tools were utilized: video-recordings of the RPG meetings, the researcher's field-notes, visual artefacts produced in the meetings (posters), two semi-structured interviews, two reflective essays, and a focus group meeting at the end of the process. The multimodal data collected from these sources were analysed using the qualitative data analysis method suggested by Saldana & Omasta (2018). More specifically, emergent patterns and their relationships were analysed to the end of formulating interconnected meanings. The pathway of our data analysis can be found below:

- Condensing data.
- Noticing patterns.
- Unifying different things.
- Understanding action, reaction, and interaction in human behavior.
- Interpreting routines, rituals, roles, and relationships (Saldana & Omasta 2018, p. 30).

To pattern the data, 'in vivo coding' was used by Saldana & Omasta (2018, p. 182), which is using the participants' own language as symbols of analysis. At the end of the analysis, the patterns were merged to reach wider meaning clusters that constituted the emergent themes of the study and their interrelationships. As to the credibility of the study, some triangulation and confirmation strategies were adopted such as utilizing different sources of data collection, applying member checks, and working with a co-researcher to ensure and confirm the outcomes (Creswell, 2007; Merriam, 2009).

4.3.4. Researcher Reflexivity

As a language instructor and teacher trainer working at the site school, the researcher was also a colleague of the participants. However, for this study, he rather took a researcher role, thereby developing another professional identity alongside teaching/training. In order to initiate and sustain the process, first, the researcher took the role of facilitator in presenting the tenets of reflective practice and structuring the process at the very beginning (in the pre-RPG meetings). Then, from RPG Meeting 1 onwards, he took a more peripheral role (Saldana & Omasta, 2018) and acted as a guide, not interfering with the discussions unless necessary, and only wrapping up the sessions at the end.

Apart from his roles within the study process per se, the researcher also stayed reflective and reflexive personally in order to grasp the meaning of the whole process, by avoiding pre-assumptions and surface understanding of issues. In fact, he reflected on the events when meanings came into play (Dahlberg, 2009) and developed a purpose, belonging, and meaning out of his immersion in the process as a researcher, a teacher (trainer), and a person (Saldana, 2018).

4.4. FINDINGS

Figure 4.3 depicts the emergent themes from our case study and their interrelationships in response to our research questions, namely how teachers are engaged in RPG and how the components of our model address the visionary understanding of PD. Specifically, the figure manifests that the RPG of this research was composed by the interplay of such factors as 'affect,' 'collectivity,' 'action orientation,' and 'exploration,' which was qualified by 'reflection,' an impactful catalyst within the process.

In detail, the primary force behind our RPG seemed to be the affective well-being of the group, which entailed friendship that ensured openness and additionally therapeutic effect. Due to the high affective bonds among the participants, collectivity was obviously generated, incorporating a culture of help and shared wisdom. Action orientation, not necessarily ensured by affect, seemed to be another cornerstone for this reflective PD process, with the sub-factors of teacher agency and practicality. Teachers seemingly reached reflective conclusions, in the form of explorations, through the continuous interplay of their collective and action-oriented work. That is to say, teachers performed in a cycle of actively constructing improvement and reinforcing it collectively in the meetings. As a result, explorations can be interpreted as the ultimate outcome of this RPG construct, and in this study, teachers were able to reach in-depth resolutions about teaching and learning. Finally, reflection was obviously the catalyst for these RPG factors to operate, and it acted in a variety of patterns as collaborative reflection in collectivity; as reflective practice cycle and tools in action orientation; and finally, as critical reflection in teachers' explorations. At this point, each theme and sub-theme needs to be clarified and exemplified for better understanding.

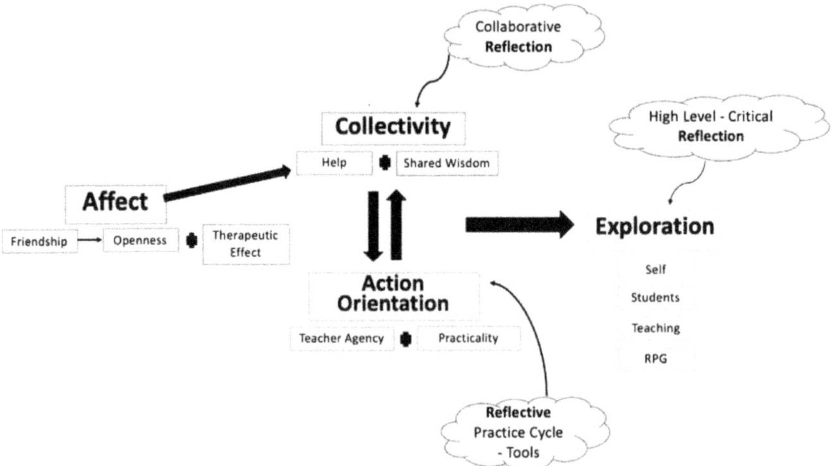

Figure 4.3. Emergent meanings surfacing from the RPG process (Aydın, 2020, p. 103).

4.4.1. Affect

The specifics of the themes are worth analysing through the collected verbal and visual data. Firstly, 'affect' was the leading theme, which was obvious from its impact on the conduct of the RPG and its promotion of collaboration. Affective elements have been a powerful determinant of teachers' collaborative work and Teacher M clearly stresses how much emotions are integrated in teachers' PD in RPG:

> I always thought there was a strict line between being a human and being a teacher. I felt if something bad happens and if I cry in my office about something, that would make me unprofessional. But in these meetings, it made me see that actually they are together, our emotions and our ways to teach. (Teacher M – Interview 1)

The teachers were clearly able to create a close relationship in the RPG process and it was fundamentally facilitated by their existing 'friendship' – a sub-theme of affect – in the school, which was traceable through Teacher B's lines:

> It was a big plus for us to work with not just our colleagues but friends. Because we are close friends and know each other very well, we felt more comfortable while we were giving feedback or advice. Also, this made these meetings less formal. (Teacher B – Reflective Essay 2)

As can be noted from Figure 4.3, this friendship eventually promoted 'openness' that helped teachers reveal their thoughts and reflections, according to Teacher B; and this was valuable for them, as Teacher J noted:

> If I don't know somebody very well, maybe I cannot be that much honest to them, or sometimes I can refrain myself from giving some kind of feedback to them. But when we are friends, we are closer, more honest to each other because we know that they will not get offended because of our opinions. (Teacher B – Interview 2)

> This process helped me realize that I need an environment where I can freely talk about issues that arise during teaching and ask for assistance without the fear of being judged. (Teacher J – Reflective Essay 1)

In fact, openness was truly appreciated by the teachers and it was an essential part of working in RPG, which is quite clear through the phrases 'don't judge' and 'be open-minded' in the poster (see Figure 4.4) which teachers created in Pre-RPG Meeting 2 while noting some ground rules for their group.

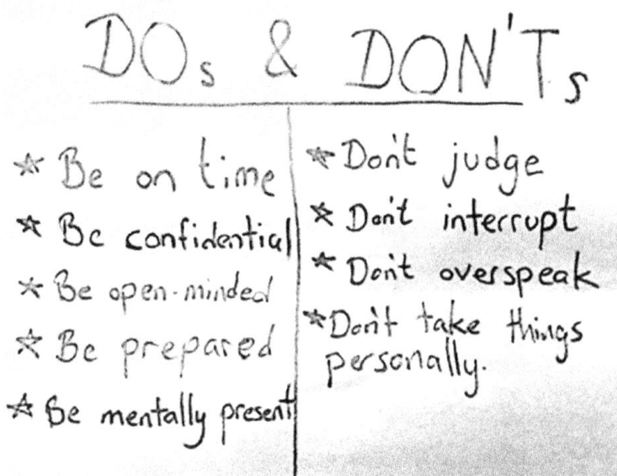

Figure 4.4. Poster on ground rules for RPG meetings.

In terms of affective bound, teachers also emphasized the 'therapeutic effect' of RPG meetings. In other words, these meetings were seen as sites for therapy in which teachers could share emotionally, as Teacher S noted:

> It is both professional and at the same time it helps me more emotionally. Well, being here, five people sitting here and talking. Talking like this is just another form of therapy for me. We talk and we try to better ourselves and it gives me a feeling of wholeness in the institution. (Teacher S – Interview 1)

4.4.2. Collectivity

Based on the affective strength of the RPG construct, the participating teachers were able to work through 'collectivity' by forming a unified body of decisions, supporting each other, and exchanging ideas and experiences. Teacher J perfectly described how collectivity mattered for her in this RPG:

> I am also amazed by how well we work together assisting each other despite having very different personalities. It made me aware that I should not refrain from asking my colleagues for assistance. (Teacher J – Reflective Essay 1)

As a highly affect-oriented factor within collectivity, 'help' was found to be an upfront theme which was an integral part of teachers' responsibility for one another in the act of professional development. Teacher S mentioned the value of help:

> Sitting here, talking with my friends and trying to help with their problems in the class. I realize then actually I do know something, then I can help these people as well as they can help me, so it feels pretty good. (Teacher S – Interview 1)

She also said that help was created out of the necessity arising from the commonality of teachers' problems:

> When the thing she (Teacher J) said about class management. I was shocked. I didn't think she would ever have a problem like that and when she said it, I was shocked. I said OK, we have the same problems [...] Right, I wanna help her, so I looked and checked and I couldn't

> find anything. But still I wanted to help her, that's why I checked. (Teacher S – Interview 1)

In fact, the commonality in teachers' problems was clearly traceable from the poster they designed in Pre-RPG Meeting 2 (brainstorming meeting), which manifests the source from which the culture of help originated (see Figure 4.5).

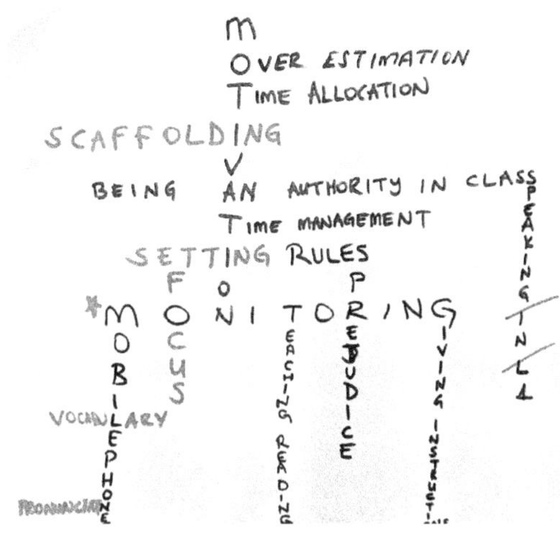

Figure 4.5. Poster on common teaching problems.

'Shared wisdom' was observed to be another sub-theme of collectivity, which prioritized the teachers' appreciation for exchanging perspectives and experiences in RPG meetings. The teachers were able to gain practices and perspectives from one another during the process, which is manifest in Teacher M's comparison between RPG and peer observation:

> I think it is actually better than peer observation and such things, because in peer observation only one person sees you and you only get one perspective. But here, you tell about your lesson from your own perspective and you hear many other ideas from many other level teachers. (Teacher M – Interview 2)

Apart from sharing perspectives and practices, the teachers also found chances to work jointly in RPG meetings, as they did in collaborative lesson planning:

> I really liked preparing a lesson plan together [...] I really liked seeing the reflection of another teacher. (Teacher M – Interview 2)

The above-mentioned collective work of teachers entailed 'collaborative reflection' – an essential element of putting heads together – which facilitated their efforts in creating learning through RPG meetings. In our case, reflection was appreciated to be a collaborative act, through Teacher B's words:

> I am used to reflect on my lessons because I do it from time to time [...] but again it is an individual thinking for me [...] This time, we all bring some data to the table and then we share and we take out from them [...] so it is not individual anymore when you share it. We can use it as collective thing, so this is different than any other reflective cycles. (Teacher B – Interview 2)

4.4.3. Action Orientation

Alongside working collectively, the teachers also enjoyed the 'action orientation' of the RPG process, meaning that their development was fostered by classroom realities and the reflective data were directly derived from teaching practice – as opposed to their being passive recipients of training events. In particular, the teachers stressed the importance of 'teacher agency' and 'practicality' as the major components of this action-oriented PD.

For one, teachers seemingly favored being the active constructors of their own development, through teacher agency, as noted by Teacher B and Teacher G:

> In the workshops or in the seminars, conferences, we are mostly inactive. But in RPG meetings, we are the main elements that follow the procedures and that do the meetings together, so this was an active action for all of us. (Teacher B – Interview 2)

> I think everyone is taking something out of this. You know we are not just coming here, waiting for the time to pass. Everyone is taking some information and I see outside the meetings [...] Everyone is very motivated to take some things out of it and try out. So, everyone is using it very efficiently. (Teacher G – Interview 1)

In addition to being the active agents of their development, teachers also appreciated the practicality, the fact that the meetings were informed by classroom happenings and critical incidents and that the outcome would be better teaching practice. At this point, Teacher J stated:

> Every time I leave the meeting, I have something to do. And I have something to realize, to work on and to think about for my next classes. And that gives a feeling of responsibility which makes me more aware in the class about what I am going to do and [how] to view things that happen in class. (Teacher J – Interview 1)

To better portray practicality, a critical incident from RPG Meeting 2 is worth analysing. In this instance, teachers were finalizing the meeting after considerable reflection on the literature and surveys of student motivation. They then decided to prepare some action plans to be tried in class for motivating students in the interval until the following meeting:

> Teacher B: I will have a session with them. I want make them realize their mistakes in speaking English, what their problems are in English.
>
> Teacher M: I will try focusing on the upcoming quiz with the students. One at a time. I will see how it motivates them.
>
> Teacher G: I will have a pair system to motivate students. Whenever one [of a] pair is stuck, their partner has to jump in. Maybe they will be more comfortable to talk that way.
>
> Teacher S: I will work on making students feel OK when they make mistakes.
>
> Teacher J: There are things that I am already working on but maybe working on materials to make reading classes more enjoyable or tolerable. (RPG Meeting 2)

As in collectivity, reflection played a huge role in qualifying action-oriented RPG discussions. Specifically, it helped the teachers inquire about their classrooms and collect reflective data from them. This was possible by reflecting in, on, and for actions, through 'a cycle of reflection' and utilizing 'reflective practice tools.' The quotations below demonstrate the effects of reflection on teachers' thinking and practices in RPGs:

> I wasn't a person who did reflection, even on my own. I like to think about my lessons but now I realize that I looked at it in a wider perspective that I need to get into details. (Teacher M – Interview 2)

> When you don't have data when you come to those meetings, it is just your idea, you know. And it is just your memory combined with what you think about what you got through. But when you have these reflective tools, it's evidence of so much going on. (Teacher J – Interview 2)

4.4.4. Exploration

Setting off with affective strength, then developing through collectivity and action-orientation, and qualifying this improvement with the help of reflective practice, the participating teachers finally reached major 'explorations,' which proved the achievement of critical reflection at the end of the RPG period.

First of all, they reached '(re)explorations about their teacher self,' although they had already been considerably experienced teachers prior to the RPG work. They seemingly put their ongoing classroom practices under scrutiny:

> I got used to doing the same things. I have been using Book E (the course book used in the school) for four years now and it was just automatic. I was doing everything automatically. But with the journaling, I just stopped and take a look at myself. And why do I do that? Why did I say that? (Teacher S – Interview 1)

> I found out that I was wrong to think that students want me to speak Turkish in class all the time. (Teacher J – Reflective Essay 2)

Their second major point of exploration was related to the 'student aspect of teaching,' which gave them an opportunity to put themselves in students' roles:

> It made me realize my own actions in the classroom, journaling especially. Before, I was just on my own in the class. I was the teacher and I was interacting with the students, but with journaling, I started being the student and the teacher at the same time. I started like 'OK, what would I do if I were the student?' 'What would I react when my teacher said this to me?' So, it made me realize the student aspect of the classroom. (Teacher S – Interview 1)

Figure 4.6 presents a good visual from RPG Meeting 1, a poster that teachers designed on (de)motivational factors for students, which shows the depth of teachers' reflections – in this particular instance, about the student side of teaching.

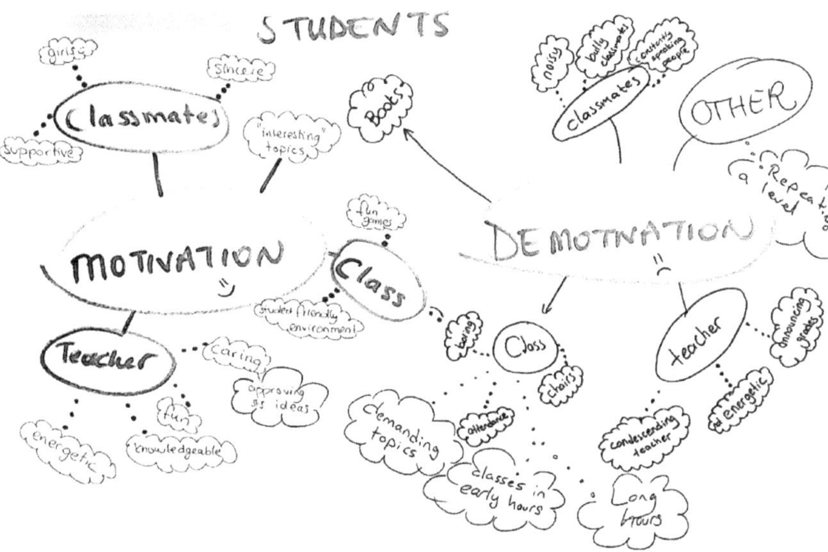

Figure 4.6. Poster on the analysis of (de)motivational factors for students.

Another exploration emerged about the nature of the 'teaching profession.' In this category, the teachers articulated a variety of realizations ranging from the practicality of teaching to the necessity of reflection and the probability of failure in the classroom, noted in the quotations below respectively:

> I am not an ELT graduate. I feel bad on this because I realize all big words like ELT words like interpretation, generalization and planning. These words scared me usually because I don't know them. I know them but I didn't study them. Well, in these meetings, I learned a lot of them and besides learning I realized that I don't have to know all of them because I use them in my class. (Teacher S – Interview 1)

> While we were discussing about specific situations, different suggestions came up, yet, they did not work out the same as expected in all classes. Therefore, I now think that teaching contains a continuous reflection. (Teacher G – Reflective Essay 1)

> It (RPG) helped me see that failing is okay and that it actually helps us find better ways of implementing our lesson plans. (Teacher M – Reflective Essay 1)

Finally, the teachers explored the 'RPG process' itself, reflecting on its parameters and delivering suggestions for further practice. Below are nine reflections distilled from their reviews that can offer implications for future RPGs:

(1) RPGs should be voluntary.
(2) The participants should have rapport and come from different backgrounds.
(3) The meetings should not involve more than four or five teachers.
(4) The frequency of RPG meetings should depend on content and period of study.
(5) Freedom of choice is an important aspect of RPGs.
(6) Facilitators (as a rotational duty) have an important role in these meetings – the roles teachers assigned for their facilitators are listed on the poster in Figure 4.7.
(7) A leading coach is necessary in RPGs, with a professional and friendly attitude.
(8) Teachers need time to dedicate to RPG meetings to benefit from them.
(9) RPGs can be versatile and be used functionally.

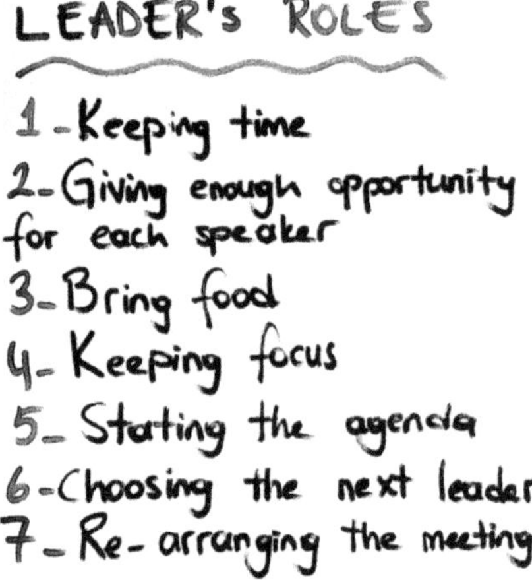

Figure 4.7. Poster on facilitators' roles in RPGs.

4.5. DISCUSSION

The findings of the study shed light on the nature of RPGs as well as their value in terms of language instructors' PD. The detailed account of the emergent themes and their interconnections clearly portrayed the intrinsic workings of the construct and answered the research questions with solid thematic outcomes.

4.5.1. Research Question 1: How do teachers engage in RPG?

Clearly, the trajectory of themes presented in Figure 4.3 demonstrates how teachers engaged in this RPG work. Firstly, the project was initially promoted by high affective bonds, that is, teachers' friendship in particular or rapport in general. This supports the idea that teachers' good relationships with each other and a low affective state are integral parts of the RPG form of development (Farrell, 2003, 2013). It also accords with Farrell's (2019) principle that reflection is a 'holistic' activity in which the non-cognitive side of reflection, namely teacher well-being, is an essential component to be noted. Supporting this argument, Mercer & Gregersen (2020) suggest that teachers' personal and professional lives inform each other, thus making their spiritual and mental well-being a reference point for PD. Therefore, answering the first research question, teachers clearly engage in RPG and build momentum from an affectively strong state. This fact is also observable from how friendship created openness and how this RPG eventually turned out to be a site of therapy for our teachers.

Another observation point is that teachers' strong rapport led to collective behavior thanks to which teachers could support each other and share their perspectives. This proves how reflection is qualified through collaboration (Rodgers, 2002). As Farrell (2019) notes in one of his six principles, reflection involves dialog with self and others. This way, he believes, teaching assumptions can be challenged and questioned easily, which also occurred in our case. In this RPG, teachers appreciated their high-level collaboration and positive interdependence, which is actually the core of any collaborative reflection activity (Farrell & Jacobs, 2016). As such, this RPG case could also present an embodiment of the social constructivist learning paradigm, through which our teachers were able to create personal understanding of things supported by the perspectives of others, through intersubjectivity (Tudge, 1992). Correspondingly, our RPG can be called a 'community of practice' (Wenger et al., 2002) because the participating teachers seemingly engaged in a dialogic process of sharing common concerns in a continual manner – for 10 meetings in three months. In other words, our RPG teachers engaged in a co-learning experience to build bottom-up development as opposed to accumulating expert knowledge.

Besides working by putting their heads together, our teachers also engaged in action-oriented PD by which they could act as the agents of their improvement as well as learn from their classrooms. As Distad & Brownstein (2004) note, in RPGs, teachers are the active constructors of knowledge that translates into enhanced student learning. In our study, the teachers continually connected past actions with future actions through a data-driven approach, supporting Farrell's

(2019) idea that reflective practice is 'evidence-based' and it 'bridges principles and practices.' At this point, Farrell (2019) claims that a 'stronger' form of reflection takes place when it is an informed activity (being evidence-based) and when teachers reveal their hidden teaching conceptions to be compared with classroom happenings (bridging principles and practices).

Facilitating this evidence- and action-based process, the most important components of this RPG were apparently reflective practice cycles (in, on, for) and tools (journaling, reading literature, surveying, recording). This underpins the centrality and functionality of reflective practice in developmental teacher meetings. Empirically supporting this argument, Burhan-Horasanlı & Ortaçtepe (2016) found in their study that reflection works efficiently within an embedded cycle of reflecting in, on, and for actions. As to the reflective practice tools, our teachers adopted a variety, with journaling being the most preferred – as in Fakazlı & Kuru-Gönen's (2017) study. In sum, it is noteworthy that future RPGs should seek ways to embed a reflective process in which teachers take data from the classroom and reflect on it in a cycle to inform future practices.

Finally, after setting off with a high affective setup and developing through collectivity and by taking actions, our RPG teachers seemingly reached the level of critical reflection, which is reconsideration of teaching assumptions in a maintained process (Brookfield, 2017). At the end of the RPG process, the teachers could notably explore a variety of professional domains such as teacher self, students, teaching, and the RPG process itself, which proves the achievement of high reflectivity and reflexivity conducive to enhanced teacher efficacy aimed at in any RPG (Distad & Brownstein, 2004). In this sense, Farrell's (2015) idea of 'reflection beyond practice,' which is the ultimate level of reflective practice in his framework, is actually obvious from our results since the teachers' realization points were clearly elaborated beyond the constraints of classroom walls. These ultimate deep explorations can also be identified with Farrell's (2019) two other principles about RP, namely reflection 'requires an inquiring disposition' and it is 'a way of life.' In other words, our teachers clearly showed a positive attitude to change and would apparently continue to adopt a reflective approach to their teaching, given all the deep conclusions they were able to make after just 10 meetings.

4.5.2. Research Question 2: What insights can we gain about RPG as a visionary PD model?

Apart from the specific depiction of meanings emerging out of our RPG, it is also worth discussing to what degree RPG is actually congruent with visionary understanding of teachers' PD. As discussed in the introduction of this chapter, visionary

PD is a school-based (Craft, 2000), teacher-centered (Fullan & Hargreaves, 1992), process-oriented (Johnstone, 2006), reflective (Bailey, 2006), and collaborative (Knight, 2002) activity. Therefore, our RPG case can be evaluated through these factors for its PD value to be gauged.

First of all, our RPG was a school-based activity since it was a situated practice involving a specific cohort of teachers, based on the contextual realities and needs of a specific school of foreign languages. Second, our group was highly teacher-centered, with the freedom of choice in terms of discussion points, facilitators, and reflective practice tools. In visionary PD understanding, it is true that teachers should be active constructors of their own development (Diaz-Maggioli, 2004) and also their needs and purposes should be paramount in the endeavor (Fullan & Hargreaves, 1992). Actually, these realities were obvious from the action-oriented (agency and practicality) aspect of our RPG. Also, it regarded teacher well-being as inherently critical for this group and this is manifest in how teachers' affective state facilitated the whole process and how motivated they were throughout the whole program.

In addition, our RPG was a process-oriented developmental program as opposed to one-off PD events. For Guskey (2000), effective PD is an intentional, ongoing, and systemic process and our RPG was a longitudinal opportunity for teachers to fine-tune their teaching in time, through conscious progress. As another point of discussion, our group was highly reflective, as its name suggests, congruent with the fact that effective PD assumes teacher autonomy that is shaped through reflection (Bailey, 2006). Correspondingly, according to Day & Sachs (2004), PD should be evidence- and inquiry-based, which was the case for our group since it was an informed activity in which teachers took data in and data out throughout the meetings. Lastly, our RPG was clearly aligned with the fact that effective PD should be collaborative. As Knight (2002) puts it, PD should be practiced in communities of practice, which our teachers adopted due to the presence of socially constructed learning. With all the mentioned compatibility, RPGs can evidently be regarded as a visionary model of professional development for language teachers.

Reflective Break

- What do you think is the value of RPGs in teachers' professional learning?
- Which component(s) of visionary PD do you think RPGs address the most/the least?
- Our RPG case surfaced several themes that can set a model for future practices (see Figure 4.3). Which of these themes do you consider the most important to teachers' professional learning?

4.6. CONCLUSION

In short, our study yields emergent insights into the understanding of language teachers' PD by clearly portraying how an RPG actually works and how much development it can promote. From the collected data, our case can set a model for further RPG projects with its details about the intrinsic workings of our group and its developmental effect as articulated by our teachers. More particularly, their critical reflection about the RPG process itself can be noted by other practitioners in the field. We hope to see more RPG cases, especially in different teaching and learning contexts, in order to reach a wider understanding of such a way of professional development.

REFERENCES

Atay, D. (2006). Teachers' professional development: Partnerships in research. *Teaching English as a Second or Foreign Language, 10*(2), 1–15. http://www.tesl-ej.org/pdf/ej38/a8.pdf

Aydın, B. (2020). Professional development of prep school EFL instructors through reflective practice groups. Master's thesis, Dokuz Eylul University, Turkey. https://tez.yok.gov.tr/UlusalTezMerkezi/TezGoster?key=fl0Kw4p1rmMDotyKRdYv1DJq9SvMTXC-LUTW8ewSZR7E2bJ8VWsBbADfxqT3EL1wb

Bailey, K. (2006). M. *Language teacher supervision: A case-based approach.* Cambridge University Press. https://doi.org/10.1017/CBO9780511667329

Berkey, R., Curtis, T., Minnick, F., Zietlow, K., Campbell, D., & Kirschner, B. W. (1990). Collaborating for reflective practice: Voices of teachers, administrators and researchers. *Education and Urban Society, 22*(2), 204–232. https://doi.org/10.1177/0013124590022002006

Brookfield, S. D. (2017). *Becoming a critically reflective teacher.* Jossey-Bass.

Burhan-Horasanlı, E., & Ortaçtepe, D. (2016). Reflective practice-oriented online discussions: A study on EFL teachers' reflection on, in and for-action. *Teaching and Teacher Education, 59,* 372–382. https://doi.org/10.1016/j.tate.2016.07.002

Certificate in TESOL, SIT Graduate Institute, accessed February 15, 2021, https://graduate.sit.edu/programs-of-study/certificate-in-tesol/

Christodoulou, N. (2013). The impact of guided reflective practice on the teaching of English as a foreign language in higher education in Cyprus. PhD dissertation, University of Nottingham, UK. http://eprints.nottingham.ac.uk/13635/1/Thesis-Niki_Christodoulou.pdf

Craft, A. (2000). *Continuing professional development: A practical guide for teachers and schools.* Routledge Falmer.

Creswell, J. W. (2007). *Qualitative inquiry and research design: Choosing among five approaches.* Sage Publications.

Dahlberg, K. (2009). The essence of essences – The search for meaning structures in phenomenological analysis of lifeworld phenomena. *International Journal of Qualitative Studies on Health and Well-being, 1*(1), 11–19. https://doi.org/10.1080/17482620500478405

Day, C., & Sachs, J. (2004). Professionalism, performativity and empowerment: Discourses in the politics, policies and purposes of continuing professional development. In C. Day & J. Sachs (Eds.), *International handbook on the continuing professional development of teachers* (pp. 3–32). Open University Press.

Dewey, J. (1933). *How we think: A restatement of the relation of reflective thinking to the educative process*. DC Heath and Company.

Diaz-Maggioli, G. (2004). *Teacher-centred professional development.* Association for Supervision and Curriculum Development, Virginia.

Distad, L. S., & Brownstein, J. C. (2004). *Talking teaching: Implementing reflective practice in groups.* Scarecrow Education.

Eitington, J. E. (2002). *The winning trainer: Winning ways to involve people in learning.* Butterworth-Heinemann.

Fakazlı, Ö., & Kuru-Gönen. S. I. (2017). Reflection on reflection: EFL university instructors' perceptions on reflective practices. *Hacettepe University Journal of Education, 32*(3), 708–726. https://doi.org/10.16986/HUJE.2017025118

Farrell, T. S. C. (1998). *Reflective practice in an EFL teacher development group.* 32nd TESOL Conference, Seattle, USA. https://eric.ed.gov/?id=ED426615

Farrell, T. S. C. (2001). Tailoring reflection to individual needs: A TESOL case study. *Journal of Education, 27*(1), 23–38. https://doi.org/10.1080/02607470120042528

Farrell, T. S. C. (2003). Reflective teaching: The principles and practices. *English Teaching Forum, 41*, 14–21. https://www.researchgate.net/publication/265539985_Reflective_Teaching_The_Principles_and_Practices

Farrell, T. S. C. (2013). *Reflective practice in ESL teacher development groups: From practices to principles*. Palgrave Macmillan. https://doi.org/10.1057/9781137317193

Farrell, T. S. C. (2015). *Promoting teacher reflection in second language education: A framework for TESOL professionals.* Routledge. https://doi.org/10.4324/9781315775401

Farrell, T. S. C. (2019). *Reflective practice in ELT*. Equinox Publishing. https://doi.org/10.4324/9781315659824-5

Farrell, T. S. C., & Jacobs, G. M. (2016). Practicing what we preach: Teacher reflection groups on cooperative learning. *The Electronic Journal for English as a Second Language, 19*(4), 1–9. https://eric.ed.gov/?id=EJ1092795

Fullan, M., & Hargreaves, A. (Eds.). (1992). *Teacher development and educational change.* Routledge.

Glazer, C., Abbott, L., & Harris, J. (2004). A teacher-developed process for collaborative professional reflection. *Reflective Practice, 5*(1), 33–46. https://core.ac.uk/download/pdf/235401547.pdf. https://doi.org/10.1080/1462394032000169947

Guskey, T. R. (2000). *Evaluating professional development*. Corwin Press.

Harvey, M., Lloyd, K., McLachlan, K., Semple, A., & Walkerden, G. (2020). *Reflection for learning: A scholarly practice guide for educators*. https://s3.eu-west-2.amazonaws.com/assets.creode.advancehe-document-manager/documents/advance-he/Adv_HE_Reflection_for_Learning_Guide_1580298564.pdf

Johnstone, R. (2006). Language teacher education. In A. Davies & C. Elder (Eds.), *The handbook of applied linguistics* (pp. 649–671). Blackwell Publishing. https://doi.org/10.1002/9780470757000.ch26

Killion, J. P., & Todnem, G. R. (1991). A process for personal theory building. *Educational Leadership*, *48*(6), 14–16. http://www.ascd.org/ASCD/pdf/journals/ed_lead/el_199103_killion.pdf

Knight, P. (2002). A systemic approach to professional development: Learning as practice. *Teaching and Teacher Education*, *18*, 229–241. https://doi.org/10.1016/S0742-051X(01)00066-X

Kolb, D. A. (2015). *Experiential learning: Experience as the source of learning and development*. Pearson Education.

Kuh, L. P. (2015). Teachers talking about teaching and school: Collaboration and reflective practice via critical friends groups. *Teachers and Teaching*, *22*(3), 293–314. https://eric.ed.gov/?id=EJ1090993. https://doi.org/10.1080/13540602.2015.1058589

Mercer, S., & Gregersen, T. (2020). *Teacher wellbeing*. Oxford University Press.

Merriam, S. B. (2009). *Qualitative research: A guide to design and implementation*. Jossey-Bass.

Oldfather, P., West, J., White, J., & Wilmarth, J. (1999). *Learning through children's eyes: Social constructivism and the desire to learn*. American Psychological Association. https://doi.org/10.1037/10328-000

Richards, J. C. (2008). Second language teacher education today. *RELC Journal*, *39*, 158–177. https://doi.org/10.1177/0033688208092182

Richards, J. C., & Farrell, T. S. C. (2005). *Professional development for language teachers: Strategies for teacher learning*. Cambridge University Press. https://doi.org/10.1017/CBO9780511667237

Richards, J. C., & Lockhart, C. (1996). *Reflective teaching in second language classrooms*. Cambridge University Press.

Rodgers, C. (2002). Defining reflection: Another look at John Dewey and reflective thinking. *Teachers College Record*, *104*(4), 842–866. https://www.researchgate.net/publication/240645823_Defining_Reflection_Another_Look_at_John_Dewey_and_Reflective_Thinking. https://doi.org/10.1177/016146810210400402

Saldana, J. (2018). Researcher, analyze thyself. *International Journal of Qualitative Methods*, *17*, 1–7. https://doi.org/10.1177/1609406918801717

Saldana, J., & Omasta, M. (2018). *Qualitative research: Analysing life*. Sage Publications.

Schön, D. A. (1983). *The reflective practitioner: How professionals think in action*. Basic Books.

Schön, D. A. (1987). *Educating the reflective practitioner: Toward a new design for teaching and learning in the professions*. Jossey-Bass.

Tudge, J. R. H. (1992). Processes and consequences of peer collaboration: A Vygotskian analysis. *Child Development*, *63*, 1364–1379. https://doi.org/10.2307/1131562

Van Gyn, G. H. (1996). Reflective practice: The needs of professions and the promise of cooperative education. *Journal of Cooperative Education*, *32*(2–3), 103–131. https://eric.ed.gov/?id=EJ524110

Vygotsky, L. S. (1978). *Mind in society: The development of higher psychological processes*. Harvard University Press.

Wallace, M. J. (1991). *Training foreign language teachers: A reflective approach*. Cambridge University Press.

Wenger, E., McDermott, R., & Snyder, W. M. (2002). *Cultivating communities of practice*. Harvard Business School Press.

ABOUT THE AUTHORS

Burak Aydın is a Lecturer at Izmir Katip Celebi University, Turkey, and a licensed teacher trainer for the SIT TESOL Certificate Course. He teaches in a tertiary-level preparatory English program and is also involved in mentoring and supervising language teachers. In the field of teacher training, he has been conducting research, facilitating courses, and presenting for ELT conferences, INSET PD events, and various educational institutions.

İrem Çomoğlu is an Associate Professor in the Faculty of Education, English Language Teaching Department, Dokuz Eylül University, Izmir, Turkey. She has published widely in national and international journals and books. Her research focuses on teacher learning and development in TESOL and teacher research mainly from a qualitative research paradigm.

Chapter 5

Mediating Reflective Practice through Lesson Study: The Case of an EFL Teacher

Özgehan Uştuk & İrem Çomoğlu

5.1. INTRODUCTION

Professional development (PD) can be considered a compulsory part of every teacher's professional practice as their subject knowledge base is in constant growth, alongside the transformation of their pedagogical principles. In this sense, their initial teacher education is not capable of providing all the professional capital that will suffice till the end of their careers. Teaching English as a foreign language (EFL) is not exempt from this observation. In light of the ever-bourgeoning language education research, EFL teachers need to engage in continuous PD so that they can stay relevant in terms of their expertise.

The problem, though, is the approach to PD that frames its form as well as its content (Tanış & Dikilitaş, 2018). What happens when teachers need to follow a very busy teaching schedule in an institutionalized teaching context, as in universities, colleges, or K-12 schools? Their main PD opportunities are oftentimes one-off, top-down events that are delivered by outside experts with little (if no) idea regarding their teaching situations. Farrell (2013) calls for a more situated, reflective, and most importantly a bottom-up approach to language teacher PD that is 'more focused towards classroom realities, based on the knowledge that is co-constructed through engagement with experience, and systematic reflections' (p. 8). In this chapter, we intend to follow Farrell's call for moving *from practices to principles*, focusing exclusively on teacher experiences to understand what a bottom-up professional practice in a lesson study (LS) (Dudley, 2013, 2015) can illuminate in regard to transformative principles that may impact 'the small culture' (Holliday, 1999) of the activity. That being said, we also aim to present a case study that underscores the transformative value of one teacher's reflective practice (that is enacted in bottom-up PD) in an institutional context, drawing on the conceptual framework of the multifaceted nature of language teaching and learning developed by the Douglas Fir Group (2016).

Since 2016 when it was first published in the *Modern Language Journal*, the Douglas Fir Group's seminal work presenting a transdisciplinary framework has inspired many studies in applied linguistics with a sociocultural perspective to language pedagogy. This framework was a response to the prevailing 'monolithic view of both content and language' (Hawkins, 2019, p. 12). In their model, the Douglas Fir Group proposed three nested circles as seen in Figure 5.1, showing micro-, meso-, and macro-levels of language learning and teaching. The micro-level of social activity hosts individuals engaging with others, their actions, and interactions. This inner circle is surrounded by the meso-level of sociocultural institutions and communities, which may include schools, neighbourhoods, families, workplaces, and so on. On this level, we can also observe how individuals engage in their activities in a given context through the exercise of their investment, agency, and power. This whole system, though, is surrounded by the macro-level of ideological structures (e.g., beliefs, religion, culture, politics, and so on) that have a fundamental influence on the meso-level institutions, and also on the micro-level individuals enacting their identities within these institutions.

Originally intended 'to help multilingual users to thrive with and through their very multilingualism by the kind of research and practice it advocates' (Douglas Fir Group, 2016, p. 25), the framework has been upcycled and applied to various areas in language pedagogy. Analysing the framework, De Costa & Norton (2017) proposed several themes and their implications related to language teaching. Even though their analysis of the framework focused primarily on language teaching as identity work, these themes are also closely related to teacher PD. They underscored that 'language teaching is situated and attentionally and socially gated' and 'agency and transformative power are means and goals for language teaching' (p. 8). That being said, language teachers' PD activities are not exempt from this sociocultural understanding. The activities emerging in the inner circle of this system, as well as the agency of teachers initiated/sustained in these activities, are closely related to the institutional context of the activity as well as the macro-level *cultural system* of PD. Likewise, Gao (2019) reflected on the Douglas Fir Group's framework from a language teacher education perspective and suggested that the framework could 'inform the language teacher education programs by asking anew why we teach languages, what languages we teach, and how we teach languages' (p. 165). These critical questions go well beyond the *best* methodological choices of language education but pose an agenda to make teachers more aware of the context in which they teach, in other words, their 'small culture' of teaching practice (Holliday, 1999).

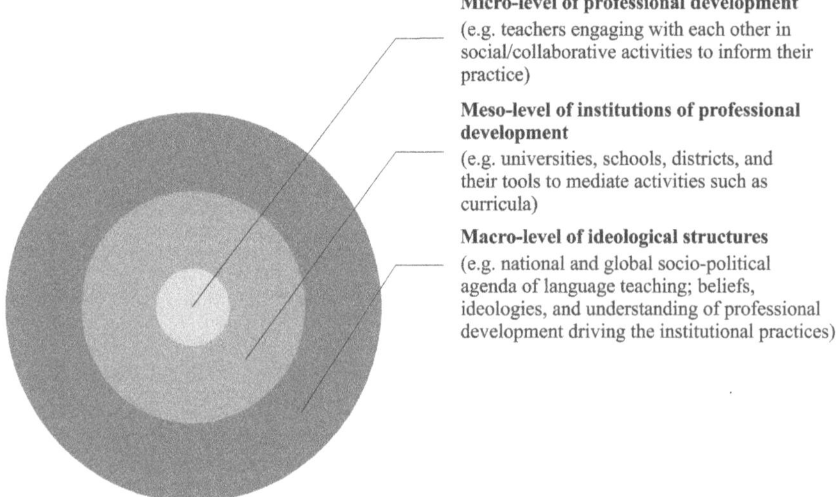

Figure 5.1. The Douglas Fir Group's framework of multifaceted nature of language learning and teaching, re-illustrated for teacher professional development.

Reflective Break

- How do you think your everyday teaching practice in a particular classroom might be embedded in wider contexts such as school or country settings and related to them?
- Do you think your everyday teaching activities can inform national or even global ideologies surrounding language education?

In response to Gao's call for teacher educators to promote teacher education and PD practices, we investigate LS as a model that supports in-service and pre-service teachers to reflect on the context of language teaching and the critical issues surrounding it. With this in mind, we approach LS, as reported in the current chapter, as a critical teacher PD activity initially emerging in the micro-level context of language teaching due to its bottom-up nature. Moreover, we show how reflective practice can help teachers to position themselves and to understand, develop, and exercise their agency within this nested system (see Figure 5.1).

5.2. LITERATURE REVIEW

Traditionally, PD practices in institutionalized settings have been criticized for their top-down approach, which entails short sit-and-get events such as seminars or workshops (Dikilitaş, 2015) that are often administration-mandated (Farrell, 2013) and delivered by outside experts (Wyatt & Ončevska Ager, 2016). These one-off events are seldom situated in classroom realities and usually lack reflective opportunities for teachers (Farrell, 2013). Alternatively, in PD with a bottom-up approach, the form and content of the PD activities are based on the local-institutional needs (Atay, 2006); therefore, they are often teacher-initiated and inquiry-based (Tanış & Dikilitaş, 2018). While top-down PD is transmissive and transitional in terms of the delivery of form and content, the bottom-up approach is transformative (Dikilitaş, 2015; Farrell, 2013). It has also been shown that bottom-up PD affords more opportunities for reflective practice because it is relevant to teacher-participants (Farrell, 2013; Uştuk & De Costa, 2020). Besides, as the bottom-up approach prioritizes actual teacher needs, it affords voice and agency to teachers.

5.2.1. LS: A Bottom-up Model of Reflective Professional Development

Lesson study is a bottom-up PD model (Saito et al., 2020) that is driven by a community of practice (Lave & Wenger, 1991) towards a common goal of the activity (Uştuk, 2020). In LS-modelled PD practice, the content is typically identified by the participant-teachers. Instead of a topic imposed by outside experts or administrators, teachers decide the goal of the activity as they are the 'subjects' of this activity (Uştuk & Çomoğlu, 2021). Moreover, the teachers have the opportunity to decide on the form of the activity itself as well actions within the LS, through mediatory practices such as LS protocols (Dudley, 2015), division of labour (Tasker, 2014), effective facilitation (Akiba et al., 2019), and mentorship (Dudley, 2015; Næsheim-Bjørkvik et al., 2019). To this end, LS can be regarded as a bottom-up activity due to its ability to project teacher voice so that they can *have a say* in both the content and form of PD.

LS is also closely associated with reflective PD for various reasons. First of all, in this activity, a group of teachers engage in 'critical reflective analysis' of the research lessons regarding 'the learning challenges faced by pupils' (Cajkler & Wood, 2019). The research lessons are the model lessons that teachers design collaboratively to overcome the situated learning challenge. Furthermore, the reflective value of LS goes beyond these analyses. The identification of this learning challenge also requires a high level of understanding of one's teaching practices. To identify a learning challenge that the community of practice would like to focus on, the teachers need to 'reflect on [the] elements of the curriculum in which their students appear to show poor understanding' (Wood et al., 2017, p. 204). Finally, the process-oriented learning experience in LS helps teachers to focus on their teaching practice over 'LS cycles' (Cajkler et al., 2014). These cycles include repeated actions after the identification of the learning challenge: such as devising the research lesson to overcome this challenge, teaching it to a class and observing the student-learning, reflecting on the experience, revising the research lesson, and going to an equivalent class to repeat the process until the group feels satisfied (Dudley, 2015).

As the process goes on, teachers find opportunities to reflect-*in-*, *-on-* (Schön, 1983), and *-for-action* (Killion & Todnem, 1991). It was also shown that in the later stages of this process (e.g., in later LS *cycles*), teachers grew more reflective towards their teaching practice (Hui & Yan-jun, 2016) especially during intensified LS meeting sessions (Vermunt et al., 2019). That being said, we argue that LS is a model to operationalize 'reflection-as-action' (Farrell, 2018). In addition, as the reflection permeates throughout LS activity, cycles, and actions in these cycles, and it emerges in both the individual and collaborative planes, we perceive it as 'reflection-as-*meta*-action' (Uştuk & De Costa, 2020). Relatedly, LS is also in line with the principles of reflective practice that were proposed by Farrell (2019b). LS allows teachers to reflect both on themselves and on the context(s) of their practices more holistically and systematically (Dudley, 2015), in an evidence-based inquiry to investigate and solve instructional problems (Wood et al., 2017), through critical dialog and systematic collaboration (Cajkler & Wood, 2019).

Though LS is considered a form of reflective practice of PD, few studies have associated its bottom-up characteristic with the reflective opportunities it brings (e.g., Mon et al., 2016; Saito et al., 2020). To this end, a multifaceted contextual analysis of reflection and its influence on teacher agency in the LS practice is needed to understand how reflective practice can help teachers exercise their agency across micro, meso, and macro contexts of language teaching practice. In tandem with this, we draw on the Douglas Fir Group's framework and re-conceptualize reflective PD in LS by investigating the following research questions:

- How does an EFL teacher engage in LS as a reflective practice?
- What insights can we gain about how reflective practice in LS influences teacher agency across micro, meso, and macro contexts of language teaching practice?

5.3. METHODS AND MATERIALS

In this chapter, we report a case study of an EFL teacher who participated in LS as a PD activity. As a part of Ozgehan's doctoral dissertation work, which was supervised by Irem, the methods in this study are derived from a larger ethnographic study (Uştuk, 2020) with a specific focus on one teacher's experience with a different conceptual set of understandings. We adopted an instrumental case study design since we aimed at interpretation and evaluation in addition to the description of the case (Yazan, 2015) to explore how reflection in LS as a PD activity influences teacher agency across micro, meso, and macro contexts of language teaching practice.

5.3.1. The Research Setting

This study took place at the School of Foreign Languages (SFL) at Western University (WU, a pseudonym), in a metropolitan city located in the western part of Turkey. The SFL hosts around 3,150 EFL learners as students and 118 EFL instructors along with the administrative personnel. The students come from 104 different programs and 14 different faculties/institutions. The SFL's main function is to plan and administer the preparatory year of intensive foreign language education for WU's undergraduate candidates before they commence study in their departments. As most undergraduate programs are either entirely or partially in English at WU, EFL education plays an important role as a part of the university's educational policy. This policy issue creates relative pressure on the administration of this massive school, given the large number of students with various academic needs and an insufficient number of instructors.

In this challenging situation, it is critical for the instructors to engage in continuous PD at WU SFL; therefore, the school has a professional development unit that offers seasonal seminars, workshops, and initiatives for all instructors at the school on various topics. These activities include experienced instructors sharing knowledge with others, with experts especially from the faculty of education to introduce some methods and techniques, as well as hired outside experts mostly sponsored by press houses as part of commercial agreements between them and the school.

In the 2017–2018 academic year, Ozgehan approached the school administrators with an idea for his doctoral research: to investigate the implementation of PD with a bottom-up approach and its influence on teachers, teaching practice, and school transformation. After negotiating the logistics, the administrators decided to support Ozgehan in initiating his fieldwork at WU SFL and pledged to respect the bottom-up characteristics of the process. After an open call for participants in the school, an introductory meeting was organized, and Ozgehan introduced the concept of LS as well as the research timeline. A question-and-answer session was also facilitated so that the volunteering participants could understand the research they might choose to participate in. As a result, five teachers volunteered to participate in this study, among whom one inspired the current study.

5.3.2. The Participant

In our study, the focal case is an EFL teacher, Oya (a pseudonym), who participated in the larger LS practice with four of her colleagues from the same institution. Oya was an active member of the PD unit at WU SFL. This means that she was familiar with PD events from both the organizing and the participant point of view. She was a veteran teacher with 20+ years of EFL teaching experience when the current study was conducted. Moreover, she also had experience as a teacher trainer, and was distinctive in this sense.

In her own words, she had 'the hunger' for personal and professional growth, and believed that a teacher needs to engage in continuous PD not only to increase her knowledge of the subject content and the pedagogy but also to be able to inspire her students so that they can appreciate their teacher's 'growth mindset.' She believed that as long as the teacher is 'open and ready for learning,' her students can 'transform their mindsets,' too. Building her teacher belief in the quoted vocabulary, it is fair to say that she was not only motivated but also professionally invested to participate in this research. She had ample experience in various PD events, and she was also familiar with the small culture in WU SFL in terms of PD practices.

Oya mentioned her previous experience of a PD event in which she first encountered the word 'reflective practice.' To her, the experience was still a 'stressing' memory because she was required to video-record herself while teaching and to comment on her teaching in a stimulated recall (Gass & Mackey, 2017). Due to this experience, she said she was at first doubtful about participating in the current study, but when she heard that she would be observed by other LS group members rather than being video-recorded, she decided to participate. In light of her particular experience, her reflective practice in LS meta-activity became the *case* in this study.

5.3.3. Researcher Reflexivity

Ozgehan was a PhD candidate when he initiated the current study at WU SFL. As a doctoral student, he observed how the existing top-down approach mainly drove PD practice in the research setting. Believing that such practices ignored teachers' voices and jeopardized their agency, he decided to introduce a new model devised according to the local needs in a participatory way, in which all local stakeholders could have a say. With this in mind, he wanted to create a situated and collaborative model of PD drawing on LS that might foster reflective practice.

Irem was Ozgehan's doctoral supervisor, and she was the vice-chair at WU SFL when the current study was conducted. As a school administrator, she was also aware that the existing culture of PD was highly top-down and created few situated learning opportunities that could influence the practices behind classroom doors at WU SFL. Therefore, Irem welcomed this initiative at the school and provided administrative support to work out the practices as well as affording autonomy for the study group. This support was vital as the lack of administrative support could disturb the process of teachers' professional growth (Lee & Tan, 2020) and intimidate them given the higher workload (Chong & Kong, 2012) especially in the Turkish tertiary-level EFL education context (Karabuğa & Ilin, 2019). Moreover, with relative anonymity, the study group could truly focus on the situated learning challenges instead of meso- and macro-level teaching agendas and policies, so that LS's bottom-up characteristics could be secured (Gero, 2015).

5.3.4. Ethical Concerns

Holliday (1999) states that the small culture paradigm associates culture to 'social groupings or activities wherever there is cohesive behaviour' (p. 237). As a part of a larger ethnographic study, the present case study focused on interpreting PD practices and processes, with specific focus on the smallest micro context of the activity (i.e., the LS) and the meso context of the institution (i.e., the cultural and historical background of PD practice at WU SFL). Thus, the study was conducted in a relatively small context in which careless acts of research could jeopardize the participants' integrity.

With this in mind, we took both macro and micro ethics into account (De Costa, 2015). Relatedly, we obtained the necessary institutional review board approvals from WU. In addition, we maintained our constant reflexive stance towards the research project throughout the fieldwork. In terms of micro ethics, we were very careful to be open with the participants regarding the research agenda and made sure that they were aware of the research aims, procedure, and scope of the study. After all, this was not only doctoral research but also a PD practice for the participants. This openness was also an act of respect in recognizing the participants as the central part of the study group and of the study as a social practice itself.

We used pseudonyms to protect the rights of the participants as well as the institution. We also used member-checking while processing the data, in that Oya read all the data related to her, and she was allowed to edit, omit, and change the transcriptions as she liked. She was also encouraged to elaborate on the excerpts when she felt that her opinions or experiences were misrepresented. This way, we intended her to feel that her voice was heard not only in the relation of her LS experience but also through the research project.

5.3.5. Research Process

The fieldwork for the current study was started at the beginning of the 2017–2018 academic year's fall semester with the researchers' immersion into the research context. However, the case study reported in this chapter began in January 2018 with the starting phase activities such as the introductory meeting for the participant candidates. As this was the first time Oya appeared in the study group, we focus here on the period of Oya's participation from January 2018 through the end of LS activities in June 2018 until her final consent after the data analysis and reporting in October 2018.

After Oya agreed to participate in the study group, the process began with a preliminary meeting in which the participants identified a learning challenge. The learning challenge in this specific LS was to create an engaging EFL reading class that aims to teach reading strategies to make inferences. The group members all agreed that this was a common problem in their everyday teaching practice and showed interest in working on this challenge collaboratively. After this meeting, the group engaged in a two-week self-study period in which they shared their readings, self-inquiries, and reflections in a synchronous communication group. They decided that they needed this time so that they would not be overwhelmed in their already very busy teaching schedule and so that they could reflect on the issue with selective attention. In the third step of the LS process, the group met and discussed their challenge in light of the self-study experience, and they created the first draft of their research lesson. They needed another preparatory period to refine their draft collaboratively and to develop materials. At this juncture, Oya volunteered to teach the first research lesson in her class and invited peers to observe her teaching. After the research lesson, the group gathered and elaborated on their experiences, both as the teacher and as the observers. As is a common characteristic of LS (Dudley, 2015), the meeting was facilitated by Ozgehan in a way that supported the teachers in focusing on student learning rather than the teacher's performance. Based on their collective reflections and decisions, they revised the research lesson and initiated another LS cycle. The whole process, which is illustrated in Figure 5.2, included three LS cycles.

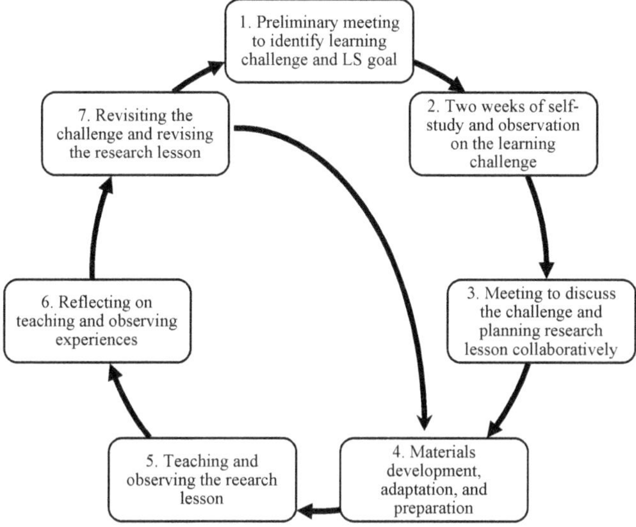

Figure 5.2. LS model illustrating the professional development action steps (Uştuk, 2020, p. 86).

5.3.6. Data Collection and Analysis

The case study featuring Oya's LS-oriented reflective practice drew on qualitative data that were collected through (1) researcher's field-notes, (2) audio-diaries, and (3) semi-structured interviews. The field-notes included annotations specifically featuring Oya's engagement as well as the other factors at WU SFL to make sense of the practice across the nested contexts. Audio-diaries included Oya's reflective voice memos that she was asked to record and submit throughout the LS steps. Last, data from two semi-structured interviews were utilized in this case study. First, a group interview was facilitated by Ozgehan to enable the study group to reflect on the experience collectively after the entire LS process was concluded. Later, Oya was interviewed about the whole experience. In total, we had (1) 62 journal entries in the researcher's field-notes covering the time from January to June 2018, (2) 32 minutes of voice memos comprising Oya's audio-diary, and (3) 125 minutes of interview data. We varied the data sources to triangulate the data so that the credibility of our research could be maintained by shoring up the internal validity of this case study (Merriam & Tisdell, 2016).

In this case study, we adopted a discourse analytic approach to examine the language produced by Oya in her reflective practice experience. Unlike the doctoral dissertation study (in which a thematic analytic approach was utilized to analyse the data), in this case study, we chose to adopt a discourse analytic approach to explore how the reflective understanding across micro, meso, and macro contexts of Oya's classroom practice was portrayed. We focused on 'selected nuances of language, conversation, and images to assess how elements such as vocabulary, grammar, intonation, topics, and so on work together in intricate combination to impart meaning about human relationships and big-picture ideas' (Saldana & Omasta, 2018, p. 107) such as culture, agency, and power. In line with the Douglas Fir Group's conceptual framework, we explored how power and Oya's agency in response to power was represented in her reflective discourse.

The data were analysed by using MAXQDA™, a qualitative data analysis software (VERBI Software, 2019). Once the data were coded through multiple rounds, the discourse marks in Oya's reflections were analysed in the light of our conceptual framework. Finally, we followed a rigorous procedure of external audit (Yazan, 2015) to increase the trustworthiness of this study. We invited two external auditors with whom we shared the anonymized data with the consent of our participants and the approval of the institutional review board.

5.4. FINDINGS

In this study, we reported a case of EFL teacher professional development and explored this case in terms of the reflective practice in LS. In addition, we investigated how the participant's discourse could inform our understanding of teacher agency and reflection in the micro, meso, and macro contexts of language teaching. To do that, we drew on a case participant's language use in her audio-diary entries, one-to-one interview, and group reflections after the LS process. We also used our field-notes to triangulate our analysis.

Utilizing a discourse analytic approach, we explored how Oya used language to communicate her understanding and reflection on the nested contexts surrounding her teaching practice. We found that LS activities created reflective opportunities for Oya to make sense of her doxa related to her classroom, her institution, and her beliefs about being a language teacher. She adopted an array of linguistic resources to communicate these reflections. Accordingly, she created both discourse marks with a small 'd' and *Discourse* with big 'D' (Gee, 2015) to refer to her micro-level and wider contexts of practice.

5.4.1. Representation of Power and Oppression in Oya's Language

Gee (2015) claims that one needs to understand social languages and *Discourses* to understand language; in other words, 'reading the word requires reading the world' (p. 418). Analysing Oya's language use enabled us to understand not only her classroom but also how this classroom and her teaching practice are heavily oppressed by the forces coming from the meso- and macro-levels of her teaching context.

In LS, Oya seemed to develop linguistic and discursive tools to determine and verbalize her doxa. In the data, a distinctive word was chosen repeatedly by Oya to express her understanding of the issues that surround her teaching practice: 'coursebook.' With this word, she referred to an entity that permeates wider levels of her teaching context, rather than the actual coursebook that she used in her everyday practice:

> There are some students with huge potential but sadly they spend their potential here in vain by sleeping during the class or by their mobile phones and so on. It would make me very happy to earn them back ... So I wish our EFL teaching could be more practical. I really wish to get English we teach out of the coursebooks and drag it back to real life. Perhaps LS can do that because it creates common sense. (Interview)

At WU SFL, both the curriculum and the syllabus are designed centrally by the Materials Design and Development Unit for each level, and the various levels of the same coursebook are followed by every teacher. Although the teachers are allowed to use any other appropriate materials that match the objectives, the contents page of the coursebook still shapes the *de facto* curriculum for the majority of these teachers who prefer to follow the coursebook and cover the entire syllabus with no deviation or improvisation. As the SFL's main function is to have learners pass a proficiency test so that they can continue to their programs, the curricular goals are perceived as most important. Here, Oya talked about her wish to 'get English [and] drag it back to real life.' This expressed her perception that teaching English depending only on the coursebook was unauthentic for her students. She chose the word 'coursebook' to refer to her teaching practice at the SFL, in which she had to follow the coursebook content and had little voice in her practice. Thus, the coursebook signifies the oppressive nature of the top-down decision-making processes that abduct her agency and power to determine the content of her practice, and that also lead to her colleagues' blindly following the coursebook content. The following excerpt displays a similar discursive use of the word.

> ... in that way [LS], it is possible to create a whole curriculum. I believe this is possible providing that sufficient time is given, maybe a pilot study. And perhaps we no longer have to follow the coursebook. (Audio-diary)

In her audio-diary, Oya reflected on the process of LS as a way to get free of the oppressive system that is expressed by the word 'coursebook'. In her use of the word, she referred to multiple contexts. The above excerpt refers to the institutional practice of coursebook over-dependency or oppression.

During the group interview, Oya explained why she likes it better when she can take ownership of her teaching materials.

> For example, there were comics that I gathered for teaching models. This was the way I enjoyed teaching, and it was nice. I used them later as well, students really liked it. Isn't this the essence of [collaboration in LS] after all? This is what I can bring. I enjoyed creating it. I know it works. When ideas like this come together, isn't it more fun than saying 'let's go to page 63 and exercise 5' at the beginning of the class? (Group interview)

In a culture where teachers are used to following the main coursebook with little agency in shaping content for their instruction, Oya struggled to 'bring' something unique to her class. The agentic space that was afforded by LS was a liberating and empowering factor for her. She later elaborated on the issue as follows:

> I think coursebooks passivize teachers. All the activities and their answer keys are in the teacher's book; even quizzes and pictures or videos to use, and the workbook. You do not produce when you have all that. You can even write a sentence in your book and use this same sentence as the example for years because you are so lazy to give one authentic example there and then while teaching in the classroom ... This is what I meant by the limiting coursebooks. The teacher does nothing except for the coursebook. I find it very disturbing. (Interview)

In the excerpt above, Oya explained the impact of the oppressive teaching practices that were represented by the word 'coursebook'. According to her, coursebooks are not just an institutional problem; at the macro-level, she also believes that coursebooks 'passivize' teachers. She reflected that coursebooks not only passivized her in her classroom but also her colleagues at the SFL, and all teachers alike. It was noteworthy that she considered LS as an agency source for her to claim back her classroom because in LS, she had the power to choose the content and materials of research lessons, and research lessons were directly related to her curricular goals. In this way, LS was perceived by her as a way to initiate a transformative curricular change that is driven by the teacher.

5.4.2. Representation of Position and Agency in Oya's Language

According to Gee (2015), Discourse with capital 'D' refers to the ways people use language while enacting and recognizing socially and historically significant identities or 'kinds of people' (p. 420). On the other hand, discourse with a small 'd' is related to the analysis of language in use 'across time and the patterns and connections across this flow of language make sense and guide in interpretation' (p. 420). In line with Gee's conceptualization, we found both discourse and Discourse remarks in Oya's reflective language.

One of LS's main characteristics is that it allows reflecting on teacher learning experience collaboratively (Vermunt et al., 2019), which fosters reflection on a collaborative plane (Uştuk & De Costa, 2020). Therefore, it may sound natural for Oya to refer to the LS group with the pronoun 'we.' However, 'we' meant more than the teacher group in LS in Oya's language use. Oya adopted a dynamic positioning (Kayi-Aydar, 2019) by using the first-person plural pronoun 'we' while referring to a positional identity that she based on all contextual levels. After the whole process, she reflected on the experience. At the micro-level of their professional development activity, she used the pronoun 'we' accordingly:

> In the meetings, I believe everyone is equally involved, I mean all the team members; also the facilitator is helping us. We can consult anytime we cannot move further. The meetings have quite a warm atmosphere. (Audio-diary)

In this entry, she framed an LS 'team,' and she included herself as a team member. Thus, Oya posited a community of teacher-learners by using the word 'team' and by creating an agentic entity that could consult the 'facilitator' anytime they needed. Even though the facilitator was a resource for them, it seemed that the team consisted only of the teachers engaging in the micro-level of the meta-activity.

Secondly, Oya used the first-person plural pronoun also to refer to the teachers working at WU SFL. However, she used this pronoun to refer to an agentic group of teachers with transformative intentions about an aspect of the school culture that she perceived negatively:

> I wish we could create a variety of lessons and alternatives to what coursebooks provide collaboratively and somehow put them together to create a plan, which is content-wise and time-wise realistic. Probably we could also overcome the timing problem by [LS]. I realize that we, as the school, have problems covering the schedule but this is because we do not use the time we have wisely. This is probably the biggest realization about myself and my institution. (Interview)

According to Oya, teachers at the SFL had problems with time management; she mentioned that during a regular semester it seemed like everybody was running around from lesson to lesson frantically to cover all the content that was served to them. She felt that she was putting a lot of her energy into trying to catch up with the yearly plan. In the excerpt given above, she reflected on this culture, and she asserted that she realized those problems more clearly. She stated that teachers at WU SFL could overcome this problem if given the power to create content collaboratively.

Finally, Oya's discourse after she participated in LS reflected how her beliefs on PD and the teaching profession had become more assertive. She used the first-person plural pronoun to create a discourse, in which she referred to an idea of 'good teacher,' a teacher identity that engages in PD:

> As a teacher, I had this feeling of satisfaction. I believe this is the same for all teachers when we see that our students are actually getting what we offer to them. This feeling is very nice. All the effort was worth it. They benefit from all [LS activities]. (Group interview)

In this excerpt, one may identify two major positions in her discourse. She used 'we' to remark on the LS team and 'they' to remark on the students. In LS, she participated in activities that afforded her that feeling of 'satisfaction' due to its hands-on nature. The process included her as actively involved in understanding what her students needed, getting into action to meet these needs, and teaching a research lesson to improve her actual classroom practice. This situatedness made sense to her as she reflected on her 'nice feeling.'

> I feel as if I am in a kind of helplessness, kind of a vicious circle. I wish we had LS here. This has got the potential to activate the teachers, who are less active due to this feeling of helplessness and the comfort zone

> created by the years of routine. This system can change it. Because this system [LS] made me say 'yes, I can contribute it. I can create content that also has the potential to change the class'. This may have similar effects on them. This system also supports collaboration. I mean, we all had our strengths and weaknesses as teachers. Some have wonderful warm-up ideas; some are good at forming tasks or group works. This is good but one by one, their effect is limited and students in the other class cannot reach the individual effects. In a collaborative meeting, you can say 'I have a great activity specifically for that topic, and I have good results'; this is the essence of [collaboration] isn't it? You are a hundred percent in the activity, yet you are not doing it alone. This may also help to support this healthy communication among teachers in this school. When we organize extracurricular meetings, people are mostly very reluctant to remain at the school. Not many people take ownership of the school, and we, unfortunately, do not have this culture. This is the way we can create commitment and healthy communication. (Interview)

In this excerpt, we hear Oya revealing an aspect of the school culture while reflecting. Oya had negative feelings such as helplessness but these feelings, signalling the absence of power, were replaced by the agentic and strong assertions given later such as 'I can contribute,' 'when we organize meetings,' or 'we can create commitment.' Starting with her own experience and feeling at the beginning, her agentic behavior is expanded through the end of the excerpt. Her self-positioning is an example of how micro-level activity can inform the meso-level institutional culture when teachers engage in reflective practice that includes both their practice and institutional practice. Thus, Oya's use of pronouns in her discourse had a dynamic meaning demonstrating her agency across the contextual levels of the reflective practice.

5.5. DISCUSSION

Farrell (2019a) suggests that experienced teachers may have to develop their own strategies to overcome the initial theory-practice gap to 'survive' professionally (p. 3). To this end, the teachers need to engage in a situated PD practice so that they can truly comprehend the teaching context that surrounds their practice. With situated PD, their understanding of content and (new) methods can stay relevant to their classroom reality. In achieving this, bottom-up PD models such as LS play an important role because they mediate reflective practice not only throughout different stages of a longitudinal, processual teacher learning activity (Karlsen & Helgevold, 2019; Uştuk, 2020; Vermunt et al., 2019; Yalcin Arslan, 2019), but also at both individual and collaborative planes of reflection (Uştuk & De Costa, 2020). In this study, we focused on an additional aspect of the reflective practice afforded by LS. More specifically, we investigated the contextual levels of an EFL teacher's reflections and explored how these levels are represented and intersected in her reflective language.

In our discourse analysis, we borrowed the conceptual framework from the Douglas Fir Group framework illustrating the nested micro, meso, and macro contexts of language teaching. Analysing Oya's reflections on the LS process that she participated in as a part of Ozgehan's doctoral dissertation project, we focused on her reflective trajectory as a case. Our findings showed that Oya used both the first-person plural pronoun 'we' and the word 'coursebook' at multiple levels. What is more, her language use showed the agentic positioning at both discourse and Discourse levels (Gee, 2015).

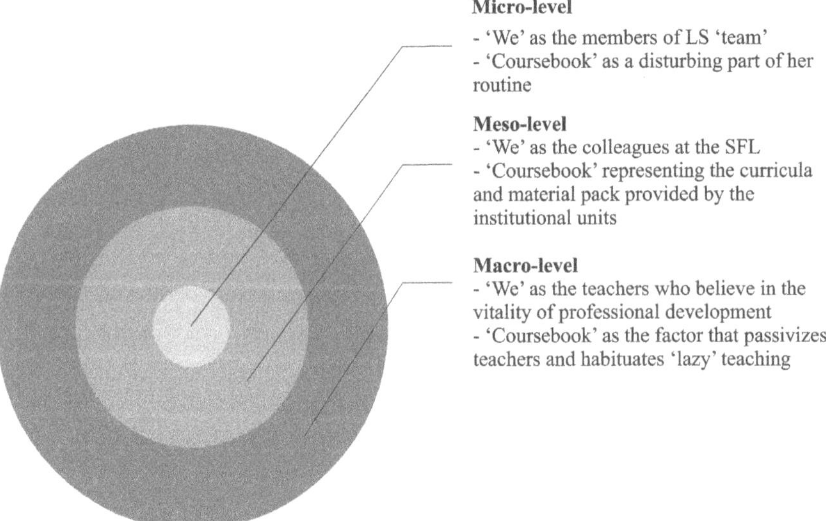

Figure 5.3. The reflective levels and the intersected language permeating through Oya's context(s).

In light of this, we propose that reflective practice in LS is an effective teacher learning and PD practice because it provides and/or fosters understanding of one's teaching practice with respect to different contextual levels. With the dynamic use of 'we' and 'coursebook,' Oya showed an increased understanding of not only her classroom, but also how this classroom and her practice informs and is informed by the wider contexts. In this sense, reflective practice afforded a permeability for Oya to see what she does and why she does it. Figure 5.3 illustrates how her reflective language permeated multiple contextual levels surrounding her everyday practice.

Our findings are in line with previous works that found that LS is effective in reflecting on and internalizing curricula and curricular reforms (Akiba & Wilkinson, 2016; Zhang et al., 2019), or in transforming teacher beliefs such as identity (Lieberman, 2009), teacher roles (Coenders & Verhoef, 2019; Ni Shuilleabhain & Seery, 2018), and pupil voice (Warwick et al., 2019). These are all macro-level entities that are *above* individual teachers or institutional practices. Nevertheless, as shown in these studies, LS affords participant-teachers an increased understanding of how these entities are represented in their everyday practice. Building on these findings, our study demonstrated a shared discourse that emerged in LS. This shared discourse provides the LS team with an understanding of their immediate culture (Saito et al., 2015) as well as the macro-level entities represented in their immediate culture. As suggested by Farrell (2013), when a group of teachers create a shared discourse based on a common experience, it becomes easier for them 'to articulate their reflections of teaching by making the tacit explicit' (p. 125). Specifically in the LS context, Dudley (2013) also reported discourse showing that collaborative LS processes 'unmask' the unknown in teaching practice (p. 107). We also further propose that LS creates reflective practice that allows groups of teachers to build a reflective space in which teachers can make associations of their classroom practices, institutional 'small cultures' (Holliday, 1999), and macro-level beliefs and policies. These levels can be called the reflective levels of LS.

Our findings also show that reflective practice in LS helped Oya to enact her agentic position in her discourse. Regardless of her previous negative feelings regarding reflective practice, she re-positioned herself from a powerless position to a capable one many times in her LS reflections. We suggest that this is related to the bottom-up characteristic of LS. This model can create opportunities in school-based learning communities which may create more sustainable school reform, beginning from teachers (Saito et al., 2015). In LS, teachers become the agents of their activity (Dudley, 2015; Johnson, 2009) by determining the form and content of their PD practice. As we saw in Oya's language, when she was invested with this power and voice, she was also able to associate her expansive PD experience to inform a sustainable school transformation. Re-positioning herself from 'helpless' to the position of 'we can create commitment and healthy communication [at the SFL]' is discursive proof of her improved agency afforded by her reflective practice experience in LS.

5.6. CONCLUSION

In short, we found that LS helped Oya to engage in bottom-up reflective practice that created a transformative teacher learning experience in terms of her agency. We also demonstrated that LS enabled Oya to better understand how her classroom practice is nested in the wider contexts surrounding her everyday teaching. These reflective levels of her teaching helped her to make sense of her doxa. This increased awareness of the reflective levels provides some implications for teacher educators to take into consideration. As in Oya's case, effective teacher education and PD should draw on the situatedness of one's practice with a bottom-up perception. More specifically, we, as teacher educators, should facilitate teacher PD in such a way that they can claim their agency over their learning practices by being responsible for choosing the content and form. However, this does not mean that teacher PD should not be facilitated. Oya's experience showed that teacher learning can afford increased agency when it is not fixed only on the micro-level of teaching experience. Teacher education and PD activities should help teachers to understand their classrooms as nested in levels driving practices and even sometimes 'passivizing' them. In this sense, reflective practice should include reflective levels so that situated PD can help teachers *situate* what happens beyond their classroom doors in *the bigger picture*.

This case study also showed the discursive potential of teacher learning in reflective practice and more specifically in LS. More studies adopting a discourse analytic approach can shed further light on how teachers' language can be used to understand their learning processes. Oya's language also provided evidence that may inspire prospective studies to approach teachers as oppressed professionals whose professional voices are often abducted. In light of this, we also call for more critical discourse analytic studies to explore *if-and-how-and-why* professional development practices create injustice for teachers, and *if-and-how-and-why* reflective practice can support teachers to grow as agentic practitioners.

Reflective Break

- How important is it do you think to reflect on the micro-, meso-, or macro-levels of your teaching practice? Do you believe LS or any other type of PD model can help you achieve this?
- What do you think is the value of collaborative reflection created in the LS context in teachers' professional learning?
- What opportunities do you think could result from empowering teachers to use their agency?

REFERENCES

Akiba, M., Murata, A., Howard, C. C., & Wilkinson, B. (2019). Lesson study design features for supporting collaborative teacher learning. *Teaching and Teacher Education, 77*(1), 352–365. https://doi.org/10.1016/j.tate.2018.10.012

Akiba, M., & Wilkinson, B. (2016). Adopting an international innovation for teacher professional development. *Journal of Teacher Education, 67*(1), 74–93. https://doi.org/10.1177/0022487115593603

Atay, D. (2006). Teacher research for professional development. *ELT Journal, 62*(2), 139–147. https://doi.org/10.1093/elt/ccl053

Cajkler, W., & Wood, P. (2019). The wider perspective on lesson study: Developing a holistic view of practitioner development through pedagogic literacy. In P. Wood, D. S. L. Lynn, N. Helgevold, & C. Wasyl (Eds.), *Lesson study in initial teacher education: Principles and practices* (pp. 189–201). Emerald Publishing Limited. https://doi.org/10.1108/978-1-78756-797-920191014

Cajkler, W., Wood. P., Norton, J., & Pedder, D. (2014). Lesson study as a vehicle for collaborative teacher learning in a secondary school. *Professional Development in Education, 40*(4), 511–529. https://doi.org/10.1080/19415257.2013.866975

Chong, W. H., & Kong, C. A. (2012). Teacher collaborative learning and teacher self-efficacy: The case of lesson study. *The Journal of Experimental Education, 80*(3), 263–283. https://doi.org/10.1080/00220973.2011.596854

Coenders, F., & Verhoef, N. (2019). Lesson study: Professional development (PD) for beginning and experienced teachers. *Professional Development in Education, 45*(2), 217–230. https://doi.org/10.1080/19415257.2018.1430050

De Costa, P. (2015). Ethics in applied linguistics research. In B. Paltridge & A. Phakiti (Eds.), *Research methods in applied linguistics: A practical resource* (pp. 245–257). Bloomsbury.

De Costa, P., & Norton, B. (2017). Introduction: Identity, trans disciplinarity, and the good language teacher. *The Modern Language Journal, 101*(1), 3–14. https://doi.org/10.1111/modl.12368

Dikilitaş, K. (2015). Teacher researchers in action. In K. Dikilitaş, R. Smith, & T. Trotman (Eds.), *Professional development through teacher research* (pp. 47–55). IATEFL, UK.

Douglas Fir Group, The (2016). A transdisciplinary framework for SLA in a multilingual world. *The Modern Language Journal, 100*(S1), 19–47. https://doi.org/10.1111/modl.12301

Dudley, P. (2013). Teacher learning in lesson study: What interaction-level discourse analysis revealed about how teachers utilised imagination, tacit knowledge of teaching and fresh evidence of pupils learning, to develop practice knowledge and so enhance their pupils' learning. *Teaching and Teacher Education, 34* (August), 107–121. https://doi.org/10.1016/j.tate.2013.04.006

Dudley, P. (2015). *Lesson study: Professional learning for our time*. Routledge.

Farrell, T. S. C. (2013). *Reflective practice in ESL teacher development groups: From practices to principles*. Palgrave Macmillan UK. https://doi.org/10.1057/9781137317193

Farrell, T. S. C. (2018). *Reflection-as-action in ELT*. TESOL Press.
Farrell, T. S. C. (2019a). 'My training has failed me': Inconvenient truths about second language teacher education (SLTE). *TESL-EJ*, *22*(4), 1–16.
Farrell, T. S. C. (2019b). *Reflective practice in ELT*. Equinox Publishing. https://doi.org/10.4324/9781315659824-5
Gao, X. A. (2019). The Douglas Fir Group framework as a resource map for language teacher education. *The Modern Language Journal*, *103*(1), 161–166. https://doi.org/10.1111/modl.12526
Gass, S., & Mackey, A. (2017). *Stimulated recall methodology in applied linguistics and L2 research*. Routledge.
Gee, J. P. (2015). Discourse, small d, big D. In K. Tracy (Ed.), *The international encyclopaedia of language and social interaction* (pp. 418–422). Wiley Blackwell. https://doi.org/10.1002/9781118611463.wbielsi016
Gero, G. (2015). The prospects of lesson study in the US: Teacher support and comfort within a district culture of control. *International Journal for Lesson and Learning Studies*, *4*(1), 7–25. https://doi.org/10.1108/IJLLS-02-2014-0007
Hawkins, M. R. (2019). Plurilingual learners and schooling. In D. C. De Oliviera (Ed.), *The handbook of TESOL in K-12* (pp. 9–24). John Wiley & Sons, Ltd. https://doi.org/10.1002/9781119421702.ch2
Holliday, A. (1999). Small cultures. *Applied Linguistics*, *20*(2), 237–264. https://doi.org/10.1093/applin/20.2.237
Hui, T., & Yan-jun, Y. (2016). *Study on the development of teachers' reflection ability in lesson study*. The 11th International Conference on Computer Science & Education (ICCSE), Nagoya, Japan.
Johnson, K. E. (2009). *Second language teacher education: A sociocultural perspective*. Routledge.
Karabuğa, F., & Ilin, G. (2019). Practicing lesson study in a Turkish education context. *International Journal for Lesson and Learning Studies*, *8*(1), 60–78. https://doi.org/10.1108/IJLLS-05-2018-0036
Karlsen, A. M. F., & Helgevold, N. (2019). Lesson study: Analytic stance and depth of noticing, post-lesson discussions. *International Journal for Lesson and Learning Studies*, *8*(4), 290–304. https://doi.org/10.1108/IJLLS-04-2019-0034
Kayi-Aydar, H. (2019). *Positioning theory in applied linguistics*. Palgrave Macmillan.
Killion, J., & Todnem. G. (1991). A process for personal theory building. *Educational Leadership*, *48*(7), 14–16.
Lave, J., & Wenger, E. (1991). *Situated learning legitimate peripheral participation*. Cambridge University Press.
Lee, L. H. J., & Tan, S. C. (2020). Teacher learning in lesson study: Affordances, disturbances, contradictions, and implications. *Teaching and Teacher Education*, *89* (March), 102986. https://doi.org/10.1016/j.tate.2019.102986
Lieberman, J. (2009). Reinventing teacher professional norms and identities: The role of lesson study and learning communities. *Professional Development in Education*, *35*(1), 83–99. https://doi.org/10.1080/13674580802264688

Merriam, S. B., & Tisdell, E. J. (2016). *Qualitative research: A guide to design and implementation*. Jossey-Bass.

Mon, C. C., Dali, M. H., & Sam, L. C. (2016). Implementation of lesson study as an innovative professional development model among Malaysian school teachers. *Malaysian Journal of Learning and Instruction, 13*(1), 83–111. https://doi.org/10.32890/mjli2016.13.1.5

Næsheim-Bjørkvik, G., Helgevold, N., & Østrem, S. (2019). Lesson study as a professional tool to strengthen collaborative enquiry in mentoring sessions in initial teacher education. *European Journal of Teacher Education, 42*(5), 557–573. https://doi.org/10.1080/02619768.2019.1641487

Ni Shuilleabhain, A., & Seery, A. (2018). Enacting curriculum reform through lesson study: A case study of mathematics teacher learning. *Professional Development in Education, 44*(2), 222–236. https://doi.org/10.1080/19415257.2017.1280521

Saito, E., Khong, T. D. H., Hidayat, A., Hendayana, S., & Imansyah, H. (2020). Typologies of lesson study coordination: a comparative institutional analysis. *Professional Development in Education, 46*(1), 65–81. https://doi.org/10.1080/19415257.2018.1561495

Saito, E., Murase, M., Tsukui, A., & Yeo, J. (2015). *Lesson study for learning community: A guide to sustainable school reform*. Routledge.

Saldana, J., & Omasta, M. (2018). *Qualitative research: Analyzing life*. Sage Publications.

Schön, D. (1983). *The reflective practitioner: How professionals think in action*. Temple Smith.

Tanış, A., & Dikilitaş. K. (2018). Turkish EFL instructors' engagement in professional development. *Eurasian Journal of Applied Linguistics, 4*(1), 27–47. https://doi.org/10.32601/ejal.460628

Tasker, T. (2014). Exploring EFL teacher professional development through lesson study: An activity theoretical approach. Unpublished doctoral dissertation, Pennsylvania State University, University Park, Pennsylvania, USA.

Uştuk, Ö. (2020). A critical ethnographic understanding of lesson study as an EFL teacher professional development strategy. Doctoral dissertation, Dokuz Eylul University, Turkey.

Uştuk, Ö., & Çomoğlu, İ. (2021). Reflexive professional development in reflective practice: What lesson study can offer. *International Journal for Lesson & Learning Studies, 10*(3), 260–273. https://doi.org/10.1108/ijlls-12-2020-0092

Uştuk, Ö., & De Costa, P. (2020). Reflection as meta-action: Lesson study and EFL teacher professional development. *TESOL Journal*, June. https://doi.org/10.1002/tesj.531

VERBI Software (2019). 'MAXQDA 2020.' https://www.maxqda.com/

Vermunt, J. D., Vrikki, M., Van Halem, N., Warwick, P., & Mercer, N. (2019). The impact of lesson study professional development on the quality of teacher learning. *Teaching and Teacher Education, 81* (May), 61–73. https://doi.org/10.1016/j.tate.2019.02.009

Warwick, P., Vrikki, M., Karlsen, A. M. F., Dudley, P., & Vermunt, J. D. (2019). The role of pupil voice as a trigger for teacher learning in lesson study professional groups.

Cambridge Journal of Education, *49*(4), 435–455. https://doi.org/10.1080/0305764X.2018.1556606

Wood, P., Fox, A., Norton, J., & Tas, M. (2017). The experience of lesson study in the UK. In L. L. Rowell, C. D. Bruce, J. M. Shosh, & M. M. Riel (Eds.), *The Palgrave international handbook of action research* (pp. 203–220). Palgrave Macmillan.

Wyatt, M., & Ončevska Ager, E. (2016). Teachers' cognitions regarding continuing professional development. *ELT Journal*, *71*(2), 171–185. https://doi.org/10.1093/elt/ccw059

Yalcin Arslan, F. (2019). The role of lesson study in teacher learning and professional development of EFL teachers in Turkey: A case study. *TESOL Journal*, *10*(2), e00409. https://doi.org/10.1002/tesj.409

Yazan, B. (2015). Three approaches to case study methods in education: Yin, Merriam, and Stake. *The Qualitative Report*, *20*(2), 134–152.

Zhang, H., Yuan, R., & Liao, W. (2019). EFL teacher development facilitated by lesson study: A Chinese perspective. *TESOL Quarterly*, *53*(2), 542–552. https://doi.org/10.1002/tesq.480

ABOUT THE AUTHORS

Ozgehan Uştuk (PhD) is an EFL teacher, teacher educator, and research assistant at Balikesir University, Turkey. He is the chair-elect of the TESOL International Association's Research Professional Council. His research interests include reflexivity and reflective practice in TESOL, language teacher education and professional development through practitioner inquiry, identity work, and tensions.

İrem Çomoğlu is an Associate Professor at Dokuz Eylül University, Faculty of Education, English Language Teaching Department, Izmir, Turkey. She has published widely in national and international journals and books. Her research focuses on teacher learning and development in TESOL and teacher research mainly from a qualitative research paradigm.

Chapter 6

Payoffs and Pitfalls of Reflective Practice as Perceived by Novice EFL Teachers

İlknur Bayram & Özlem Canaran

6.1. INTRODUCTION

The initial years in the teaching profession are memorable, but these years might also bring disappointment for novice teachers. Holding an English language teaching diploma tightly in hand with achievement certificates and intention letters, newly-graduate language teachers can hardly wait for the first lesson where they will meet their students. During pre-service training, they have been lectured about what a good language teacher is like, what constitutes quality teaching, how to teach English, and so forth. Some of their courses included great lectures giving them inspiration for practice, some were hard to follow due to the complexity of the content, and some were very pleasing to attend while some others left no mark on the formation of their professional identity. Fired with enthusiasm, but with little or no idea about the 'transition shock' (Corcoran 1981, p. 19) of the early years on the job, novice teachers believe they can finally realize their dreams in their own classes when they find employment. Moir (1999) has coined this stage as 'the anticipation phase' when novice teachers idealize teaching and feel committed to the profession. This stage starts from the teachers' first days at school and lasts until they accommodate themselves to the routines of teaching. Although several shared factors in education (students, parents, curriculum, testing, paperwork, administrative requirements, etc.) are likely to pose considerable stress and anxiety to all teachers, novice teachers can experience very particular problems during this 'anticipation phase,' besides having to deal with the same problems as more experienced teachers, often without receiving adequate support and guidance from the school (Farrell, 2012).

There is no common agreement on the definition of the term 'novice' and at what point this stage ends for teachers. For some, two years' (e.g., Haynes, 2011) or three years' teaching experience (e.g., Barrett et al., 2002) suffices to complete this initial stage, while for others (e.g. Kim & Roth, 2011) it is experience of five years. Farrell (2012) defines 'novices' as 'newly qualified teachers' who have completed a pre-service education program and have been teaching English in an educational institution for less than three years. Despite the different perceptions of the term, the early years of teaching are described as a 'sink or swim process' (Huberman, 1992) and it is stated that most teachers receive 'a reality shock' (Veenman, 1984) when they begin teaching in real classrooms (Farrell, 2019a). Pitton (2006) highlights that teachers' early experiences and the opportunities provided by schools are crucial for their success, but unless they are offered guidance and support for coping with challenges, they might start feeling ineffective and end up quitting their jobs.

Due to the complexities of being on-the-job immediately after university, novice teachers can experience increased levels of exhaustion (Chaplain, 2008; Voss & Kunter, 2020) and attrition (Darling-Hammond et al., 2016; Farrell, 2012), issues of inadequate support, identity development, lesson planning, and delivery (Farrell, 2012; Karataş & Karaman, 2013), problems of classroom management and discipline (Lundeen, 2004), and a lot of stress due to the workload and paperwork (Goldrick, 2016). Scholars in the field of general education mostly attribute these problems to the gap between pre-service teacher preparation and in-service teacher development (Darling-Hammond, 2010; Farrell, 2012; Peercy, 2012; Robinson, 1998). The argument is that teacher education programs do not adequately form a link between 'what is known in the field' and 'what is done in the classroom' (Freeman, 2016, p. 9). Farrell (2012) argues that after graduation many novice teachers immediately lose support from their teacher educators and are left alone with problems as if they were experienced professionals. Regarding the field of second language teacher education (SLTE) and the gap between theory and practice, Farrell (2019a, p. 3) notes that

> ... something is not working in the field of second language teacher education. Indeed, many experienced TESOL teachers may also attest to this dysfunction in second language teacher education after they have had to survive on their own to develop successful teaching careers. We must thus tackle this inconvenient truth in SLTE that there is still a serious disjuncture between what learner teachers are being presented with in teacher education courses and the reality of

what they experience in real classrooms when they graduate from their SLTE programs.

To this end, reflective practice (RP) can form a link between theory and practice, and serve as a 'compass,' guiding teachers when they are trying to find what they should do in their classrooms (Farrell, 2012). Engaging in RP, teachers can look at what is actually happening in the classroom and compare this experience with the learning and teaching theories they hold. This practice and theory comparison provides them with the opportunity to 'systematically look at their practice so that they can deepen their understanding of what they do and thus come to new insights about their students, their teaching, and themselves' (Farrell, 2012, p.14). Despite this, during initial teacher training, the contribution of RP to the professional development of teachers and to the improvement of teaching and learning processes might be overlooked due to a great emphasis being put on the development of subject knowledge and technical aspects of teaching (Kelchtermans, 2000; Penso et al., 2001). Without proper guidance or a 'compass' in their early years, they might feel lost in the classroom, hardly knowing which direction to take.

6.1.1. A Holistic, Evidence-Based, and Collaborative Approach to RP

Reflective practice is highly welcome in second language teacher education, although there is no agreement about what constitutes RP and what kind of RPs can stimulate teacher development (Farrell, 2007, 2012, 2020). After its appearance in the field of SLTE in 1990s, RP grew more in popularity in the post-methods era when the general tendency was towards teachers' adapting their own methods in line with the contextual factors without depending on prescribed techniques or procedures (Farrell, 2019b; Kumaravadivelu, 1994). Despite its popularity and various attempts to define it, RP is still a vague term used comparably with other terms such as reflection and reflective inquiry, which sometimes leads to confusion and misunderstandings.

Farrell (2014, p. 123) has defined RP as 'a cognitive process accompanied by a set of attitudes in which teachers systematically collect data about their practice, and, while engaging in dialog with others, use the data to make informed decisions about their practice both inside and outside the classroom.' He suggests engaging in *reflection-as-action*, where the teacher, the problem, and the reflective process are handled with a more holistic approach. In his holistic approach, Farrell (2014) emphasizes technical, internal (i.e., the teacher's teaching philosophy), and external (i.e., contextual factors) aspects of teaching with five stages of reflection:

philosophy; *principles*; *theory*; *practice*; and *beyond practice* (Farrell & Kennedy, 2019). Although the approaches and techniques to implement RP are abundant in the field of general education, Farrell (2018a, 2019b) has stated that either some might be placing restrictions on reflection, turning RP into a mechanical activity by a set of questions and checklists, or some might ignore the teacher-as-person, neglecting her personal and emotional aspects and solely focusing on solving instructional problems. To this end, Farrell (2019b) suggests that the teacher may stick to a set of principles which can stimulate the process of reflection. He outlines the six principles of RP:

- Principle 1: Reflective Practice Is Holistic
- Principle 2: Reflective Practice Is Evidence-Based
- Principle 3: Reflective Practice Involves Dialog
- Principle 4: Reflective Practice Bridges Principles and Practices
- Principle 5: Reflective Practice Requires a Disposition to Inquiry
- Principle 6: Reflective Practice Is a Way of Life

The Reflective Teaching and Learning Program (RTLP) in the present study was designed in the light of the first three principles of RP, its *being holistic, evidence-based*, and *involving dialog*. The holistic principle is based on the idea that RP should not be reduced solely to the cognitive, intellectual, and metacognitive capabilities of teachers; instead, the teacher should be valued as a person with personal, spiritual, and emotional aspects (Farrell, 2014, 2018a). It places stress on providing teachers not only with improved instruction but also with a better understanding of themselves, their actions, and the reasons behind their actions inside and outside the class. According to Farrell (2019b, p. 60), unless teachers' 'inner lives' are valued, they will end up in 'burnout' with a feeling of having to 'do' reflection instead of living it.

Based on the first principle, the second principle, that RP is evidence-based, suggests taking reflection further from simply thinking about a situation to a more careful and thorough examination, leading teachers to systematic investigation of a problem. With an evidence-based approach to reflection, teachers can express the what, how, and why of their actions as well as researching the impact of these actions on student learning. This can also provide the opportunity to improve or change their current practices. Further, systematic data collection helps teachers find answers to such questions as: *What do I do?, How do I do it?, Why do I do it?, What is the result?, Will I change anything based on the answers to the previous questions?* (Farrell, 2019b, p. 62).

The third principle, that RP is a 'collaborative process of dialoguing' (Farrell, 2018a, p. 1) is centered on the teacher's inner dialog as well as their dialog with other educators and teachers through critical friends groups, team teaching, peer coaching, and group discussions. Dialog is an essential component of RP, and it is highly unlikely that a teacher will experience a sense of community, a deeper level of reflection, and effective professional development without dialoging (Cordingley, 2006; Farrell, 2019b). The collaborative dialog process is primarily initiated by the teacher's inner dialog with herself. Drawing on the teacher's beliefs, assumptions, and values about teaching and learning, inner dialoging can provide the teacher with an opportunity to explain: *What do I do?, How do I do it?, Why do I do it?, What is the result?, Will I change anything based on the answers to the previous questions?* The dialog can be developed into a reflection group by collaborating with other teachers and educators with the aim of encouraging reflection and dialog as well as improving the quality of teaching and learning.

Although it might be hard to attain at the beginning of the profession without proper and sufficient guidance, reflection can make way for quality teaching and professional development. However, not until teachers review their individual philosophies and principles as a whole, systematically investigate their practices, and collaborate with colleagues for reflection would they be able to develop deeper reflective skills which will guide them onto the right road when they feel lost in the classroom. We are further aware of the significance of supporting novice teachers in overcoming the challenges of a theory and practice divide in their first years, besides helping them adapt to the classroom practice in a new workplace. To this end, this study aims at presenting the implementation of a Reflective Teaching and Learning Program (RTLP) designed in accordance with Farrell's (2019b) *holistic, evidence-based*, and *dialoging* principles of RP and implemented with a group of novice teachers in a foreign languages department of a foundation university in Turkey. We set out to explore the novice teachers' reflections on the RTLP held for 24 weeks in 2018–2019. The following research questions were addressed in this study:

1. How do novice teachers reflect on the RTLP in terms of its perceived benefits and challenges?
2. What modifications do novice teachers suggest for better implementation of RTLP?

6.2. METHOD

In order to investigate the novice EFL teachers' reflections on RTLP, we employed a mixed-methods research methodology for data collection and data analysis procedures. To achieve this, convergent parallel design was chosen where two strands of data were simultaneously collected, analysed, and merged for better interpretation of the findings (Creswell & Plano-Clark, 2011).

6.2.1. Context and Participants

The study was conducted in the 2018–2019 academic year at the department of foreign languages of a foundation university in Turkey. The implementation lasted 24 weeks – 12 weeks in the Fall semester and 12 weeks in the Spring semester.

The department where the study took place has a well-established professional development (PD) philosophy which values active teacher participation in every stage of PD activities. The department wants teachers to take ownership of their own PD, so they adopt a bottom-up approach to meet teacher needs. PD practices are supported by the department's administration. Teachers are offered PD practices such as team teaching, lesson study, action research, RTLP, and article and book discussion clubs; and they are encouraged to pick a model to support their PD. These practices require teachers to spend a lot of time in planning and teaching, so the administration helps arrange their teaching timetables, temporarily reducing their compulsory teaching hours. The department does not have a separate training unit for PD; instead, there are PD facilitators in charge of supporting teachers by helping with their needs and problems as well as guiding them through the PD program. PD facilitators are chosen among relatively experienced teachers with a keen interest in PD.

In RTLP, each facilitator is assigned to work with a group of maximum six teachers each semester. They are in charge of introducing RTLP, explaining the procedures to be followed throughout the program, and guiding new teachers with any academic problems they may encounter in and outside the class.

The participants in the present study were 12 EFL teachers with 1–3 years' teaching experience. Of the participants, 11 of them were female and held a major in English Language Teaching; the 12th was a graduate of the department of translation and interpretation. None of them had been involved in any kind of RTLP before.

6.2.2. RTLP Implementation

RTLP in the context of the study was implemented for 12 weeks each semester. The whole process will be explained under three headings; before an RTLP cycle, RTLP cycle, and repeating an RTLP cycle.

Before an RTLP Cycle: Before an RTLP cycle began, facilitators held an orientation meeting with all the novice teachers, where they introduced themselves, explained the goals of the PD in the department, and introduced RTLP procedures. At the first meeting, novice teachers also got to know their peers with whom they would be working the whole academic year. Next, each teacher video-recorded a lesson of their choice, watched the recording afterwards, and made a checklist of their strengths and areas that needed further consideration. Later, the teacher and the facilitator arranged a meeting where they viewed the video together and discussed the lesson's strengths, teacher's concerns, and learners' behavior, thus identifying the focus areas to be dealt with during RTLP. This was followed by a focus group meeting where all novice teachers and facilitators met in order to determine the content of the RTLP.

At the time when this study was conducted, the focus areas agreed by teachers and facilitators were as displayed in Figure 6.1.

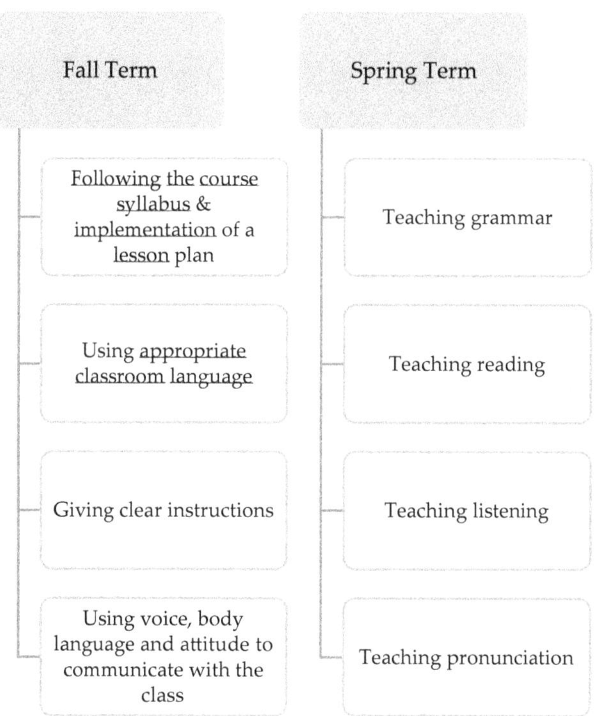

Figure 6.1. Focus areas decided by teachers and facilitators.

Finally, the teacher prepared a PD plan where they noted the focus areas, PD goals, expected learning outcomes, as well as activities that might help achieve the goals. Figure 6.2 indicates the procedures that the teachers went through before an RLTP cycle.

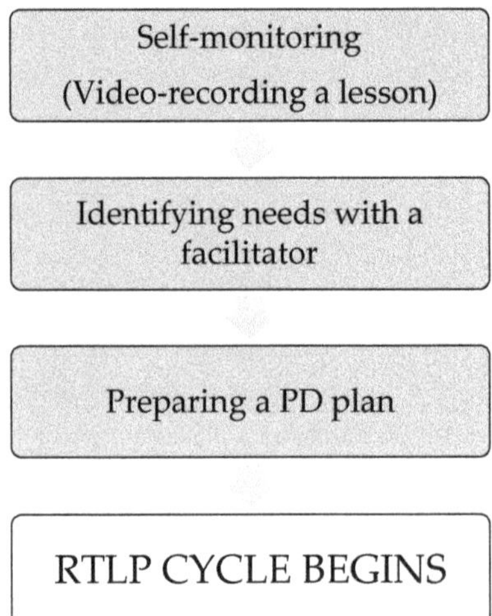

Figure 6.2. Steps to follow before an RTLP cycle.

RTLP Cycle: When all these steps were completed, the RTLP cycle was initiated. Each RTLP cycle was performed three times each semester. In each cycle teachers spent 2 weeks for preparation and 1 week for implementation. Upon the completion of one cycle in 3 weeks, another cycle began. For each RTLP cycle, teachers followed certain steps as displayed in Figure 6.3.

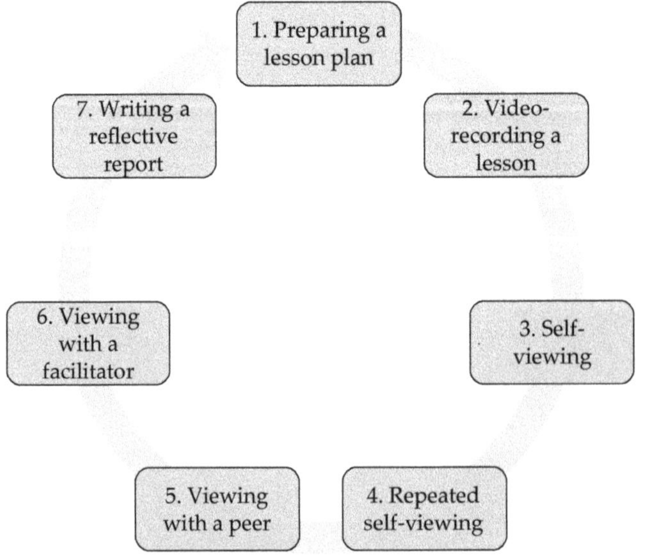

Figure 6.3. Steps to follow in an RTLP cycle.

As shown in Figure 6.3, each cycle began with lesson planning. At this stage, the teacher prepared a lesson plan with a focus area in mind. During the application of the lesson plan, the teacher video-recorded the lesson. Then the teacher watched the video-recording on their own without taking any notes. One or two days later, the teacher watched the video-recording of the lesson again, this time filling in the 'Repeated Self-Viewing Checklist' (see Appendix 6.1).

The fifth stage of the cycle was watching the video with a peer. The teacher and their peer viewed the recording together, using a set of 'Reflection Questions' (see Appendix 6.2) to facilitate their conversation. Once the viewing was over, an 'Evaluation Form' (see Appendix 6.3) was filled in separately by the peer and by the teacher.

The next stage in the cycle was to watch the video with the facilitator. The facilitator and the teacher viewed the recording together, talking about the positive aspects of the lesson as well as the further steps toward making teaching more efficient. The facilitator filled in a 'Facilitator Feedback Form' (see Appendix 6.4). Based on the feedback from the facilitator and insights gained from self- and peer-viewings, the teacher wrote a 'Reflective Report' (see Appendix 6.5) to complete the cycle.

Repeating an RTLP Cycle: Having completed an RTLP cycle, the teacher repeated it a second and third time with the same or a different focus area. The teacher and the facilitator decided together whether to study the same focus area or to work on a different one during the repeated cycles. The teacher then prepared a new lesson plan in accordance with the focus area and went through all the stages displayed in Figure 6.3.

Teachers repeated an RTLP cycle another three times in the second semester. In the second semester, the facilitator formerly assigned to the teachers was changed, and each teacher worked with the new facilitator and different peers.

Reflective Break

- How would you feel if in your school all newly hired teachers – regardless of their experience – had to go through the RTLP?
- Your school is looking for facilitators for RTLP and seeks your advice about what makes a good facilitator. What would you say?
- Do you think RTLP as outlined above is feasible in your school context? What makes it feasible? What makes it infeasible?
- How do you feel about the documents teachers have to fill in or prepare as they engage in RTLP (see Appendices 6.1–6.8)? What else would you include? What would you exclude?

At the end of the two semesters, teachers wrote an 'End-of-Year Reflective Report' (see Appendix 6.6), considering their experience, teaching practice in and outside the class, their beliefs and opinions about teaching, their students, and their PD before and after the RTLP.

6.2.3. Data Collection Tools

We collected data in three different forms: reflective reports, RTLP experience questionnaire, focus group interview.

Reflective Reports: As explained in the implementation of RTLP, teachers were required to write 'reflective reports' after each RTLP cycle, and at the end of the academic year. Since teachers repeated an RTLP cycle six times, they wrote six reflective reports, plus an 'end-of-year reflective report.' These seven reflective reports per teacher were collected and archived by the researchers.

RTLP Experience Questionnaire: At the end of the academic year, we gave the teachers the 'RTLP Experience Questionnaire' (see Appendix 6.7) to explore how participation in RTLP affected them. We modified the questionnaire developed by Cerbin (2011) for our purposes. The questionnaire consisted of two parts, and contained multiple choice and open-ended questions.

Focus Group Interview: A 'Focus Group Interview' was conducted with teachers at the end of the academic year. The main aim of this interview was to encourage teachers to elaborate on their reflections about RTLP (see Appendix 6.8). All 12 teachers participated in the interview conducted in Turkish. It lasted for about an hour and conversations mainly revolved around teachers' experiences of RTLP, how they felt during the process, what they achieved in terms of their PD, and what could have been modified for a smoother implementation of the program.

6.3. FINDINGS

The findings of the study are presented under two main headings: positive aspects of RTLP, and potential pitfalls of RTLP.

6.3.1. Positive Aspects of RTLP

We asked teachers how effective they found RTLP as a way to improve teaching. While 75% of teachers reported that they found it very effective, 25% of them found it somewhat effective. We also asked them to rate their overall RTLP experience: 66.7% of the teachers found it very positive, and 33.3% found it somewhat positive.

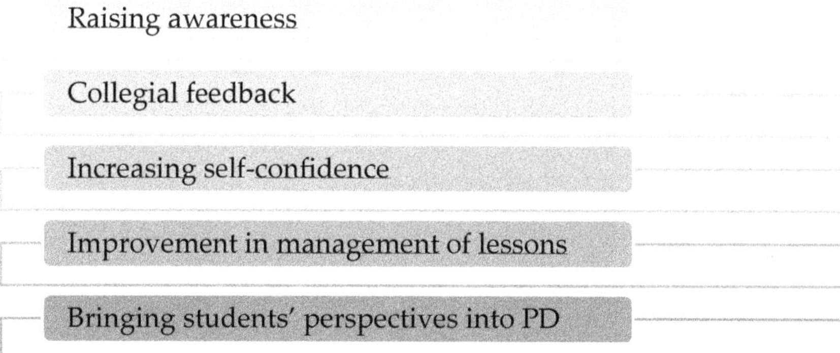

Figure 6.4. Positive aspects of RTLP.

As seen in Figure 6.4, the reasons why teachers considered RTLP to be a positive PD experience fell into five categories: raising awareness, collegial feedback, increasing self-confidence, better management of lessons, and thinking about students.

Teachers were of the opinion that RTLP benefited their PD in terms of *raising their awareness* about themselves as individuals professionally engaged in the teaching business. Underlining the various ways RTLP helped him become aware of himself and his classroom practices, one of the teachers commented as follows:

> You can also evaluate yourself in many aspects like, giving instructions, classroom management, intonation, activity variety. There were lots of things that I didn't even realize when I was doing them like walking back and forth all the time and after watching myself, I could see that this can be distracting for the students.

Facilitators' encouraging comments reportedly had a positive influence on teachers' beliefs about teaching, and stimulated their PD. Feedback from the facilitator helped broaden their knowledge and turn negative ideas about teaching practices into positive ones by showing them how 'to see the glass half full rather than half empty.' One teacher thought she had a more accurate picture of herself now, and built up a more favorable self-image as a teacher thanks to RTLP. She had previously tended to think 'everyone was better' than her, but she felt relieved upon seeing that they were all 'not that different from each other.'

Another category among the positive aspects of RTLP was found to be *collegial feedback*. Teachers found peer meetings fruitful because they included the mutual exchange of ideas. As stated by one: 'I especially enjoyed the peer meetings and discussions where I could learn what other colleagues thought and did about the same issue. They were quite beneficial.' Teachers thought feedback from different sources enabled them to gain a completely different perspective on their teaching practices 'because each person in the process means a different style for teaching and a different perspective that I may not be even aware of.' Feedback from peers and facilitators was regarded as a valuable asset of RTLP, as mentioned by one of the teachers:

> I peered up firstly with X and secondly with Y. Their feedback is precious to me since it is my first professional year in a university, and I believe I can learn something from any person. Getting some feedback not only from our facilitator but also from our peers helped me realize different ways of teaching.

Increasing self-confidence was another category established as a result of teachers' comments. The comments of the teacher below indicate how the peer-viewing stage of RTLP enhanced teachers' confidence in themselves:

> We had a great time with my colleagues whose videos I watched and who watched my videos. We don't hesitate to talk about mistakes and learn the correct versions of them from one another because we know that they also make the same or similar mistakes. This certainly boosted our confidence.

In addition to viewing their recorded lessons with peers, teachers also watched them with their facilitators, and they regarded this as contributing to their self-confidence. As stated by one of the teachers: 'The meetings with my mentor improved my teaching obviously. When I received feedback about the things I did well, I started to feel more confident as a teacher.' Modifications made in lesson plans and classroom activities based on teachers' discussions with their peers and facilitators were found to reflect well on teacher morale and confidence: 'The more I learn from feedback sessions, the better I teach in class. When I notice that the things we focused on RTLP work with my students, my confidence increases.'

The fourth theme we came up with as a result of data analysis was *improvement in management of lessons*. Teachers reported that their engagement in RTLP made it possible for them to ensure that their classes ran more smoothly than before because they were 'discussing different ideas with a peer' thereby enhancing their 'creativity.' With the help of discussions with a mentor, they felt that they gained 'a richer understanding of classroom management.' One of the teachers said that

RTLP sharpened her classroom management skills, thus leading to a more successful learning environment: 'This year has been a great start for my teaching career. RTLP taught me how to look and behave like a teacher, where to stand during the lessons, how to approach the students, and many other stuff.' Additionally, teachers' delivery of instruction was reported to be positively affected during the process. By raising awareness about teacher talking time and different teacher roles, RTLP helped teachers maintain control of their classes:

> Before RTLP, I had my own beliefs about teaching, students, teachers, and etc. For example, I thought the more I talked, the more my students were exposed to the language, so I had to talk non-stop. I myself was the lead, director, and the cast. I never thought this would mean less student talking and letting them insufficient time to produce something real and creative.

Last but not least, teachers had a high opinion of RTLP because they believed it enabled them to *bring students' perspectives into their PD*. Looking at themselves through the eyes of their students, teachers could specify their strengths and weaknesses: 'It helped me realize how I am seen by students and see clearly what goes well or wrong.' One of the teachers highlighted that by considering student reactions during a lesson, he could improve his attitudes towards students as RTLP has encouraged him to see and think about 'what perceptions students have' of his lessons; and besides, 'I could observe my students and could find solutions for my wrong attitudes.' RTLP was also reported to make visible the otherwise overlooked link between teacher behavior and student learning. Another teacher stated: 'I have realized that my position and attitudes are so significant in the classroom that they can affect students' learning. I also learned that I didn't check students' comprehension.' Thinking about students and considering their needs before the lesson made it possible for the teachers to start using the book as a guide rather than a master, leading to more student-centered instructional approaches:

> I start to think and see the lesson from the students' point of view. At first, I followed the book line by line, but now before the lesson, I check the book and I think about how I can make this activity, reading or grammar topic easier for students. I realized that I am becoming a more student-centered teacher.

6.3.2. Potential Pitfalls of RTLP

Teachers were engaged in several different activities during RTLP implementation, such as writing reflective reports, preparing a lesson plan, video-recording of lessons, etc. We asked teachers to indicate to what extent they found each activity difficult during their RTLP experience. The results are shown in Figure 6.5.

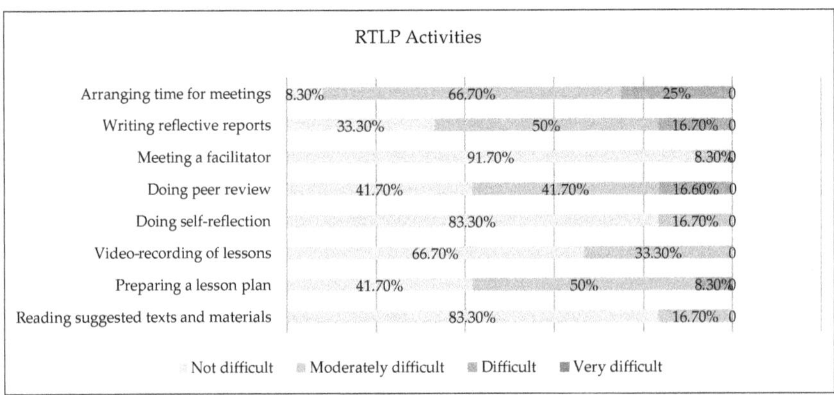

Figure 6.5. Teachers' opinions regarding the difficulty of RTLP activities.

None of the activities were regarded as 'very difficult.' However, 25% of teachers thought that 'arranging time for meetings' was difficult, 16.60% of them found 'peer reviews' difficult, 16.70% regarded 'writing reflective reports' as difficult, and 8.3% of teachers found 'preparing a lesson plan' difficult.

An analysis of tasks considered to be moderately difficult by teachers indicated that 66.70% of teachers found 'arranging time for meetings' moderately difficult, 50% of them thought 'writing reflective reports' was moderately difficult, and 50% of them reported that 'preparing a lesson plan' was a moderately difficult task, which was followed by 41.70% of teachers indicating that 'peer reviews' were moderately difficult. While 33.30% of teachers reported 'video-recording lessons' to be moderately difficult, 16.70% of them considered 'self-reflection' as moderately difficult, and 16.70% thought that 'reading suggested texts and materials' was moderately difficult. A small minority of teachers (8.30%) regarded 'meeting a facilitator' as moderately difficult.

It can be seen from Figure 6.5 that a great majority of teachers found 'meeting a facilitator' (91.70%), 'reading suggested texts and materials' (83.30%), and 'self-reflection' (83.30%) not difficult. More than half of the teachers (66.70%) thought that 'video-recording lessons' was not difficult. The percentage of teachers who regarded 'peer review' and 'preparing a lesson plan' not difficult was the same

(41.70), while 33.30% regarded 'writing reflective reports' not difficult. Just 8.30% of them found 'arranging time for meetings' not difficult.

Teachers were asked if they would participate in RTLP again in the future under the right circumstances. All 12 (100%) teachers reported that they would. We also wanted them to describe the 'right' circumstances. Their descriptions fell under two categories: more support from the administration and facilitator, and new areas for improvement.

Teachers commented that they needed *more support from the administration and facilitator*. No matter how satisfied they were with the amount of support they received from both parties, teachers declared that they wanted this support to be more extensive. For one thing, as they found 'arranging time for meetings' to be difficult, they reported that administration could make their jobs easier by arranging RTLP practitioners' schedules in advance so that they could have a free slot for meetings. One teacher commented: 'It is almost impossible for us to meet. The administration could have fixed this before the semester began.'

In terms of facilitator support, teachers thought that they were in need of more guidance especially when they prepared lesson plans and when they attempted to put them into action. This is reflected in their comments, e.g.: 'Lesson plans were like a pain in the neck to me. I wished I could receive more help from my facilitator in that sense.' Another teacher also mentioned her need for guidance in lesson planning: 'I think writing lesson aims, finding activities, and designing a lesson were so difficult. I definitely needed more help in those areas and implementing them was another story.'

Teachers also underlined that they would like to take part in RTLP in the future provided that they would focus on *new areas for improvement*, 'but in a different way' and concentrating 'on new topics.' Our analysis of the qualitative data also showed that teachers wanted some modifications to take place for RTLP to be a more effective PD practice. First, teachers complained about *ineffective peer reviews*. One teacher expressed that she did not benefit from peer reviews either by observing a peer's lessons, or 'getting feedback' from a peer about her own lessons. Since they 'did not know how to give proper feedback to each other,' peer feedback sessions were found unhelpful and 'not fruitful.' One of the teachers voiced her concerns about peer review and suggested that the way it is done should be modified in the future:

> I don't like peer review at all. There should be a change in it. Maybe for future practices, our advisor could pick one of the videos to be analysed and everyone could watch that specific video and we could get our mentor's feedback about the video as well.

The second modification suggested by teachers was about *observing other colleagues*. One teacher commented that before implementing RTLP, peer observation would help them a lot to assess the teaching/learning situation, because they 'were very inexperienced about both the curriculum and the learner profile' of the school and they felt 'very nervous in the first video recording.' Through peer observation, they would be able to see 'how certain things are implemented in their peer's classroom' and would feel more comfortable before RTLP began. They further suggested observing a more experienced colleague's class as it could make them feel more at ease, and ready for RTLP. One teacher said: 'Seeing a model would make me feel more secure and confident about myself. Thus, I would like to attend experienced teachers' lessons to observe them teach in class.'

For RTLP to produce better results in terms of PD, teachers recommended that they should have *a more flexible schedule* and *fewer recordings and reports*. In their view, RTLP should be implemented every other week, rather than every week. If they could 'have a gap week after each video and feedback session,' they believed it would be more helpful 'to internalize' what they learned from the experience. One teacher stated: 'Sometimes we don't have enough time between reflective teaching videos. There can be more time between the videos.' Additionally, reducing the number of video-recordings and reflective reports was suggested to facilitate the process: 'Fewer video-recordings could be better for us to have some time to relax and not rush.' RTLP was considered to be more effective with 'more free time' and 'reduced paperwork' for the teachers who 'can't write the reports properly' under time pressure.

Reflective Break

- Considering your school context, what aspects of RTLP would present the most benefits and challenges?
- Have you ever received feedback about your teaching from your colleagues? What was the experience like?
- Do you think students might help teachers become better reflective practitioners?
- Why do you think teachers find conducting peer reviews and writing reflective reports difficult?
- How could the effectiveness of peer reviews be increased?

6.4. DISCUSSION

The aim of this study was to investigate novice English language teachers' reflection on a Reflective Teaching and Learning Program (RTLP) implemented at a foreign languages department of a foundation university in Turkey for 24 weeks. The results to emerge from the data were grouped under three categories: positive aspects of RTLP, its potential pitfalls, and teachers' recommendations for better RTLP implementation.

Regarding the positive aspects of RTLP, we believe the findings indicated the significance of peer and mentor or collegial feedback for teacher PD. Through both forms of feedback in RTLP, the novice teachers believed their awareness of themselves as professional individuals increased. RTLP seemed to provide them with more consciousness of teaching theories and practices besides a more favorable self-image about themselves as teachers. While having dialogs with peers in feedback sessions, the teachers seemed to be relieved upon noticing they had some shared problems, and similar strengths and weaknesses, with their colleagues. The teachers found peer meetings and discussions a very important opportunity for evaluating one's self and learning from each other and also realizing that different ways of teaching could exist. This finding fits with Silberstein (1998) and Kelchtermans (2000) who argued that constant reflective feedback leads to a higher level of self-evaluation and ultimately to PD for teachers. Further, peer and facilitator meetings where they could share opinions and exchange ideas with great comfort were considered to boost their confidence as well as contributing to their skills in managing lessons. It appeared that dialoging with other colleagues not only developed their knowledge and ideas about their teacher selves but also improved their classroom practice. We believe there is substantial agreement between our findings and the arguments made by Farrell (2018a) who has emphasized that the 'collaborative process of dialoguing' among teachers and other educators is a very important principle of reflective practice where they can examine their beliefs, develop practices, and create alternative solutions to problems.

Our findings further led us to believe that the novice teachers were encouraged to gradually perform a systematic examination of theories and practices through the cycles of RTLP. Completing one teaching practice in the classroom, they engaged in reflection both individually and with other colleagues and sought ways to take further actions for future practice. We believe that self-observation, collegial dialog, and peer feedback in RTLP could help teachers become involved in systematic study, or as suggested by Dewey (1933, p. 18), help them give 'active, persistent and careful consideration' to teaching problems and resolving these problems in future lessons (reflection-in-action). This systematic work might reinforce the emergence of new ideas and practices resulting in better lesson management skills. This could be regarded as an important step at the start of a teacher's career. On the other hand, we are also aware that the teachers focused mostly on technical aspects of their teaching, which could be regarded as their immediate need at the time of the study. Therefore, RTLP in our context could have remained at a basic level without much concentration on social, cultural, and emotional aspects of reflection, underlined by Farrell (2018a) in his six principles as crucial elements of reflective practice.

Acknowledging that viewing their lessons through video-recording was a good chance to see themselves through the eyes of learners, the novice teachers agreed that they started to plan lessons considering students and their needs more, in addition to taking up more learner-centered methods. This might imply that RTLP had an influence on teachers' assumptions and beliefs about students. It seemed that they tended to pay little consideration to learners when making their lesson plans, and selected their instructional approaches and methods accordingly. We believe that reflective practice helped teachers better appreciate the significance of learners, making room for better classroom practice and teacher development. This might imply that RTLP helped change their beliefs and practices and encouraged them to select, design, and apply more student-centered activities in the classroom. This finding ties in well with Farrell (2018a) who recommends that effective reflective practice should bridge principles and practices. We think RTLP facilitated the creation of this link. After the teachers came to realize they were not involving learners in their teaching as much as they should, they began taking up new teaching practices paying more attention to students' voices.

When it comes to the potential pitfalls of RTLP, the teachers agreed on the difficulty of arranging time for meetings. What's more, half of them believed that writing reflective reports presented them with some kind of challenge, which could be attributed to their tight schedule at school and RTLP requiring them to do regular planning, teaching, peer meetings, evaluation, and reflection almost every week. This showed us that RTLP should be revised in regard to its schedule and paperwork. Considering the challenges most novice teachers face in the initial years of the profession, we strongly believe that the program must have a facilitating purpose rather than a debilitating one, and must fully support teachers in overcoming the difficulties they might have inside and outside the classroom, instead of placing a heavy burden on them with tight schedules, time limitations, and too much paperwork.

Our findings also showed that the novice teachers developed positive feelings and attitudes towards RTLP, because all of them showed enthusiasm to participate in the program again as long as they were supported more by the administration in terms of their schedules and by the facilitators about new areas to focus on. They seemed to think that they benefited a lot from RTLP but they did not want it to be repetitive. This led us to think that RTLP aroused enthusiasm among teachers for PD and working in collaboration with their peers. On the other hand, we think that particular attention should be paid to prevent RTLP from becoming a routinized practice, which does not lead to higher-level critical reflection. As the findings yielded very positive results about the teachers' willingness to continue reflective practice, we believe that RTLP should be designed with a more holistic outlook and with more attention to the 'beyond practice' stage of reflection, where teachers are encouraged to be aware of the sociocultural aspects of teaching and learning besides moral, political, and social issues affecting the context inside and outside the classroom (Farrell, 2014).

Considering teachers' recommendations for better implementation of RTLP, we believe that the program should be revised with regard to peer review sessions. The teachers considered that they did not gain as much from peer reviews as they did from facilitator reviews. Since they did not know how to give feedback to each other, they did not find peer feedback as effective as facilitator feedback. This is an important lesson to be learned from the results of the study. Without receiving any training in giving peer feedback, it must have been difficult for teachers to find what to focus on and how to express it properly. Some of them might have been too polite because of the fear of hurting a colleague's feelings, while some others might have taken a highly critical attitude, causing feelings of demotivation or discouragement in their peers. Neither of these cases contributes to PD, so RTLP needs to be reconsidered with regard to the peer feedback stage, and teachers should be given some pre-training on how to give effective feedback.

Another suggestion by the teachers about the program was inserting an additional stage before video-recordings began, where novice teachers could observe a more experienced teacher's class so that they could get some idea about or become familiar with the learners and learning context. We believe this should also be taken into consideration for better future practice. New in the profession and foreign to the learning environment, novice teachers cannot be expected to learn and practice effectively unless they are familiarized with the social, cultural, and educational realities of their teaching context.

6.5. CONCLUSION

RTLP in its current shape and form conforms to most of the essential principles of reflective practice put forward by Farrell (2019b). Its evidence-based nature and the way it engages teachers in dialog with their facilitators, peers, and students encourages teachers to question – in a systematic structure – their beliefs about teaching and how these beliefs impact on their in-class practices. However, we must also acknowledge the fact that although RTLP is a promising start in our endeavor to help novice teachers become more reflective, it may prove inadequate in making reflection a lifelong professional activity for beginning teachers, for several reasons. For one thing, in its current form RTLP is a prescriptive model, and when practiced for a long period of time, it could result in reflection being considered as a 'dull and routine' task for teachers, restricting its real potential as a PD tool. In addition, we might also criticize the model for its strong focus on, as Freeman (2016) calls it, 'post-mortem' reflection. In this type of reflection, teachers tend to consider reflection solely as a tool to fix common classroom problems and thus develop a limited understanding of it. Reducing reflection to such a mechanical tool also means ignoring one of the most essential aspects of it, the affective side. Noncognitive aspects of reflection such as teachers' inner feelings and emotions play a key role in the process of reflection and in our understanding of reflexivity as a holistic activity (Farrell, 2019b). We should adopt a holistic approach to reflection if we aim to help teachers become more integrated and self-aware (Farrell, 2018b). Holism is achieved when teachers reflect on their philosophy, principles, theory, practice, and beyond practice. RTLP enables teachers to reflect on one or – from an optimistic point of view – two of these elements, theory and practice. Though this might be a humble beginning in a context such as ours where reflective practices are rarely employed by novice teachers, we believe that RTLP needs to be transformed to incorporate as many stages as possible to make reflection a holistic and lifelong attempt.

REFERENCES

Barrett, J., Jones, G., Mooney, E., Thornton, C., Cady, J., Guinee, P., & Olson, J. (2002). Working with novice teachers: Challenges for professional development. *Mathematics Teacher Education and Development, 4*, 15–27. https://doi.org/10.1080/01626620.1993.10463161

Cerbin, B. (2011). *Lesson study: Using classroom inquiry to improve teaching and learning in higher education*. Stylus Publishing, LLC.

Chaplain, R. P. (2008). Stress and psychological distress among trainee secondary teachers in England. *Educational Psychology, 28*(2), 195–209. https://doi.org/10.1080/01443410701491858

Corcoran, E. (1981). Transition shock: The beginning teacher's paradox. *Journal of Teacher Education, 32*(3), 19–23. https://doi.org/10.1177/002248718103200304

Cordingley, P. (2006). Talking to learn: The role of dialogue in professional development. *Education Review, 19*, 2.

Creswell, J. W., & Clark, V. L. P. (2011). *Designing and conducting mixed methods research*. Sage Publications.

Darling-Hammond, L. (2010). Teacher education and the American future. *Journal of Teacher Education, 61*(1–2), 35–47.

Darling-Hammond, L., Furger, R., Shields, P. M., & Sutcher, L. (2016). Addressing California's emerging teacher shortage: An analysis of sources and solutions. Learning Policy Institute, Palo Alto, CA.

Dewey, J. (1933). *How we think: A restatement of the relation of reflective thinking to the educative process*. DC Heath and Company.

Farrell, T. S. C. (2007). *Reflective language teaching: From research to practice*. Continuum Press.

Farrell, T. S. C. (2012). Reflecting on reflective practice: (Re)Visiting Dewey and Schön. *TESOL Journal, 3*(1), 7–16. https://doi.org/10.1002/tesj.10

Farrell, T. S. C. (2014). *Promoting teacher reflection in second language education: A framework for TESOL professionals*. Routledge. https://doi.org/10.4324/9781315775401

Farrell, T. S. C. (Ed.) (2018a). Reflection as action. In *Reflection as action in ELT* (pp. 1–5). Tesol Press. http://www.reflectiveinquiry.ca/wp-content/uploads/2018/12/chapter-1-Farrell.pdf

Farrell, T. S. C. (2018b). Operationalizing reflective practice in second language teacher education. *Journal of Second Language Teacher Education, 1*(1), 1–20.

Farrell, T. S. C. (2019a). 'My training has failed me': Inconvenient truths about second language teacher education (SLTE). *TESL-EJ, 22*(4), 4.

Farrell, T. S. C. (2019b). *Reflective practice in ELT*. Equinox Publishing. https://doi.org/10.4324/9781315659824-5

Farrell, T. S. C. (2020). Professional development through reflective practice for English-medium instruction (EMI) teachers. *International Journal of Bilingual Education and Bilingualism, 23*(3), 277–286. https://doi.org/10.4324/9781003178729-3

Farrell, T. S. C., & Kennedy, B. (2019). Reflective practice framework for TESOL teachers: One teacher's reflective journey. *Reflective Practice, 20*(1), 1–12.

Freeman, D. (2016). *Educating second language teachers*. Oxford University Press.

Goldrick, L. (2016). Support from the start: A 50-state review of policies on new educator induction and mentoring. Retrieved from: New Teacher Center, https://studentsatthecenterhub.org/resource/support-from-the-start-a-50-state-review-of-policies-on-new-educator-induction-and-mentoring/

Haynes, L. (2011). *Novice teachers' perceptions of their mentoring experiences*. ProQuest Dissertations Publishing, Lamar University–Beaumont.

Huberman, M. (1992). Teacher development and instructional mastery. In A. Hargreaves & M. Fullan (Eds.), *Understanding teacher development* (pp. 216–241). Longman Publishers.

Karataş, P., & Karaman, A. C. (2013). Challenges faced by novice language teachers: Support, identity, and pedagogy in the initial years of teaching. *The International Journal of Research in Teacher Education*, *4*(3), 10–23.

Kelchtermans, G. (2000). Reflective learning from biography and content. In *Fourth Teachers Develop Teachers Research Conference Report*.

Kim, K., & Roth, G. L. (2011). Novice teachers and their acquisition of work-related information. *Current Issues in Education*, *14*, 1.

Kumaravadivelu, B. (1994). The postmethod condition: (E)merging strategies for second/foreign language teaching. *TESOL Quarterly*, *28*(1), 27–48. https://doi.org/10.2307/3587814

Lundeen, C. A. (2004). Teacher development: The struggle of beginning teachers in creating moral (caring) classroom environments. *Early Child Development and Care*, *174*(6), 549–564. https://doi.org/10.1080/0300443042000187068

Moir, E. (1999). The stages of a teacher's first year: A better beginning, supporting and mentoring new teachers. https://eric.ed.gov/?id=ED435603

Peercy, M. M. (2012). Problematizing the theory-practice gap: How ESL teachers make sense of their preservice education. *Journal of Theory and Practice in Education*, *8*(1), 20–40.

Penso, S., Edna, S., & Neomi, S. (2001). First steps in novice teachers' reflective activity. *Teacher Development*, *5*(3), 323–338. https://doi.org/10.1080/13664530100200159

Pitton, D. E. (2006). *Mentoring novice teachers: Fostering a dialogue process*. Corwin Press.

Robinson, V. M. J. (1998). Methodology and the research-practice gap. *Educational Researcher*, *27*, 17–26. https://doi.org/10.3102/0013189X027001017

Silberstein, M. (1998). Reflective teaching – Conceptual clarification for teacher-training programs. In M. Silberstein, M. Ben-Peretz, and S. Ziv (Eds.), *Reflection in teaching, the pivot in teacher development* (pp. 15–42). Levinski College, Tel-Aviv (in Hebrew).

Veenman, S. (1984). Perceived problems of beginning teachers. *Review of Educational Research*, *54*(2), 143–178. https://doi.org/10.3102/00346543054002143

Voss, T., & Kunter, M. (2020). 'Reality shock' of beginning teachers? Changes in teacher candidates' emotional exhaustion and constructivist-oriented beliefs. *Journal of Teacher Education*, *71*(3), 292–306. https://doi.org/10.1177/0022487119839700

APPENDIX 6.1

Repeated Self-Viewing Checklist

THE TEACHER	Very much	Much	Moderately	Very little	Not at all
Shows enthusiasm					
Arouses and maintains student interests					
Teaches in an organized manner					
Is good at classroom management					
Relates teaching to students' real life					
Encourages student participation					
Uses a variety of activities					
Uses appropriate activities					
Employs an appropriate level of difficulty					
Teaches at an appropriate pace					
Uses the board effectively					
Uses a variety of materials effectively (visual, technology, etc.)					
Presents clear instructions					
Shows support and concern for students					
Praises and encourages students appropriately					
Asks questions effectively (clarity, relevance, redirection, wait time, etc.)					
Provides effective feedback					
Establishes good eye contact					
Has a clear voice (pleasant, audible)					

APPENDIX 6.2

Reflection Questions (while viewing the recording with a peer)

Now view your lesson with a colleague. The following questions might help you engage in a reflective discussion with your colleague.

1. Were your instructions clear and simple?
2. Did you rephrase your instructions if your students were at a loss, or did you translate them?
3. Did you confirm the right answers?
4. How did you correct wrong answers?
5. Did you praise the students?
6. Was your use of gestures sufficient?
7. Were you monotonous? Were you emotional?
8. How will problems identified in your teaching affect your teaching next time?
9. What questions would you like to add to this list?
10. Did you try to involve the whole class?
11. What modes of interaction were used? (whole class, individual work, pair work, group work, etc.)
12. Was there a pupil in the classroom who was not involved?
13. Was the pacing too fast or too slow for the majority of students?
14. How many questions were asked for each student?
15. Can you specify the proportion of teacher talk vs student talk?
16. How effective was your use of multimedia technology?
17. Were your instructions clear and simple?
18. Did you rephrase your instructions if your students were at a loss?
19. Did you explain assignments, or did you show the pupils what to do?
20. Did you notice any serious errors in your speech?
21. Can you reflect on cases when students failed to speak English and shifted to their native language?
22. Did you implement the objectives you had planned?

APPENDIX 6.3

Evaluation Forms (after viewing the recording with a peer)

Peer Evaluation Form

Was the lesson successful? How do you know it has/hasn't been successful?
What did you like/dislike about the lesson?
Did your colleague do what s/he had planned to do?
What were his/her main strengths?
What were his/her main weaknesses?
If your colleague had the opportunity to teach the lesson again, what would recommend that s/he should do differently?
Other comments:

Self-Evaluation Form

Was the lesson successful? How do you know you have/haven't been successful?
What did you like/dislike about the lesson?
Did you do what you had planned to do?
What were your main strengths?
What were your main weaknesses?
If you had the opportunity to teach the lesson again, what would you do differently?
What did you learn from the experience of teaching this lesson?
Other comments:

APPENDIX 6.4

Facilitator Feedback Form (while viewing the recording with a facilitator)

TEACHER:	FOCUS AREA:
FACILITATOR:	DATE:
Positive aspects of his/her teaching:	Steps toward making his/her teaching techniques more efficient:

APPENDIX 6.5

Reflective Report (after viewing the recording with a facilitator)

Please answer the following questions reflecting on your experiences in the first and subsequent self-viewing, peer-viewing, and facilitator-viewing.

1. Write down something new or useful that you have learnt through video-recording.
2. Write down something new or useful that you have learnt in peer and facilitator meetings.
3. In what ways/areas do you think you have improved?
4. In what ways/areas do you think you need to improve?
5. What's one goal you would like to set for yourself for the next session?

APPENDIX 6.6

End-of-Year Reflective Report

Please reflect on your experience in RTLP this year. Provide as many specific details as you remember and answer each item below.

1. Describe yourself as a teacher (you as a teacher, your teaching practice in and out of class, your beliefs and opinions about teaching, students, professional development, etc.) before involving in RTLP and after the completion of the program. Please provide specific examples and details.
2. What *feedback*, *practice/s*, and/or *who* contributed most to you professionally? How and why? Please provide specific examples and details.
3. What are your suggestions for the future RTLP practices?

APPENDIX 6.7

Reflective Teaching and Learning Program Experience Questionnaire

This questionnaire is for RTLP practitioners who have been involved in the program for two semesters. Particularly, it aims to explore how participation in RTLP affects novice teachers. We sincerely appreciate your contribution to this effort.

Your participation in this questionnaire is voluntary. By completing it you are granting permission to us to use your responses for research purposes.

Your responses will be kept anonymous. Excerpts of responses may be used in presentations or publications, but you will not be associated with individual responses.

Thank you for your time and cooperation.

Part A

1. What is your major?
2. How many years of teaching experience do you have?
   - ELT
   - Linguistics
   - Translation & Interpretation
   - American Culture & Literature
   - English Language & Literature
3. Have you been involved in RTLP before?
   - Yes
   - No
4. How effective is RTLP as a way to improve teaching?
   - Very effective
   - Somewhat effective
   - Somewhat ineffective
   - Very ineffective
5. To what extent did you find each activity difficult during your experience?
   - Reading suggested texts and materials
   - Preparing a lesson plan
   - Video-recording of lessons
   - Doing self-reflection
   - Doing peer review
   - Meeting a facilitator
   - Writing reflective reports
   - Arranging time for meetings
6. How would you rate your overall RTLP experience?
   - Very positive
   - Somewhat positive
   - Neutral
   - Somewhat negative
   - Very negative

7. Under the right circumstances would you participate in RTLP again in the future?
    - Yes
    - No

If you answered yes, please describe the right circumstances.

Part B

8. Comment on your RTLP experience. Emphasize and explain any features you think were particularly significant, worthwhile, beneficial, or negative.
9. This section asks you to reflect on ways that RTLP has influenced your attitudes, thinking, and behavior. Influence has a broad meaning. For example, it can refer to how your RTLP experience stimulated your thinking about some aspects of teaching, led to some realization about students, or changed the way you actually teach.
10. Please offer suggestions or advice about how to improve any aspect of RTLP.

APPENDIX 6.8

Focus Group Interview Form

Welcome to our focus group interview. Thanks for taking the time to join us. Today, ____ will be moderating our discussion, and ____ will be assisting me with recording and note-taking. Our topic is the RTLP implementation we have been carrying out for the whole academic year, and more importantly your experiences as teachers. As you know, we conducted a survey to learn about what you think about RTLP. We analyzed the results, and we would like you to elaborate on your answers. The results will be used for improving RTLP. You were selected as interviewees because you recently participated in our RTLP implementation, so your ideas are valuable to us.

There are some guidelines we will follow during the interview. We would like to remind you that there are no right or wrong answers or comments. We will be recording our discussions, so we kindly ask one person to speak at a time. You do not need to agree with your colleagues, but you need to listen as they speak. We kindly ask you to turn your cell phones off, or put them in silent mode.

If you are ready, let's start with the first question.

- What would you like to tell us about RTLP?
- What do you like best/least about RTLP?

- How did you feel when you implemented RTLP?
- Survey results showed us that you found ____ difficult. Can you explain why?

ABOUT THE AUTHORS

İlknur Bayram received master's and PhD degrees from Ankara University, Turkey, in the field of Curriculum and Instruction. She currently works at the Center for Teaching and Learning, TED University, Ankara, Turkey. She also teaches at the faculty of education. Her main research interests are teacher professional development, reflective practice, lesson study, curriculum evaluation, and education for sustainable development.

Özlem Canaran is currently working as a Lecturer in the English Language Education Program at TED University, Ankara, Turkey. She has an MA and PhD in Foreign Language Education. Her research interests include language teacher education, teacher professional development, and English for academic and specific purposes.

Chapter 7

A Blended Reflection Cycle for Trainers: A Case Study

Mehmet Haldun Kaya

7.1. INTRODUCTION

Teachers suffer from higher levels of burnout than any other professionals in the service sector or in white-collar jobs (Hakanen et al., 2006); however, Farrell (2018) finds this unsurprising, as it ultimately results from following the same patterns in daily repetitive tasks. In this regard, Ur (1996) considers that teachers who have been teaching for twenty years can be divided into two categories: 'those with twenty years' experience, and those with one year's experience repeated twenty times' (p. 317). In a similar vein, having diagnosed the source of this burnout, Dewey (1933 as cited in Fazio, 2009) argues that, without reflection, teachers will become slaves to routine. Evidently, reflection could serve as an antidote, leading to breaking the chains of mundane routine that result in burnout. This clearly shows that, for teachers, being involved in reflective practice is, in fact, not only a voluntary act of self-development, but also a prerequisite for job satisfaction and strong professional identity.

With respect to the perception and definition of reflection, the extensive literature and studies display its dynamic, comprehensive, and adaptive nature. Dewey (1933 as cited in Fazio, 2009) defines reflection as an action involving 'the active, persistent and careful consideration of any belief or supposed form of knowledge in light of the grounds that support it' (p. 9). Elaborating on the concept, Schön (1987) distinguishes between 'reflection-in-action' and 'reflection-on-action.' The former refers to the ability to think on one's feet or make on-the-spot decisions when confronted with challenging and/or perplexing situations. 'Reflection-on-action,' however, refers to systematic and conscious thinking about past events in the classroom (Loughran, 2005). Underscoring the importance of the outcomes of both 'reflection-on-action' and 'reflection-in-action,' Farrell (2018) states that being involved in such reflective practice allows teachers to determine the direction of their professional plans. 'Reflection-for-action,' a related concept suggested by Killion & Todnem (1991), focuses on teaching experience following an instructional incident, and involves looking backward and forward simultaneously (Postholm, 2008); hence, it is evident that reflective practice has a cyclical nature, which requires instructors to self-observe, analyse, and revise their own teaching (Gözüyeşil & Soylu, 2014).

Reflection has proved itself as an optimum method in many teacher-training programs, particularly for second language teachers (Avalos, 2011); and numerous studies and research have been carried out in this area (e.g., Karakaş & Yükselir, 2021; Martinez, 2022; Mulryan-Kyne, 2021). There are many resources for teachers which cover the various definitions, philosophical foundations, approaches, and the challenges and benefits of reflection. Most reflective practice material focuses on teachers, providing many reflection tasks, templates, pathways to follow, best practices as models, and peers or trainers to work with collaboratively. Reflection is of equal value and use for teacher trainers, the providers of professional development. However, trainers are provided with little help or guidance; and there is a dearth of research or resources specific to trainers' self-reflection on their own work and performance. The value and use of reflection for the development of teachers, in fact, suggests its potential as a method for trainer development (Ida, 2018).

When trying to find solutions to the challenges experienced in the classroom, it is always teachers who are encouraged to engage in 'reflection-in-action.' As for trainers, they are also involved in 'reflection-in-action' but this usually occurs in the post-observation meetings, when making on-the-spot suggestions or recommendations for dealing with the challenges teachers faced in the classroom. In other words, as seen in Figure 7.1, while teachers are 'reflecting-on-action,' trainers are involved in 'reflecting-in-action.' For trainers, 'reflection-on-action' means evaluating their own work and performance as a trainer after a training event, such as a post-observation meeting, workshop, seminar, or team-teaching.

Considering the undeniable value of 'reflection-on-action' for trainer development and the lack of such research in the literature, this study aims to address the gap by proposing a 'Blended Reflection Cycle for Trainers,' created by the author of this study, and analysing the results based on an implementation of this cycle in a single case. Thus, the study addresses the following research questions:

- To what extent does the 'Blended Reflection Cycle for Trainers' improve a trainer's practice?
- To what extent does the 'Blended Reflection Cycle for Trainers' improve a trainer's reflective skills?

Figure 7.1. Teachers and trainers reflecting.

7.2. LITERATURE REVIEW

The fragmented and diverse literature on reflective practice has been closely analysed; and this section presents a concise description of reflection, its components, the key principles, various approaches, and its importance for teachers. More importantly, the current study incorporates the literature related to the development of trainers, and the role reflection plays in this.

7.2.1. Teacher Training and Reflection

The ambiguity in the perception of reflection gives rise to various definitions (Clara, 2015) and suggested implementations (Williams & Grudnoff, 2011), such as defining it as a process of remembering, contemplating, and examining an experience with a certain focus (Richards, 2004) and likening it to a compass through which teachers can locate their current position and plan their route (Farrell, 2012). Likewise, Marcos et al. (2011) state that it is a cyclical process, in which teachers solve a problem requiring awareness and professional knowledge. In a similar vein, Rodgers (2002) regards it as a meaning construction not limited to teachers' practice but involving comprehension of the theoretical basis of their actions. In order to fully discern the components of reflection, Jay & Johnson (2002) also point out its tacit characteristics, stating that it should involve uncertainty, experience, and interaction with oneself and/or with others.

Reflection has various stages or dimensions, which, according to Nelson & Saddler (2012), consist of stimulus (What causes one to reflect?), content (What is one to reflect on?), process (What are the ways to reflect?), and outcome (What is the consequence of reflection?). Dividing the reflective practice into three steps: description, comparison, and criticism, Jay & Johnson (2002) state that in the description phase, teachers identify the puzzling situation as a burning question for reflection; and in the comparison stage, they examine the situation from different perspectives and notice the key and hidden points. In the final stage, criticism, teachers consider the implications and establish a new point of view. Similarly, Zeichner & Liston (1996) focus on five dimensions or sub-phases:

1. *Rapid reflection* which involves immediate reflection-in-action.
2. *Repair* which involves elaborated reflection-in-action.
3. *Review* which involves reflection-on-action at one specific time.
4. *Research* which involves a systematic reflection-on-action over a period of time.
5. *Re-theorizing and reformulating* which involve making connections between reflection-on-action and valid theories.

The literature frequently refers to the key function of reflection as a means for change in teacher development (Avalos, 2011) and highlights that the teachers best able to make changes in their teaching are those involved in reflective practice (Salmani-Nodoushan, 2006). Similarly, Brandt (2008) proposes that an effective teacher is a reflective one; and Valdez et al. (2018) agree that by reflecting, teachers can explore their practices and values, allowing them to make adjustments if necessary. Notably, Farrell (2013) underlines this unveiled function of reflection, by stating that reflective practice is more than a mere method, helping teachers to construct and re-construct their practice. Many researchers have also analysed how reflective practice has resulted in such a change in teachers' work, focusing on the link between reflection and its aspects such as professional identity (Korthagen, 2004), formative evaluation (McAlpine, et al., 2004), different perspectives on the evaluation of teaching experiences (Postholm, 2008), reflexive analysis of professional environments (Bolton & Delderfield, 2018), and adaptable teaching (Thorsen & DeVore, 2013).

Owing to the various understandings of reflection and the various types of reflective practice, numerous methods and tools have been used in the reflection process, including reflective diaries (Gallego, 2014), reflective video analysis (Tripp & Rich, 2012), peer coaching (Garber, 2014), peer observation (Lakshmi, 2014), peer collaboration or discussions (Johnson, 2003), narrative inquiry (Johnson & Golombek, 2002), critical incident analysis (Mann & Walsh, 2015), stimulated-recall interviews (Kane et al., 2004), and action research (Leitch & Day, 2000).

7.2.2. Trainer Training and Reflection

Describing 'teacher trainers' as highly qualified professionals, Diadori (2013) characterizes them as using their extensive background as language teachers and learners to guide those with less experience and/or less expertise to gain new knowledge derived from theory, practice, and research. Like 'village elders' among teachers (Kerr, 1979 as cited in Hayes, 2004), trainers often start their trainer career through attending teacher development programs, gaining knowledge as a result, and thus being selected as trainers (Kiely, 1996). In line with this, Wright (2009) refers to trainer development as a transition from 'teacher' to 'trainer'; thus, trainers' qualities and knowledge are similar to those of effective teachers (Leach, 1996) in that they are expected to have effective communication, organization, and leadership skills, as well as high emotional intelligence (Stronge, 2007). Yuk-Kwan Ng & Lam (2015) identified the following competencies and psychological needs of teacher trainers: facilitation skills, pedagogical knowledge, rich experience, good understanding of teachers' expectations, and self-regulation of emotion.

Knowledge about trainers and their development usually depends more on experience than formal research (Cambridge English & NILE, 2016); there are, however, various ways for trainers to develop themselves, such as through workplace learning (Fuler & Urwin, 2003), engaging in communities of practice (White, 2014), or developing interpersonal skills and formal learning (Morgan, 2015). The great majority of trainers continue developing themselves based on their own experience, rather than through a formal program (Diadori, 2013), which makes informal sharing the key factor in trainer development (Boyd et al., 2011).

Teachers can gain new perspectives, improve their professional work, and increase the quality of their teaching through reflection (Fatemipour, 2013); and reflecting on their own practices has become an equally popular method of development among trainers (Izadinia, 2014). When exploiting reflection for trainer development, trainer training often involves documenting teaching practices, analysing beliefs and values, and evaluating teaching practices with a reflective eye (Richards & Farrell, 2005) since an open and reflective mind is regarded as the key characteristic of a trainer (Yuk-Kwan Ng & Lam, 2015). In this regard, Hayes (2004) points out the importance of 'reflection-on-action' in trainer development. Kaya & Adıgüzel (2021), for example, showed that trainers who participated in an e-reflection course that focused on online 'reflection-on-action' increased both their teaching and teacher-training skills. The potential success of this type of formal trainer training courses and programs mainly relates to the principles of reflective teaching (Kandiller & Özler, 2015). Considering both theoretical and practical knowledge, Farrell (2019) identifies six principles for use as criteria for effective reflective practices: reflective practice (1) is holistic, (2) is evidence-based, (3) involves dialog, (4) bridges principles and practices, (5) requires a disposition for inquiry, and (6) is a way of life.

7.3. METHOD

Considering that no previous study in Turkey has investigated reflective practice as a method to develop trainers' professional work and reflective skills, it is appropriate to conduct an instrumental single case study with qualitative data. Instrumental case studies help to draw generalizations or provide solutions for a problem (Stake, 2005), with the case acting as a tool intended to foster the understanding of a particular phenomenon. This qualitative research involves three distinctive features: it is '*particularistic*,' being built on a particular case, '*descriptive*,' giving a rich and thick description of the case, and '*heuristic*,' helping to better comprehend the phenomenon under study (Merriam, 2009). Thus, in this research, the case of one trainer is a tool to gain insight into how trainers can improve their activities and reflective skills through the Blended Reflection Cycle Form (the BRC Form), specifically designed to allow comprehensive reflection-on-action. As a common characteristic of instrumental case studies, this research has implications for other trainers in different institutions (Mills et al., 2010).

7.3.1. Participant and Context

The research was conducted in a school of foreign languages at a foundation university in the west of Turkey in the 2020–2021 academic year. The seven trainers of the Teacher Development Unit were responsible for providing in-service support and development to enable the school's language instructors to achieve their full potential. The types of activities offered were usually determined by the trainers themselves, as well as by the school administrators, taking into consideration the needs of the teachers.

The participant, a 41-year-old teacher trainer, has a BA in ELT with an MA on 'Curriculum and Instruction,' a PhD on 'Educational Technologies,' and the Cambridge Diploma in Teaching English to Speakers of Other Languages. As well as successfully finishing a formal trainer training course at an international training center, at the time of the study he had concurrently 19 years of teaching and 10 years of training experience at the same institution, and its CELTA center. He has been involved in teacher training activities such as

- conducting lesson observations along with feedback sessions,
- presenting face-to-face and online workshops and seminars,
- designing and delivering training courses,
- being involved in team teaching,
- working as a mentor,
- assisting the instructors with their action research,
- guiding and helping the instructors with their individualized professional development studies.

7.3.2. Data Collection

In order to provide a rich and thick description of the case and increase the reliability of the findings, various triangulated data sources were involved in this study, including two post-observation meetings, two online training sessions, and two rounds of interviews with two different teachers: the first round was conducted after the trainer delivered an online training session, and the second, before delivering a hybrid training course; both teachers were participants in these events.

The qualitative data were collected through a specially designed form (Appendix 7.1) called the Blended Reflection Cycle Form (the BRC Form). In the process of creating this form, the researcher collaborated with a colleague who is an expert teacher trainer. All the data sources were recorded to allow the participant trainer to conduct meticulous and elaborate reflection-on-action. The reflection was conducted on training activities throughout the course of one academic year, which enabled him to assess over time how being involved in this Blended Reflection Cycle influenced his reflective skills and training activities.

The International Society for Technology in Education (ISTE), an organization designed to set standards and professional development for effective uses of technology for teaching, states that teachers 'use technology resources to engage in ongoing professional development and lifelong learning' (Kelly & McAnear, 2002, p. 308), an objective that is equally valid and applicable for trainers. This process is called 'blended' because it involves both '*pen-and-paper*' and '*digital resources*' in the process of reflection-on-action. In this study, the audio- and video-recordings provided concrete and convincing data for trainer reflection (Walsh & Mann, 2015), enabling him to notice easily-missed, but important incidents in the data. As for the traditional pen-and-paper dimension, reflecting on the training activities through the BRC Form enabled the trainer to closely analyze his behavior as a trainer, achieve in-depth reflection, evaluate his training from different perspectives, and make action plans accordingly.

7.3.3. Data Analysis

Through open, axial, and selective coding, the trainer's responses to the questions in the BRC Form were analysed to identify certain common themes. Rather than waiting for the end of the data collection, the researcher conducted qualitative analysis concurrently (Morrison et al., 2002), constantly revising the analysis in the light of newly emerging information.

Throughout the study, the researcher himself acted as the qualitative data collection instrument. Conscious that he was engaging in 'the process of reflecting critically on the self as researcher, the human instrument' (Lincoln & Guba, 2000, p. 183), he was careful to engage in reflexivity and thus remain credible and transparent. He made efforts to analyse the data with an objective lens, and conducted peer debriefing, defined as 'the review of the data and research process by someone who is familiar with the research' (Creswell & Miller, 2010, p. 129). Another teacher trainer viewed the data, confirming that it reflected the researcher's findings, which contributed to the credibility of this study.

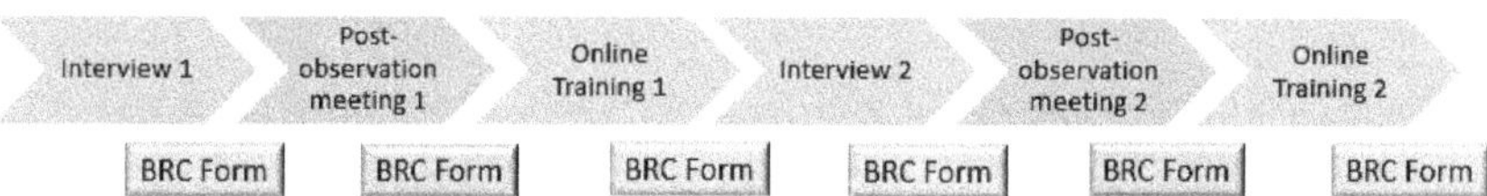

Figure 7.2. Flow of the study.

Table 7.1. The research layout.

Research Questions	**Data Sources**	**Data Collection Instrument**	**Data Analysis**
To what extent does the 'Blended Reflection Cycle for Trainers' improve a trainer's a. training activities? b. reflective skills?	The recordings of • two interviews • two post-observation meetings • two online trainings	The BRC Form	Content Analysis

Table 7.1 displays the outline of the research, while Figure 7.2 shows the flow of the study. There were two-week intervals in between the training events, during which the trainer completed the BRC Form.

7.4. FINDINGS AND DISCUSSION

Having been meticulously analysed, coded, categorized, reviewed, and re-ordered, the qualitative data presented comprehensive and richly descriptive findings and generated common themes. The second research question was more straightforward; however, the first one, whether the BRC form led to improvement in the training activities, was highly complex and multifaceted. Improvements were found in three areas: (a) in the trainer's identity, (b) in the engagement and involvement of the participants in the training events, and (c) in the trainer's management of his affective domain. Thus, throughout this blended reflection cycle, all the previous trainings and reflections functioned as an investment for the following ones. The themes which were aligned with the two research questions of this study are given as follows:

a. the changes in the trainer's identity (RQ 1),
b. the increasing engagement and involvement of the participants in the training events (RQ 1),
c. the trainer's better management of his affective domain (RQ 1),
d. the increasing depth in the trainer's reflections (RQ 2).

7.4.1. The Changes in the Trainer's Identity

Identity is a dynamic sense of self, socially constructed, and situated in a particular context (Goh, 2015). This reflective study helped the participant trainer to carefully examine his real identity as a teacher trainer in his social and idiosyncratic context, particularly via the last two questions in the BRC Form, '(11) What did you learn from this training experience? How do you think this training could contribute to you as a teacher and trainer?' and '(12) What analogy would you suggest for this training?' Farrell (2019) sees reflective practice as holistic (Principle 1); therefore, rather than reflecting exclusively on the specific activities or the participant teachers, the trainer took a wider perspective on the process of self-reflection, and the components of a training event. The analysis of the trainer's reflections showed a gradual awareness and improvement in his perception of himself as a trainer, the implications of which were also visible in the training events, indicating that such a holistic approach contributed to his trainer identity.

According to Gee (2000), identity refers to a 'kind of person in a given context' (p. 99), which was reflected in the responses given in BRC Form 2 (*a trainer with a PhD in educational technologies*) and BRC Form 3 (*a person competent in using technology*). Obviously, the trainer saw himself as the main source of support for the development of the teachers in his current institution; however, in Forms 5 and 6, he denoted a new aspect of his trainer-self, openly stating that he was, in fact, a language instructor who shared his own best practices with his colleagues in order to foster language learning. Corresponding to this new sense of trainer-self, in the second online training session, he recognized that he had begun to attach more importance to the value of his teacher colleagues, and the new tools that they introduced in his training. During the session, in the chat box, the teachers agreed to meet after the training event to learn from each other, which convinced him that a good trainer needs not only to 'know-what' or 'know-how' but also, as these teachers showed, to 'know-where,' referring to the learning context itself. He became aware that it was important to create 'learning communities' of instructors desiring to improve their practice in an ongoing and collaborative way (Mitchell & Sackney, 2000) and that his responsibility as a trainer, involved exploiting a variety of knowledge sources beyond the scheduled training events. Clearly, he had shifted his perception of a trainer away from being the 'source of knowledge' towards becoming a 'learning community organizer.' It is important to note that, from a sociocultural point of view, such a change is not unexpected, since identity is dynamic and shifting; in other words, it is constructed and reconstructed based on an individual's experiences (Norton, 2006). The identity shift was also reflected in the analogies he used in the BRC Form at various stages; for example, though involving togetherness and cooperation, the first analogies he had chosen demonstrated that he was the source of the development, like 'a coach of a marathon runner' (BRC 1) and 'a driving instructor' (BRC 2); however, the final analogy suggested a shift to allowing the participants to take the stage, in the same way as 'an orchestra conductor' (BRC 6).

Barkhuizen (2016) proposes that once a teacher understands his own identity, this has an impact on his professional practice. Similarly, in this research, there is an equally clear link between 'identity development' and the 'quality of teaching/ training' since teacher trainer identity development is parallel to teacher identity development (Dinkelman, 2011). Owens et al. (2010) strongly argue that identities function as the source of action plans; and in this study, the new roles and dimensions added to the trainer's identity could be regarded as the driving force of later improvements. Released from the burden of being a 'sage on stage,' the trainer discovered new responsibilities, including supporting the instructors in creating their own learning communities, fostering connectivism, and spreading the learning/training phase beyond a single session time. This indicates that his new trainer-self has become more likely to adopt training events that are more collaborative and process-based.

7.4.2. The Increasing Engagement and Involvement of the Participants in the Training Events

One crucial point that the trainer realized through this reflective study was that, regardless of the training event, one of the keys to achieving success is keeping the participant(s) involved, active, and engaged. As Bayrakçı (2009) stated, in-service instructors benefit more from a training event situated in their authentic context, and being engaged in finding solutions for their self-identified problems. The trainer also adopted this principle in his training sessions, as shown by the following comment in the first reflection form: '*That was good that the well-formulated questions intrigued the instructor, and I left the floor to him in most part of the interview*' (BRC 1). Once confirming the value of the engagement and involvement, he made plans for the following training activities accordingly.

> As I had expected, the instructors both learned better and enjoyed the session when they were given the chance to work with the Google Docs in breakout rooms. I will find innovative ways to make them more active through cooperation and competition in my following sessions. (BRC 3)

Based on his previous reflections, the trainer devised various strategies and methods to increase the participants' engagement and involvement; for example, in the second interview, he provided the instructor with questions to encourage figurative thinking that activated the right hemisphere of his brain, rather than the reasoning, more analytical, left hemisphere. Also, in the second post-observation meeting, the trainer presented a different case to elicit further comments, encouraging the instructor to take an innovative perspective on the issues in his teaching. In the second online training session, the instructors were encouraged to cooperate with their group members, and compete with the other groups, through miscellaneous activities and apps like puzzle completion, online quizzes, and games. In order to increase the cognitive presence and involvement of the participant instructors, the trainer exploited technological tools such as audience response systems (e.g., menti and pollev), online boards (e.g., padlet), and games (e.g., quizziz). The trainer also noted in the last BRC Form that the introduction of innovations in such an engaging way also helped the instructors to use these tools with their students; and thus, ensured their pedagogical development (Comas-Quinn, 2011).

7.4.3. The Trainer's Better Management of His Affective Domain

The trainer's reflective practice in this study increased his awareness of the importance of his own feelings, and the impact of his affective domain on the training events, which was clearly visible in some of his statements in the BRC forms: '*I did not know that my facial expressions and posture (even if I was sitting before the computer) were that obvious when giving an online session. I looked like a novice trainer*' (BRC 3). He tried to take action on his analysis of his own feelings and appearance, by remembering to control negative feelings, and adopt a positive and smiling expression in the following trainings; however, he stated: '*No matter how many times I reminded myself not to look tense, I am not happy how I looked. Better than the previous session, though. Maybe I will never get rid of feeling uptight before a show*' (BRC 6). As Hannafin (1999) states, it is difficult to change feelings or emotions; even such improvements as the trainer would be able to make in his feelings were likely to be small. However, a major achievement for the trainer, through this blended reflective practice, was that he was able unveil the underlying reasons behind such feelings. The biggest source of feeling uneasy, especially at the beginning of the training sessions, stemmed from the pressure he felt, as apparent in his responses in the BRC Form: '*As a trainer with a PhD on educational technologies, I was a bit worried about my ability to provide actionable solutions for the issues that the instructor had experienced*' (BRC 2) and '*Everyone believes that I am good at technology so I felt there could be no room for even a slightest mistake*' (BRC 3). Such statements clearly revealed that, in his mind, the instructors were expecting him to be the role model; and as this source of worry remained, his feelings of apprehension before the training sessions were little changed despite his efforts at reflection-on-action and reflection-for-action.

One significant point to note is that the trainer recognized the necessity of harnessing his affective domain when involved in reflective practice. This was because the trainer's affective domain not only led him to appear uneasy and lacking confidence, but also negatively influenced his behavior in the post-observation meetings, as seen in the comments: '*I should have firmly declined what the instructor suggested*' (BRC 2) and '*I should have stopped him as he diverted the main point*' (BRC 5). These reflections unveiled the cause of his submissive attitude as his fear of giving offence, and explained why he refrained from confrontation. Apart from the contributions of the technological affordances of the reflective tools employed, another key factor in allowing the trainer to understand how his feelings impacted on his trainer role was the non-threatening environment of this self-reflection process (Rich & Hannafin, 2009). There was no risk of embarrassment or shame, as he was voluntarily involved in this process on his own, interacting with himself, without the pressure of external judgment or appraisal.

7.4.4. The Increasing Depth in the Trainer's Reflections

The analysis of the trainer's responses in the BRC Forms clearly displayed that his training skills and his reflective eye improved over the course of the study, shown by the depth of his reflective statements and the width of his reflective spectrum toward the end of the study. As an experienced trainer at the beginning of the study, his reflections were already beyond the superficial level, involving more than mere descriptions. In the first three BRC Forms, his reflections covered a range of issues, including critical thinking: '*I should not have asked the seventh question as the instructor had already referred to it in the previous one. No need to stick to the rubrics that much.*' (BRC 1); action plans: '*Obviously, I exaggerated the wait time especially, which made the instructor uncomfortable. Next time, I will give some cues or options to prevent such long silence*' (BRC 2); and justification for his actions: '*The instructors were willing to learn how to use quizziz. That's why, I added this to the content of the session, which really worked well*' (BRC 3). In all the BRC Forms, he was able to demonstrate high-quality reflections with explanation, evaluation, and solutions (Leijen et al., 2012); however, in the last three, there was a noticeable increase in the concentration of such in-depth reflective statements. In addition to the increasing frequency of such reflections, it was difficult to ignore the variety of the points reflected on. In the first three BRC Forms, the reflections, although high-quality, were often focused on himself or on the participants; however, towards the end of the study, these were more focused on the environment of the training event, the training itself, and theoretical foundations of his practice: '*It was quite satisfactory to see that the principles of constructive learning are successful with the instructors, even on online platforms*' (BRC 5). This also shows that being involved in reflective practice through BRC forms helped the trainer see the intertwining of theoretical and practical knowledge, concurring with Farrell's (2019) Principle 4: reflective practice bridges principles and practices.

The trainer's thorough reflections on his training events were enabled by the technical affordance of re-watching or listening to certain moments, gaining a different perspective each time (Postholm, 2008). He openly stated the value of the recordings: '*If I had not watched myself, I could not have guessed how stern I looked at the beginning of the meeting*' (BRC 2), '*Till I listened to it again, I was not aware that I had interrupted the instructor abruptly and stopped him talking*' (BRC 4). The reflective practice enriched with multimodal resources eliminated the dependency on memory and enabled the trainer to self-reflect with specific concrete information and evidence (Walsh & Mann, 2015).

> If I had not watched it again, I would say that everything went well. However, I noticed that my tone of voice and facial expressions were too formal and set a barrier between the instructor and myself. That was not necessary at all. (BRC 3)

Such awareness-raising reflective comments highlight the importance of data-led information to build reflections on. This also supports Farrell's (2019) principle that 'reflection should be evidence-based' (Principle 2).

7.5. CONCLUSION

This study clearly showed that reflection is a method of professional development for teachers and trainers alike, being 'central to all learning' (Bruner, 1960 as cited in Ray & Coulter, 2008, p. 7). Markedly, this research also highlighted the key characteristics of such PD, in which successful reflection is attributed to following Farrell's (2019) principles. Throughout the research, the trainer gained a wider and comprehensive perspective on his actions, how and why he acted as he did, along with who he was as a trainer, which contributed to improving his training activities and trainer identity (Principle 1: holistic). The course taken also provided tangible and concrete proof of the progress in his training activities and reflective skills (Principle 2: evidence-based), which increased the depth and reliability of his reflections and established a sound basis for improving his professional practice. He interacted with himself when listening to and watching the videos of his training events to complete the BRC Forms (Principle 3: involving dialog) and was also able to review these self-reflections based on experience in the light of theoretical knowledge (Principle 4: bridging principles and practices). The nature of the reflection process was exploratory throughout the project (Principle 5: requiring a disposition for inquiry) due to the approach taken, which was inductive, rather than assumption-testing. Farrell (2019) also stated that reflective practice is a way of life (Principle 6), and by making reflection an integral component of his own professional development, the trainer benefited, as shown in his preparation of action plans for the following training events and as clearly reflected in the BRC forms.

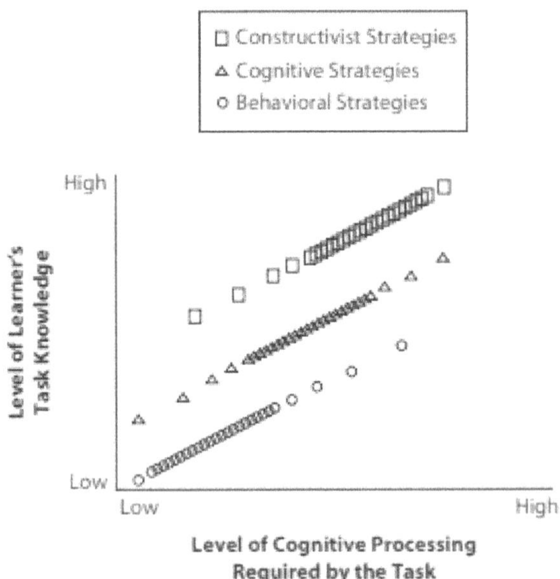

Figure 7.3. Comparison of learning theories (Ertmer & Newby, 1993).

In addition to following Farrell's (2019) principles, for trainers or teacher educators aiming to be involved in training through reflection, another key implication is that it is important to build such reflective studies on strong philosophical foundations. Trainers need to increase their understanding of reflective practice, and its elusive nature, through research, peer collaboration, or in-service trainer training. It would be useful for teacher educators to experience the reflective process from a teacher's point of view as a participant. As Figure 7.3 displays, reflective practice requires constructivist strategies, thus requiring a high knowledge level about these strategies, as well as a correspondingly high level of cognitive skill for reflection. Although a structured design involving checklists, tallies, and yes/no questions is useful for the early stages, trainers should move on to freer modes, with open-ended questions, analogies, or figurative depictions, advancing from the description level to the critique and discussion levels in reflection (Leijen et al., 2012). Considering all the above, it can be concluded that in order to achieve satisfactory results, reflective studies need to be situated in an authentic context, engage the participants, encourage them to use their higher-order thinking skills when trying to solve ill-defined problems, and allow them to make meaning of what they experience (Ertmer & Newby, 1993), as clearly seen in this study.

Reflective Break

- What is the impact of reflection on a trainer's own professional development?
- How can trainers improve the quality of training events through reflection-on-action?
- In what ways does reflective practice change a trainer's identity and affective domain?
- What characteristics of reflective practice improve the quality of a trainer's self-reflection?
- How can the six principles suggested by Farrell (2019) establish a sound foundation for trainers' self-reflection on their training events?

REFERENCES

Avalos, B. (2011). Teacher professional development in teaching and teacher education over ten years. *Teaching and Teacher Education*, 27, 10–20. https://doi.org/10.1016/j.tate.2010.08.007

Barkhuizen, G. (Ed.). (2016). *Reflections on language teacher identity research*. Taylor & Francis. https://doi.org/10.4324/9781315643465

Bayrakçı, M. (2009). In-service teacher training in Japan and Turkey: A comparative analysis of institutions and practices. *Australian Journal of Teacher Education*, *34*(1), 10–22. https://doi.org/10.14221/ajte.2009v34n1.2

Bolton, G., & Delderfield, R. (2018). *Reflective practice writing and professional development*. Sage Publications.

Boyd, P., Harris, K., & Murray, J. (2011). *Becoming a teacher educator: Guidelines for induction*. Escalate: Subject Centre of the Higher Education Academy, Bristol, UK.

Brandt, C. (2008). Integrating feedback and reflection in teacher preparation. *ELT Journal*, *62*(1), 37–46. https://doi.org/10.1093/elt/ccm076

Cambridge English & NILE (Norwich Institute for Language Education) (2016). Cambridge English Trainer Framework. Retrieved from: https://www.cambridgeenglish.org/Images/297310-cambridge-english-trainerframework-introduction.pdf

Clara, M. (2015). What is reflection? Looking for clarity in an ambiguous notion. *Journal of Teacher Education, 66*(3), 261–271. https://doi.org/10.1177/0022487114552028

Comas-Quinn, A. (2011). Learning to teach online or learning to become an online teacher: An exploration of teachers' experiences in a blended learning course. *ReCALL, 23*(3), 218–232. https://doi.org/10.1017/S0958344011000152

Creswell, J. W., & Miller, D. L. (2010). Determining validity in qualitative inquiry. *Theory into Practice, 39*(3), 124–130. https://doi.org/10.1207/s15430421tip3903_2

Diadori, P. (Ed.). (2013). *How to train language teacher trainers*. Cambridge Scholars Publishing.

Dinkelman, T. (2011). Forming a teacher educator identity: Uncertain standards, practice and relationships. *Journal of Education for Teaching, 37*(3), 309–323. https://doi.org/10.1080/02607476.2011.588020

Ertmer, P. A., & Newby, T. J. (1993). Behaviourism, cognitivism, constructivism: Comparing critical features from an instructional design perspective. *Performance Improvement Quarterly, 6*(4), 50–72. https://doi.org/10.1111/j.1937-8327.1993.tb00605.x

Farrell, T. S. C. (2012). Reflecting on reflective practice: (Re)Visiting Dewey and Schön. *TESOL Journal, 3*(1), 7–16. https://doi.org/10.1002/tesj.10

Farrell, T. S. C. (2013). *Reflective teaching*. TESOL International Association.

Farrell, T. S. C. (2018). Reflective practice for language teachers. https://doi.org/10.1002/9781118784235.eelt0873

Farrell, T. S. C. (2019). *Reflective practice in ELT*. Equinox Publishing. https://doi.org/10.4324/9781315659824-5

Fatemipour, H. (2013). The efficiency of the tools used for reflective teaching in ESL contexts. *Procedia – Social and Behavioral Sciences, 93*, 1398–1403. https://doi.org/10.1016/j.sbspro.2013.10.051

Fazio, X. (2009). Teacher development using group discussion and reflection. *Reflective Practice, 10*(4), 529–541. https://doi.org/10.1080/14623940903138407

Fuller, A., & Unwin, L. (2003). Learning as apprentices in the contemporary UK workplace: Creating and managing expansive and restrictive participation. *Journal of Education and Work, 16*(4), 407–426. https://doi.org/10.1080/1363908032000093012

Gallego, M. (2014). Professional development of graduate teaching assistants in faculty-like positions: Fostering reflective practices through reflective teaching journals. *Journal of the Scholarship of Teaching and Learning, 14*(2), 96–110. https://doi.org/10.14434/josotl.v14i2.4218

Garber, C. (2014). *Doorways and walls: Peer coaching as a means to change instructional practice*. Open Access Dissertations and Theses @ UNI, University of Northern Iowa, https://scholarworks.uni.edu/etd/8

Gee, J. P. (2000). Identity as an analytic lens for research in education. *Review of Research in Education, 25*(1), 99–125. https://doi.org/10.3102/0091732X025001099

Goh, C. C. M. (2015). Foreword. In Y. L. Cheung, S. B. Said, & K. Park, K. (Eds.), *Advances and current trends in language teacher identity research* (pp. ii–v). Routledge.

Gözüyeşil E., & Soylu, B. A. (2014). How reflective are EFL instructors in Turkey? *Procedia – Social and Behavioral Sciences, 116*, 23–27. https://doi.org/10.1016/j.sbspro.2014.01.162

Hakanen, J. J., Bakker, A. B., & Schaufeli, W. B. (2006). Burnout and work engagement among teachers. *Journal of School Psychology, 43*, 495–513. https://doi.org/10.1016/j.jsp.2005.11.001

Hannafin, R. D. (1999). Can teacher attitudes about learning be changed? *Journal of Computing in Teacher Education, 15*(2), 7–13.

Hayes, (2004). *Trainer development: Principles and practice from language teacher training.* Language Australia, Melbourne.

Ida, Z. S. (2018). Teacher trainers' self-reflection and self-evaluation. *Acta Educationis Generalis, 8*, 9–23. https://doi.org/10.2478/atd-2018-0008

Izadinia, M. (2014). Teacher educators' identity: A review of literature. *European Journal of Teacher Education, 37*(4), 426–441. https://doi.org/10.1080/02619768.2014.947025

Jay, J. K., & Johnson, J. L. (2002). Capturing complexity: A typology for reflective practice in teacher education. *Teaching and Teacher Education, 18*(1), 73–85. https://doi.org/10.1016/S0742-051X(01)00051-8

Johnson, B. (2003). Teacher collaboration: Good for some, not good for others. *Educational Studies, 29*(4), 337–350. https://doi.org/10.1080/0305569032000159651

Johnson K. E., & Golombek, P. R. (2002). *Teachers' narrative inquiry as professional development.* Cambridge University Press.

Kandiller, S., & Özler, D. (2015). From teacher to trainer: What changes? Or does it? *Procedia – Social and Behavioral Sciences*, 436–452. https://doi.org/10.1016/j.sbspro.2015.07.530

Kane, R., Sandretto, S., & Heath, C. (2004). An investigation into excellent tertiary teaching: Emphasising reflective practice. *Higher Education, 47*, 283–310. https://doi.org/10.1023/B:HIGH.0000016442.55338.24

Karakaş, A., & Yükselir, C. (2021). Engaging pre-service EFL teachers in reflection through video-mediated team micro-teaching and guided discussions. *Reflective Practice, 22*(2), 159–172. https://doi.org/10.1080/14623943.2020.1860927

Kaya, M. H., & Adıgüzel, T. (2021). Technology integration through evidence-based multimodal reflective professional training for in-service English language teachers. *Contemporary Educational Technology, 13*(4), 323–345. https://doi.org/10.30935/cedtech/11143

Kelly, M. G., & McAnear, A. (Eds.) (2002). *National educational technology standards for teachers: Preparing teachers to use technology.* International Society for Technology in Education, Eugene, OR. Retrieved from: https://files.eric.ed.gov/fulltext/ED473131.pdf

Kiely, R. (1996). Professional development for teacher trainers: A materials writing approach. *ELT Journal, 50*(1), 59–66. https://doi.org/10.1093/elt/50.1.59

Killion, J., & Todnem, G. (1991). A process of personal theory building. *Educational Leadership, 48*(6), 14–17.

Korthagen, F. A. J. (2004). In search of the essence of a good teacher: Towards a more holistic approach in teacher education. *Teaching and Teacher Education, 20*, 77–97. https://doi.org/10.1016/j.tate.2003.10.002

Lakshmi, S. B. (2014). Reflective practice through journal writing and peer observation: A case study. *Turkish Online Journal of Distance Education, 15*(4), 189–204. https://doi.org/10.17718/tojde.21757

Leach, J. (1996). Distinguishing characteristics among exemplary trainers in business and industry. *Journal of Vocational and Technical Education, 12*(2), 5–18. Retrieved from: http://scholar.lib.vt.edu/ejournals/JVTE/v12n2/leach.html. https://doi.org/10.21061/jcte.v12i2.506

Leijen, Ä., Valtna, K., Leijen, D. A. J., & Pedaste, M. (2012). How to determine the quality of students' reflections? *Studies in Higher Education, 37*(2), 203–217. https://doi.org/10.1080/03075079.2010.504814

Leitch, R., & Day, C. (2000). Action research and reflective practice: Towards a holistic view. *Educational Action Research, 8*(1), 179–193. https://doi.org/10.1080/09650790000200108

Lincoln, Y. S., & Guba, E. G. (2000). Paradigmatic controversies, contradictions, and emerging confluences. In N. K. Denzin & Y. Y. S. Lincoln (Eds.), *Handbook of qualitative research* (pp. 163–188). Sage Publications.

Loughran, J. J. (2005). *Developing reflective practice: Learning about teaching and learning through modelling*. Falmer Press.

Mann, S. J., & Walsh, S. (2015). Reflective dimensions of CPD: Supporting self-evaluation and peer evaluation. In A. Q. Howard & H. Donaghue (Eds.), *Teacher Evaluation in Second Language Education* (pp. 17–33). Bloomsbury Academic.

Marcos, J. M., Sanchez, E., & Tillema, H. H. (2011). Promoting teacher reflection: What is said to be done. *Journal of Education for Teaching, 37*(1), 21–36. https://doi.org/10.1080/02607476.2011.538269

Martínez, J. G. (2022) Action research and collaborative reflective practice in English language teaching. *Reflective Practice, 23*(1), 88–102. https://doi.org/10.1080/14623943.2021.1982688

McAlpine, L., Weston, C., Berthiaume, D., Fairbank-Roch, G., & Owen, M. (2004). Reflection on teaching: Types and goals of reflection. *Educational Research and Evaluation, 10*(4–6), 337–363. https://doi.org/10.1080/13803610512331383489

Merriam, S. B. (2009). *Qualitative research: A guide to design and implementation*. Wiley and Sons.

Mills, A. J., Durepos, G., & Wiebe, E. (2010). *Encyclopaedia of case study research*, Vols. 1 & 2. Sage Publications. https://doi.org/10.4135/9781412957397

Mitchell, C., & Sackney, L. (2000). *Profound improvement: Building capacity for a learning community*. Swets & Zeitlinger.

Morgan M. (2015). Assessing and developing English language teacher trainers. In R. Wilson & M. Poulter (Eds.), *Assessing language teachers' professional skills and knowledge*, Vol. 42 (pp. 142–175). Cambridge University Press.

Morrison, M. A., Haley, E., Sheehan, K. B., & Taylor, R. E. (2002). *Using qualitative research in advertising strategies, techniques and applications*. Sage Publications. https://doi.org/10.4135/9781412986489

Mulryan-Kyne, C. (2021). Supporting reflection and reflective practice in an initial teacher education programme: An exploratory study. *European Journal of Teacher Education*, *44*(4), 502–519. https://doi.org/10.1080/02619768.2020.1793946

Nelson, F. L., & Sadler, T. (2012). A third space for reflection by teacher educators: A heuristic for understanding orientations to and components of reflection. *Reflective Practice: International and Multidisciplinary Perspectives*, *14*, 43–57. https://doi.org/10.1080/14623943.2012.732946

Norton, B. (2006). Identity as a sociocultural construct in second language research. *TESOL in Context* [special issue], 22–33. https://doi.org/10.1016/B0-08-044854-2/00624-6

Owens, T. J., Robinson, D. T., & Smith-Lovin, L. (2010). Three faces of identity. *Annual Review of Sociology*, *36*, 477–499. https://doi.org/10.1146/annurev.soc.34.040507.134725

Postholm, M. B. (2008). Teachers developing practice: Reflection as key activity. *Teaching and Teacher Education*, *24*(7), 1717–1728. https://doi.org/10.1016/j.tate.2008.02.024

Ray, B. B., & Coulter, G. A. (2008). Reflective practices among language arts teachers: The use of weblogs. *Contemporary Issues in Technology and Teacher Education*, *8*(1), 6–26.

Rich, P., & Hannafin, M. (2009). Video annotation tools. *Journal of Teacher Education*, *60*(1), 52–67. https://doi.org/10.1177/0022487108328486

Richards, J. (2004). Towards reflective teaching. *The Language Teacher*, *33*, 2–5.

Richards, J. C., & Farrell, T.S.C. (2005). *Professional development for language teachers: Strategies for teacher learning*. Cambridge University Press. https://doi.org/10.1017/CBO9780511667237

Rodgers, C. (2002). Defining reflection: Another look at John Dewey and reflective thinking. *Teachers College Record*, *104*(4), 842–856. https://doi.org/10.1111/1467-9620.00181

Salmani-Nodoushan, M. A. (2006) Language teaching: State of the art. *The Reading Matrix*, *6*(2), 125–140.

Schön, D. A. (1987). *Educating the reflective practitioner: Toward a new design for teaching and learning in the professions*. Jossey-Bass.

Stake, R. E. (2005). Qualitative case studies. In N. K. Denzin & Y. S. lincoln (eds.), *The Sage handbook of qualitative research*, 443–466. Sage Publications.

Stronge, J. (2007). *Qualities of effective teachers*. Association for Supervision and Curriculum Development (ASCD), Alexandria, VA.

Thorsen, C. A., & DeVore, S. (2013). Analysing reflection on/for action: A new approach. *Reflective Practice*, *14*(1), 88–103. https://doi.org/10.1080/14623943.2012.732948

Tripp, T. R., & Rich, P. J. (2012). The influence of video analysis on the process of teacher change. *Teaching and Teacher Education*, *28*, 728–739. https://doi.org/10.1016/j.tate.2012.01.011

Ur, P. (1996). *A course in language teaching*. Cambridge University Press.

Valdez, P. N., Navera, J. A., & Esteron, J. J. (2018). What is reflective teaching? Lessons learned from ELT teachers from the Philippines. *Asia-Pacific Edu Res*, 27, 91–98. https://doi.org/10.1007/s40299-018-0368-3

Walsh, S., & Mann, S. (2015). Doing reflective practice: A data-led way forward. *ELT Journal*, *69*(4), 351–362. https://doi.org/10.1093/elt/ccv018

White, E. (2014). Being a teacher and a teacher educator – Developing a new identity? *Professional Development in Education*, *40*(3), 436–449. https://doi.org/10.1080/19415257.2013.782062

Williams, R., & Grudnoff, L. (2011). Making sense of reflection: A comparison of beginning and experienced teachers' perceptions of reflection for practice. *Reflective Practice*, *12*(3), 281–291. https://doi.org/10.1080/14623943.2011.571861

Wright, T. (2009). 'Trainer development': Professional development for language teacher educators. In A. Burns & J. C. Richards (Eds.), *The Cambridge guide to second language teacher education* (pp. 102–112). Cambridge University Press.

Yuk-Kwan Ng, R., & Lam, R. Y. (2015). Train-the-trainer: A study of the professional skill competencies and psychological qualities of teacher trainers. *International Journal of Learning and Teaching*, *1*(1), 38–41.

Zeichner, K., & Liston, D. (1996). *Reflective teaching: An introduction*. Lawrence Erlbaum Associates.

APPENDIX 7.1

The Blended Reflection Cycle Form

Dear Trainer,
Please watch the recording of your training event and answer the following questions.

1. What was/were the objective(s) of this training event?
2. How did you plan to achieve the objective(s) (i.e., selection of the content, method(s), strategies, activities in the preparation process)?
3. Do you think you achieved the objective(s)? Why?/Why not?
4. What worked well in the training event? Why?
5. What could have been improved? Why?
6. Which part(s) of the training event do you think the participant(s) benefited most? Why?
7. If you had been one of the participants, how would you have felt in the training event? Why?
8. How did the following affect your training event: your posture, tone of voice, body language, facial expressions, and overall mood?
9. Do you think the environment you created was non-threatening enough for the participant(s) to communicate easily? Why do you think so?

10. Did you give the participant(s) the chance of expressing, exploring, and/or reflecting by themselves?
11. What did you learn from this training experience? How do you think this training could contribute to you as a teacher and trainer?
12. What analogy would you suggest for this training?

ABOUT THE AUTHOR

Mehmet Haldun Kaya (PhD) has been working at the Izmir University of Economics, Turkey both as an English language instructor and teacher trainer for the past twenty years. He is also an approved Cambridge CELTA Tutor. He has national and international publications in the fields of ELT and educational technology.

Concluding Remarks

Bahar Gün & Evrim Üstünlüoğlu

As simply defined in many studies, reflective practice means a conscious effort to think about and develop insights into past and present actions (Leitch & Day, 2000; Schön, 1983). With this definition in mind, the purpose of this book, as pointed out in the introduction, is to demonstrate how reflective practices support teachers' professional growth by developing deeper insights into their teaching. The seven research articles on reflective practice in ELT in the Turkish context demonstrate the key role of teacher reflection in continuous professional development. These chapters have focused on different approaches to RP, including individual and collective reflection, from the perspectives of pre-service teachers and in-service teachers (novice and experienced), as well as teacher trainers. The research results led to long- and short-term implications of a collaborative and systematic nature, both for teachers and for teacher trainers in Turkey, and by extension, in EFL settings around the world.

One major focus of the book is on is RP in the pre-service EFL context. Regarding pre-service EFL teachers, an important implication is the need to revisit the EFL departmental course contents, to ensure a greater focus on reflective practices. The departmental courses, other than the practicum, can be designed to encourage reflective thinking by incorporating classroom action research, lesson study projects, critical networks, peer observation, video-based journaling, role-play, blogging, reflective journals, and online discussion questions. Additionally, the 'critical reflection' concept can be introduced to pre-service teachers in their early training stages to support the development of higher-order thinking skills such as problem-solving, critical thinking, and creative thinking. Exploiting the advantages of an increasingly digital world, EFL teacher education programs could include online components highlighting digital reflection with a focus on certain characteristics such as self-perception, self-reflection, self-assessment, self-direction, and self-adjustment. This could lead to greater professionalism and more effective reflection on teaching practices.

Another EFL setting highlighted in the book is in-service education programs. It is clear from the studies conducted that reflective practice groups could be a very valuable professional development activity, increasing engagement and promoting affective bonds among teachers while developing their reflective practices. This approach is valuable because as teachers discuss their in-/on-/for-reflection activities, they build their development from the bottom up. This practice has an ongoing, systematic, and collaborative pattern, shown to provide effective long-term professional growth. Lesson study, another form of bottom-up RP, offers an equally engaging professional learning process, allowing teachers to study their own discourse and understand their own practice.

Additionally, Reflective Teaching and Learning Programs (RTLPs) could be helpful for novice teachers to enhance reflective skills in their initial years. RTLPs designed specifically for the needs of novice teachers may include activities such as orientation, self-reflection, identifying strengths and areas to improve, preparing lesson plans with identified focus areas, self-observation, self-evaluation, and writing self-reflective reports. A very important factor in the design and planning of RTLPs is the need to consider workload, and the time teachers can invest in these programs.

One noteworthy observation from the studies in the book is teachers' apparent lack of knowledge of and training for reflective thinking and the procedural demand of the reflective tasks. Although all teachers engaged in reflective processes express a substantial number of benefits, they find it challenging to adapt to the inquiry-oriented practices required. This may be due to the teacher education program curricula, and their lack of focus on research perspectives and skills. That is, there is a need to provide reflection training for teachers before engagement in any practical reflective process for their own PD.

The in-service context studies presented in the book point to a lack of research on reflective practice in primary- and secondary-level EFL settings. As most of the current studies are from the tertiary level, it is obvious that there is room for studies with a greater focus on primary and secondary (K-12) EFL teachers.

As for teacher educators, it is obvious that there is an urgent need for further studies of trainers' reflection on their own training performance and experience. This area could be unearthed by raising trainers' awareness of constructivist strategies, as this will best help them to experience the reflective process from the teachers' perspective, i.e., that of a participant. The ways to increased consciousness of this process should, we suggest, start with a more structured design involving checklists, tallies, and yes/no questions, later giving way to a less rigid format, including open-ended questions, analogies, or figurative depictions, representing progress from the description level to the critique and discussion levels in reflection.

As noted in the introduction to the book, there is a remarkable number of high-quality RP studies in Turkish context, although there is still an ongoing need for follow-up studies across the range of EFL contexts and settings. The scope of these studies can be broadened to include the longer-term effects of PD practices, including reflective thinking, i.e., examining the extent of the retention of learning resulting from reflective practice endeavors.

We, as the editors of this book, firmly believe that reflective practice is an effective way of gaining insights into our practices, and thus becoming better able to fulfil our potential. We trust this book will be of value to pre-service teachers, in-service teachers, teacher trainers, educators, and researchers in the ELT field, and encourage them to employ reflective practice in a methodologically appropriate and ethically sound manner in their own professional contexts.

REFERENCES

Leitch, R., & Day, C. (2000). Action research and reflective practice: Towards a holistic view. *Educational Action Research*, *8*(1), 179–193. https://doi.org/10.1080/09650790000200108

Schön, Donald A. (1983). *The reflective practitioner: How professionals think in action*. Basic Books.

ABOUT THE AUTHORS

Bahar Gün holds BA, MA, and PhD degrees in ELT. Since 2003, she has been working at the İzmir University of Economics (IUE), Turkey, where she is an Assistant Professor. She served as Head of the Teacher Development Unit (TDU) in the School of Foreign Languages (SFL) at IUE between 2006 and 2021, and is currently a member of the TDU that is in charge of in-service teacher training and development programs in the SFL. Her research interests include EFL teacher education in general, and teacher cognition and reflective teaching and learning in particular. She is also a CELTA and ICELT tutor, and an Oxford Teachers' Academy (OTA) trainer. She is the founding president of TESOL Turkey, a Commission on English Language Program Accreditation (CEA) reviewer, and the coordinator of the IATEFL Teacher Training and Education Special Interest Group. She is also a board member of DEDAK, a national agency for the accreditation of language programs in Turkey.

Evrim Üstünlüoğlu received her BA and MA degrees in Teaching English as a Foreign Language, and her PhD in Educational Sciences with a special focus on program development. She has extensive experience, having served as a director, a researcher, and a lecturer for over 30 years. She is a qualified Commission on English Language Program Accreditation (CEA) reviewer, a founding member of DEDAK (a national agency for the accreditation of language programs in Turkey) and TESOL Turkey, and a board member of the IATEFL Leadership and Management Special Interest Group. She has publications in both international and national journals, on quality in higher education, pedagogical competencies of faculty members, observation/reflection, and new approaches in teaching. She has been awarded scholarships to conduct research and to teach as a visiting scholar abroad. Her expertise and interests are quality in education, program development, methodology, and design thinking. She is currently an Associate Professor at the İzmir University of Economics, Turkey.

Index

CPSIA information can be obtained
at www.ICGtesting.com
Printed in the USA
JSHW041029270623
43760JS00004B/36